HEALTH
in
BALANCE

The Essential Elements

Seasonal Cookbook

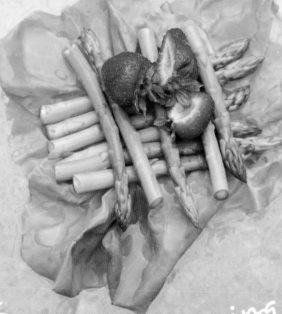

"it's what everything in life boils down to"

BY CAROL MAGLIO & DR. KEN GREY, AP,DOM

Printed in the United States of America by Jostens Commercial Printing
First Printing: October 2014
ISBN#: 978-0-9854730-7-5

Print Layout and Design by
SIR SPEEDY PRINTING
Tequesta, Florida

Cover Design by
Pitter Patter Productions and Sue Beckerman

ACKNOWLEDGEMENTS

We are extremely happy to acknowledge our blessings and give thanks to our Creator, Mother Earth, each other, Big V, our moms, our dads, our sisters, our brothers and our friends.

This compilation would not be possible without the hard work of everyone at:
DB Digital Media, Sir Speedy of Tequeta, M&K Publishing, Jostens, Professional Typing Company, and Glenn Graphics.

We are grateful for the support given to us by: Garden of Life, Macht One, L.E.T. Group, Palm Beach Post, WPBF ABC News, WJTW 103.9 FM Radio, WJNO 1290 AM Radio, Jupiter Medical Center,
The Corner Café, The Food Shack, Bice – Palm Beach, Saks Fifth Avenue, La Mer Cosmetics,
Neiman Marcus, Nutrition Wise, Willowbend Country Club, American Heart Association, The ARC, Kristen Hoke Breast Health Program, Hospice of the Palm Beaches, WZZR 94.3 FM – Real Radio, Admirals Cove, Frenchman's Creek.

Who's having more fun than us?!?!

DISCLAIMER

Contents

Introduction

Our culinary journey through life's changes enriched with the balanced principals of ancient Chinese traditions.

Sometimes people get confused about Juice & Essence. Is it a diet? Is it medicine? Is it Vegetarian or Vegan? Juice & Essence is a Movement, not a diet. It IS medicine in the truest, most basic form — therapy in the food we eat. The Juice & Essence Movement aims to heal through creative uses of food from a multicultural world. We believe you can balance your health and enjoy your life with the recipes here. The flow of energy and ideas is at the core of the Juice & Essence Movement — a natural flow that leaves us feeling as if we are sometimes just vehicles of transmission for these out-of-this-world creations! Back on Earth, we ground all our recipes with moderation and balance. Natural ingredients are chosen for their healing and therapeutic properties. We have a lot of fun cooking, and hope our love and spirit come through when you create this special food.

Our Journey

"Healthful Cuisine for the Connoisseur"

In the beginning, Juice & Essence was going to be a cookbook based on the seasons. Each season we would be using the freshest ingredients in creative ways. It has since evolved, as we have in our cooking, to include a more holistic approach. With each dish we have created, the health benefits of the ingredients we have used have come shining through. This inspired us to include references in each recipe of the many healthy attributes associated with the dish. In the end, we have created not only a delicious and visually appealing cookbook, but one that will also be used as a reference for better health through food.

Our Story Begins

Carol:

Just over two years ago, I had an irregular Pap test. Six months later, another irregular Pap test. At that time, my gynecologist performed a colposcopy. The results showed "mild dysplasia." I was told there was no real concern and they will repeat the Pap test in another six months. Well that test also had the same result. Again, I was told to come back in six months. When that test also came back irregular, my doctor recommended a cone biopsy of the cervix. She expressed that she did not feel that we would find anything since I had no other symptoms. She felt that the biopsy would remove the irregular tissue and that would take care of everything. My other option was to wait another six months and repeat the Pap test. By nature, I am proactive where my health is concerned, so I chose to have the biopsy.

My gynecologist called me with the results. She said she had good news and bad news and that I could choose which I heard first. I told her to choose because it is never good when the doctor herself calls you at 7:15pm! She said: "The bad news is that you have cancer. The good news is that we caught it." It was a good thing I did not choose to wait another six months. My outcome would have been very different since I had the aggressive type of cervical cancer. Thank God my doctor wanted to be safe rather than sorry and gave me the option to have the biopsy!

Then the "ists," as I like to refer to all of the specialists, began:

From the Gynecologist to the Oncologist, the Internist, the Radiologist, the Pathologist, the Endocrinologist, the Psychologist and of course, most importantly, my Acupuncturist, Dr. Ken Grey, DOM.

My treatments with Dr. Ken were extremely helpful during this whole ordeal. With his extensive knowledge of oriental medicine and his immeasurable guidance, he has been able to heal me both physically and spiritually. I could not have achieved the level of success I have experienced without his assistance.

As I realize the dream to help heal others through the telling of our story and the healthful recipes we have to offer, I know how truly blessed I am to have the opportunity to continue to learn from such an accomplished teacher.

Ken:

I had been treating Carol for an unexplained pain in her lower abdomen. She suffered for over two years prior to seeing me. We were successful in relieving her discomfort and in the process developed a rapport. Then she was diagnosed with cervical cancer and the treatment changed.

The treatments shifted to the acupuncture, dietary counseling, herbal supplements, and overall lifestyle change that would help Carol avoid chemotherapy and radiation. All of this would aid in her quick recovery from the radical hysterectomy she was facing. To my delight, Carol was able to stand completely upright the day after the surgery. She continued to progress in a positive manner during her recovery process.

It was her strength, focus, and love for food that connected me finally to my literary life's purpose. What we were able to do by combining treatment with her faithful following of my prescribed dietary principals prompted further investigation. I thought to myself with our combined effort we could create a compilation of international and ancient dietary principals that, when filtered through our exciting interaction, would birth a perfect, healthful approach to eating.

~ The Authors

HEALTH in *Balance*

HEALTH in *Balance* is not a program; it is a lifestyle. This is food styling personified that hooks its teeth into the multifaceted needs of the consumer. Learning to listen to the body is key here. The body gives us prompts in the forms of desire versus need. What is common and usual can become a contradiction to your body's physical and emotional requirements. Deprivation, excess, moderation, variety, and exercise are all equally important.

To put this in perspective, we are more than taste buds, calorie counters, and diet mongers. We are supreme organic vehicles spanning millennia of conscious creation. Our food is the fuel that is a tender transceiver of everything that sun, earth, and air can contribute. As we recognize the purpose, place, and energy of foods, be it medicinal or otherwise, then we can apply this knowledge as it pertains to our health and well-being. Becoming in-tune with your body and building your awareness of nature's harmony can offer a sense of peace, joy, and lightness.

When you try a new food or a new way of combining nutritional elements, you tell your mind and your body that there is more to choose from when it is looking for nourishment, energy, and healing. This is in essence the expansion of your food vocabulary. As in a verbal vocabulary, one's expression can create avenues for vast communication. The food vocabulary mirrors this in such a way as to blend color, texture, taste, and content with the nutritional resources of the foods we consume. HEALTH in *Balance* will be your aid by expanding your food vocabulary and introducing you to nature's healing code.

We live our lives by enjoying all of the foods that the world and its cultures have to offer. Because of this, we have to constantly seek the remedy to the tipping point of excess. We limit ourselves to reaching that excess. The way we do that is by not limiting what we eat but limiting the frequency. Therefore we can have a hamburger and French fries without feeling guilty because we offset the consumption of toxic foods by adding more healthful foods. Take any of our recipes and you will see that we are not pigeonholed into any particular culinary approach. We happily embrace all foods, all cultures, and promote the use of healthy, appropriate substitutions where nature permits.

HEALTH in *Balance* is about achieving physical and emotional balance. A body balance that for some may be a "detox to retox" approach and for others with chronic disease the HEALTH in *Balance* lifestyle would dictate a more strict adherence to daily consumption of the curative foods suggested in our books.

Achieving the goal of a quality life is rooted deeply in our awareness of food application. The culinary choices of today help sculpt a balanced health outlook for tomorrow. Therefore, we are in fact the living, breathing, animated proof that we are what and when we choose to eat. Come with us on an amazing journey. You will experience "HEALTH in *Balance*"!

Juice & Essence Concept

As you view our recipes, you will see that each contains something called Birth & Balance, Juice & Essence, and our newly added Complement or Contrast. This sets us apart from other cookbooks as it outlines the elements of each recipe utilizing the 3,000- to 5,000-year-old art of traditional Chinese medicine. This sheds light on the healing properties of foods along with the birth of each dish and our artfully collaborated wine pairings.

The focus on the seasons in our book is based on the human connection to seasonal foods and how each organ responds respectively to that element according to traditional Chinese medicine.

Why Seasonal Foods?

Seasonal foods meet the needs of our bodies that change energetically with the seasons and therefore have respective nutritional requirements that can be met through a properly balanced diet.

What is Birth & Balance?

Birth & Balance is how we came up with our recipes — reflecting where we were mentally, spiritually, and physically at the time. It is the birth and creation of our intuitive process in regards to what appealed to us during our "treatment pow-wows" as well as what was available seasonally and the tastes we wanted to enjoy.

What is Juice & Essence?

Inspiring a new way of viewing food combining, selection, and preparation, this is more than an educational aspect to cooking. We implement the millennia of proven traditional Chinese methods and other integrative ways of thought necessary in creating a modern gateway to "HEALTH in *Balance*" cuisine. You will see how seasonally and curatively food can play a part in each system and organ of the body. In the end, you will learn, as we have, the importance of nature's holistic code...everything is connected!

Ronnie Garcia

Creating Complement or Contrast with Ronnie Garcia

Ronnie Garcia, with over 25 years in the food industry and influences rooted in Turkish, Spanish, and Swedish heritage, brings a multicultural powder keg to any culinary establishment he touches. Ronnie truly gets the correlation, rhythm, and harmony between wine and food. He clearly understands how each can be enhanced by the other. Most attractive to him is the passionate art inherent in wine, the living elixir. Ronnie Garcia speaks plainly and therefore is fun and easy to understand. He sees the importance of the ruby and diamond threads a juicy bottle of wine can weave amongst its partakers.

His mission of deconstructing the wine barriers without discrediting the preexisting wine establishment educates from beginner to enthusiast. Ronnie creatively aids the discerning palate on their Compare and Contrast journey. Ronnie Garcia bids you to enter his less intimidating world of wine exploration.

What is Complement or Contrast?

In the endeavor to raise the bar of our creations, we wanted to include the wine combinations that would complement or contrast each dish, elevating it to its proper place. To seize the power of the living grape and combine it with a myriad of the simmered, sautéed, steamed, raw, robust, etc....opens a world of flavor otherwise locked. Each wine style recommendation will complement or contrast and in a rare occasion do both. We drink wine to complement or contrast our food. They are both enriching qualities; however, contrasting is a "breaking" between bites while complementing is a continuance and lingering between bites.

Basically...

To Complement is to select a wine that will elevate and enhance the ingredients in a dish. Example: adding a wine that has largely sweet aspects to it will enhance some inherently sweet dishes.

A Contrasting wine plays on flavors and is instrumental for breaking down the acid and fattiness of the dish. It can also fill in the gaps of taste while enhancing the dining experience and resetting the palate.

Food Group Factoids

SPROUTS

Sprouts are extremely bioavailable and have a high nutrient profile. The sprouting process is one of predigestion, which transforms fats and proteins into readily digestible forms. Sprouts initiate energy (qi) flow in a stagnant liver. They are also rich in nitrilosides, which are substances that break down in the body into chemicals that selectively destroy only cancer cells.

Sprout examples we like to use are clover, alfalfa, and sunflower.

LEGUMES

Legumes have a high protein content and do not digest easily; therefore, they are best taken in small amounts that are beneficial and easier on digestion. The most easily digested legumes are mung and aduki beans (and their sprouts). Except as a sprout, soy is not recommended in cancer treatment because of its extremely high protein and growth promoting properties.

Legumes we like: black beans, lentils, garbanzo beans (chickpeas), kidney beans, mung, aduki, and pinto beans.

ALGAE

Algae have been valuable remedies for the treatment of cancer in various oriental and western cultures. Kelp and other seaweeds are used by the Chinese to soften and reduce hardened masses in the body. They contain the range of minerals, including trace minerals, often deficient in people with degenerative diseases. Without minerals, vitamins and enzymes in the body serve no function.

Seaweeds are also concentrated sources of iodine helpful in maintaining healthy thyroid function and oxidation of cells.

In cancer therapy, it is safest to get all of one's salt from seaweeds and other foods. No salt should be added to food in this case. Also notice that sea salt in general will not contain iodine, which is essential for a healthy functioning thyroid.

WHEAT AND BARLEY GRASSES

Wheat and barley grasses have exceptional detoxification value in degenerative diseases. During cancer battles, these will soothe, help with healing crisis, and detoxification. The chlorophyll helps oxygenate tissues while promoting healthy intestinal flora. Wheat and barley grasses are also rich in the antioxidant enzyme SOD (superoxide dismutase), one of the best defenses against free-radical pathology degenerative diseases. These grasses are cooling and cleansing.

VEGETABLES

Vegetables in general are helpful in treatment of cancer. They are low in fat and protein yet abundant in minerals, vitamins, and other vital nutrients. We recommend carrots to be used most frequently. Quality carrots are very rich in the antioxidant beta-carotene and have an essential oil which kills parasites and unhealthy intestinal bacteria. According to Chinese medicine, carrots have a property of reducing accumulations such as tumors.

Carrots are the base of many of our fresh juices. Although our joy of vegetables goes on, we also promote using the following vegetables due to the healing qualities, potency, and flavor: beets, kale, spinach, peas, cabbage, sweet potatoes, eggplant, Brussels sprouts, cucumber, tomato, onion, and garlic.

FRUIT

Fruit is more cleansing than vegetables; however, the sugars and cold nature can promote yeast infections and weaken digestive energy.

Especially recommended fruit: apples, which eliminate mucus, relieve depression, and tonify the "heart-mind" which is usually depressed and weak in degenerative diseases. For those who tolerate fruit, organic apples can be recommended as the primary fruit and juice source in therapy for cancer and other such conditions.

Fruit and fruit juices should ideally be meals by themselves as they often interfere with digestion of other foods. It is best to take fruit juices in the afternoon and evening. Conscious of cancer concerns, generally beneficial fruits are: mulberry, papaya, cranberry, pomegranate, persimmon, dried cherry, grape, and mango.

GRAINS

In their whole state, grains are generally beneficial in the treatment of cancer and other serious degenerations. Whole grains are an important source of vegetable lignans (a chemical compound found in plants; one of the major classes of phytoestrogens, which are estrogen-like chemicals and also act as antioxidants). Vegetable lignans, also found in flaxseed, have anti-tumor and antioxidant properties. We recommend millet, quinoa, brown rice, amaranth, spelt, and corn for their low- or non-gluten properties and rich fiber and silica content. Grains must be thoroughly chewed to activate their healing properties.

ANIMAL PRODUCTS

Animal products such as cow's milk will be very hard on the digestive system while the fat in goat's milk is easier to digest. Goat's milk has a mildly astringent property and therefore does not cause mucus like other dairy or meats. Goat's milk is one of the least damaging of animal products and will help restore yin deficiency and weakness. In cases of weakness, these other strengthening animal meats provide omega-3 and protein: sardine, anchovy, trout, herring, salmon, and cod.

SWEETENERS

Sweeteners must be used moderately, otherwise they can cause infections and growths to spread. The best sweetener during cancer therapy is Stevia Leaf and its products. Stevia is the only sweetener tolerated in cases of candida. In non-cancer related weakened conditions, we recommend these sweeteners as an option: raw honey, maple syrup, barley malt, rice syrup, and molasses. Choose the highest quality organic varieties if possible.

SPICES

Certain spices can help with liver detox and stagnant liver energy, dry up dampness that will feed viruses, and add variety to meals. Too much spice, especially of the fiery variety, can aggravate the liver and encourage cancer and other serious diseases to spread. The following mildly aromatic spices, if taken in small amounts, favorably stimulate the qi energy of the liver therefore aiding in removing stagnation in the body: anise, dill, fennel, coriander, marjoram, sage, saffron, thyme, rosemary, black pepper, white pepper, cardamom, bay leaf, sorrel, turmeric, mace, and allspice. Turmeric is especially valuable and used widely today in cases of circulatory and arthritic disease. Parsley and chives can be used moderately as spices. They contain sulfur and other antiviral compounds.

HERBS

Bitter herbs with aromatic nature generally offer effective help in the treatment of cancer. These herbs help due to their antiviral, antifungal, oxygenating, immune-enhancing, and stagnancy cleaning qualities. Among these herbs are chaparral, pav d'arco, suma, peach seed, astragalus, ginseng, dandelion, and licorice. Herbs can have adverse reactions if taken inappropriately and physician supervision is recommended for safety and effectiveness.

DAIRY

We are fans of milk substitutes and, as discussed in our Animal Products section, goat's milk. As for milk substitutes, almond and rice milk are at the top of our list.

Eggs are a great source of yin nourishment and cholesterol along with protein which are essential for strength, overall well-being, bone marrow, and "brain" marrow health.

ALCOHOL

Alcohol helps to transport medicinal properties through the blood to the body. Cordials have been used for centuries to administer medicinal curatives to the masses. Present-day cordials are milder and rarer, however, still available. A cordial is any invigorating and stimulating preparation that is intended for a medicinal purpose. Especially beneficial to the heart, some cordials with their flecks of gold leaf and bright yellow hue, took their name from the cordial virtues of the rays of the sun which some alchemists thought they contained.

Some cordials include the family of digestifs and aperitifs, which are normally served with meals. Digestifs contain bitter or carminative herbs, which are thought to aid digestion. Common choices are amari, bitters, brandy, grappa, herbal liquor, limoncello, ouzo, tequila, and whiskey. Some fortified wines are served as digestifs, for example sherry, vermouth, port, and Madeira.

An aperitif is usually served before a meal to stimulate the appetite. Common choices for an aperitif are vermouth, champagne, and any dry, light white wine. "Aperitif" is a French word derived from the Latin verb "aperire" which means "to open."

Everyday Substitutions

Juice & Essence common substitutions include:

- Goat's, almond, or rice milk instead of cow's milk.

- Agave, stevia, or honey as a sweetener instead of processed white sugar. If we must use sugar from sugar cane, we use organic Demerara or turbinado.

- Olive oil, grapeseed oil, safflower oil, and ghee (clarified butter) are our preferred fats to margarine or other diet-based substitutes.

- Brown rice, millet, quinoa, spelt, and sprouted grains are our high protein, low carb, and gluten substitutes to processed white flour and wheat products as well as white rice.

HEART HEALTHY OILS

Coconut oil
Warming and strengthening to the heart. Scientific studies are showing that the medium chain fatty acids in coconut oil effectively kill the low-grade bacterial and viral infections associated with heart disease.

Ghee (clarified butter)
According to Ayurvedic teachings, clarified butter, with its milk solids removed, is a healing property which enhances the ojas — an essence which governs the tissues of the body and balances the hormones. Ample ojas, like the jing essence in Chinese medicine, are essential for resistance against disease and for longevity.

Grapeseed oil
Stands up to heat very well and is high in antioxidants. Grapeseed oil is influential in decreasing LDL cholesterol and raising HDL cholesterol.

Safflower oil
Safflower oil contains the largest polyunsaturated fraction of common oils. Ayurvedic teachings recommend against its use. Some health professionals recommend it as it has health benefits that include being a good source of omega-6 fatty acids and vitamin E.

Olive oil
Due to its monounsaturated properties, olive oil has less cholesterol raising effects, therefore it is highly recommended with a long history of safe, healthful use.

Sesame oil
Another highly recommended monounsaturated oil with a long history of safe, healthful use. Sesame oil relieves constipation, detoxifies, and destroys ringworm, scabies, and most fungal diseases.

Nut & Seed oils
Walnut, hazelnut, pumpkin seed, flaxseed, chia seed, and hemp seed fall under examples of polyunsaturated omega-3 rich oils. Their uses are best as medicinal oils or as a source of essential fatty acids in food preparation but not in cooking.

High Potency Superfoods

By definition these are a category of foods found in nature that are low calorie and nutrient dense. They are superior sources of antioxidants and essential nutrients — nutrients we need but cannot make ourselves. Growing concerns over foods grown in mineral depleted soil make the farming, use, and consumption of more superfoods such as goji berry, spirulina, mulberry, chia seed, açaí, quinoa, and Royal Jelly essential to healthy life and an intelligent source for a greener planet.

Terminology

The following pertains to energy balancing processes of the body:

ACIDIC
Foods that have an acidic effect are: sweets, alcohol, trans-fats, wheat, dairy, pizza, coffee, cola, biscuits, chips, white breads and pastas, beef, refined foods, and processed foods.

ALCOHOLIC THIRST
Yin deficiency due to the drying effects of alcohol on the liver

ALKALINE
Foods that create a more alkaline pH of the body are: low sugar foods, fresh dark leafy green vegetables, nuts, seeds, sea vegetables (Irish moss, dulse, wakame, bladderwrack, sea palm, arame, hijiki, kombu, kelp), and water rich foods such as melons and summer squash.

BLOOD COOLING
Foods that counteract the heat buildup in the body that may cause blood to move too vigorously in the body, increasing pressure and other hot symptoms

CHANNELS / MERIDIANS
A traditional Chinese medicine term for a path through which the life-energy known as qi is believed to flow

COLD
Yin-oriented food with closing or congealing nature and cooling to the body

DAMP HEAT
Circulation and constitution (same as dampness but with hot symptoms such as yellow mucus, burning inflammation, fever)

DAMPNESS
Sluggish, slow moving

DETOX
Ridding the body of toxic residue on a cellular, blood, tissue, and intestinal level

DIABETIC THIRST
Wasting, unquenchable thirst due to inability to transform and transport nutrients

DRY
Lacking yin, moisture, and in some cases exhibiting hot qualities

FOOD STAGNATION
Retention of food due to obstruction, intestinal moisture deficiency, or lack of energy

HARMONIZING
Restoration of balance mainly of yin and yang and where the flows of energy are concerned

HEAT CLEARING
Foods with dispersing qualities to help open pores and release heat via sweat; generally bitter and pungent in nature

HOT
Very yang, very circulating such as cinnamon and black pepper

MOISTENING
Increasing yin, assisting with producing fluid, relieving dryness

NEUTRAL
Balanced food with equal yin and yang properties

PHLEGM
Chronic dampness with slower moving circulation leading to complaints of poor digestion and sinus issues, low energy, addiction

QI
Energy, life force

STOMACH OPENING
Rejuvenating appetite, assisting with movement and digestion of food

TONIFY
Enhance, increase, benefit

WARM
Yang-oriented food helpful in soothing and circulating while warming to the body

WIND CONDITIONS
Wind is energy or qi not anchored by blood. Blood deficiency may create heat symptoms as well since blood is a factor of yin. Wind conditions may manifest as cold provided the body is weak and external pathogens invade. Includes: dizziness, common cold, tremors, seizures, spasms, itching, nervousness

YANG
Movement, warmth, heat

YIN
Moisture, essential fluids

Energetic Rule of Thumb

If it grows in the air and sunshine, it is probably yang.
If it grows in the earth and darkness, it is probably yin.
If it is soft, wet, and cool, it is more yin.
If it is hard, dry, and spicy, it is more yang.

Flavor is very important because it helps to send nutrition via the meridians to the corresponding organs. If we eat a balanced meal with many tastes, we feel satisfied and don't binge.

Digestive Support

The Eastern idea of a balanced diet is one that includes all 5 tastes. But the ratios of those tastes are going to vary according to the individual's needs and the season of the year. A person who is Yang deficient is going to need a higher proportion of foods with Yang energy than other people do. Yang energy foods such as beef, shrimp, kidneys, and liver will supply Yang energy that is lacking and help the person obtain balance. On the other hand, a person who is Yin deficient will need a higher proportion of foods with Yin energy such as millet, milk beets, and bananas. A person with dampness problems needs to go easy on the foods and herbs with sweet, salty, and/or sour tastes because these tend to be moistening. A person with dampness problems does not need an excessive amount of foods and herbs with moistening qualities adding to the dampness. On the other hand, these foods and tastes can be great for some people suffering from dryness. (There are exceptions. Everything is carefully tailored for the individual.)

Healing Your Digestion

- Temperature is important; primarily consume food at body temperature or warmer (not piping hot)

- Drink a glass of warm water before breakfast to prime your digestion

- Be sure to chew your food well

- Best to avoid damp-forming foods for breakfast such as dairy, eggs, orange juice, refined sugar, and fruit on its own. We suggest juicing and ALWAYS include ginger to aid in the digestive process as ginger also acts as a food mediator. You can play around with different grain porridges and include flavor-enhancing additions to keep it interesting. We suggest adding cinnamon and nutmeg to aid in digestive heat along with spleen/pancreas tonifying qualities. Our favorites include quinoa, cream of wheat, oatmeal, or brown rice porridge (made with rice milk, almond milk, or water). Additionally grits with a bit of butter, salt, and black pepper can be very energizing and a safe way to start your day.

- For spleen Qi-enhancing foods, go for orange/yellow vegetables of a sweet nature since the spleen resonates with these vibrations (see 5 Elements Theory). Foods with a warming or neutral thermal nature nurture a deficient spleen. Examples include:

  - well cooked rice or a congee
  - oats
  - spelt
  - sweet rice
  - mochie (pounded sweet rice)
  - winter squash
  - carrot
  - parsnip
  - turnip
  - chickpeas
  - black beans
  - peas
  - sweet potato
  - yam

Weight Management

The **three main reasons** we lose the battle so regularly fought in weight management is we abuse food and succumb to the allure of *taste, hunger,* and *comfort.*

- **Weight loss and weight gain** can consume our way of being. The trick is that it is all about balance. Even our metabolism responds to the ebb and flow of Yin and Yang. Items that one should eliminate if weight gain is a serious issue are: dairy, wheat products of any kind, excess protein (unless grass-fed beef or lamb), white rice, white sugar, processed foods (boxed or canned), caffeine, and excess alcohol.

- **Grass-fed meat is more nutritious.** Grass is also the animal's natural food versus grain, which is unnatural to them and boosts *E. coli* counts in their guts and encourages the spread of disease. Grass-fed meat has a cleaner, leaner content with higher nutrient protein strains making it more easily and efficiently absorbed. Without the hormones and chemicals to accelerate growth and production found in grain-fed meat, the meat and milk will taste better and work better with human digestion. Grass-fed meat is an environmentally conscious and ecologically lower impact food. For those concerned about the environmental or health consequences of a meat-eating diet and choose not to give up meat, this is by far the best option.

- **Grains** such as millet, spelt, and quinoa will fill you faster and alleviate a ravenous appetite quicker due to its nutrient-packed composition versus bleached, degraded, genetically-modified white flour which, no longer in its natural state, can create almost immediate weight gain, increase in sugar levels, inflammation throughout your body, irritability, and more sugar cravings.

- **The weight conscious individual** should create a diet in anti-inflammatory and circulation boosting foods such as cinnamon, ginger, turmeric, cardamom, nutmeg, as well as black and white peppers. Make sure that healthy (preferably gluten-free) grains are easy to digest and be sure to drink a teacup of warm water, broths, or soups with meals. These are all ways to stimulate metabolism and receive adequate energy from your food.

- **Creating a positive pattern** and rhythmic daily routine of energy-in/energy-out consciousness is a concept rooted at the core of all fundamental life processes. There is a tremendous gain to be had from one that is excited about quality over quantity. We can easily enjoy a long list of creative cuisine options when we put our minds and mouths to it. The key to unlocking this new world of weight management is to first accept that our approach of calorie counting and artificial processed, prepackaged foods are a dead end on a hopeless diseased and desperate road. Next we must crave knowledge more than food and begin first to consume the information available on the Internet, food labels, and in books so we know what we are putting in our bodies.

- **Juicing** can be a simple way to energize, gently detox, and replenish. We highly recommend a well-rounded morning juice with a green-based protein supplement. The key elements to a balanced, well-rounded juice include a ratio of 3 vegetables to 1 fruit and proper use of fruit flavors to sculpt the desired taste and a mindfulness to color and texture. Lemons and other citrus will offer a tartness to tone down the earthy, sweet vegetables like carrots and beets. While apples will temper the bitterness sometimes present with kale. Ginger is an absolute necessity for every juice as it adds a warming element and acts as a mediator of nutrients within the body.

We have found that a healthful balance in approaching your diet is paramount. The key is not only to avoid processed foods but to also create a balance in all that you consume. If you have a hamburger, try to use lean meat such as organic white meat turkey, chicken, or buffalo. Have it plain or on a whole grain bun. Instead of French fries, have steamed veggies or a salad that is light on the dressing. These slight changes help to balance the "bad" aspects of this particular meal. This is an easy principal to apply to your entire food intake. Balance the dish with a protein, whole grain, and vegetable whenever possible. We know that in our day-to-day lives this is not always an easy task. But if you can try to balance all your meals you will be pleasantly surprised by the results. This is not to say we do not indulge ourselves. If we feel like having French fries, we will!!! We just alter how we eat the next day and during the week by choosing more healthful foods to balance out the French fries we had earlier.

Along with the balance of the foods you consume, you must include some physical exercise. This will not only help with weight management but also physical agility. With body movement, you will find benefits in all of your day-to-day activities. By exercising your muscles, you will increase your range of motion, bone density, flexibility, and tone.

Studies have shown that this will help with a better quality of life not only by the level of physical activity but also by the foods you eat. The type of exercise you choose should be conducive to your lifestyle with all requirements and responsibilities taken into consideration. Rule of thumb suggests that 30 minutes of exercise every day should present with a consistent elevated heart rate, moderate perspiration, and focused cardio-based activity. For example: 30-minute walk, at least 30 minutes of yoga, circuit training to include some weight-bearing exercises, Pilates, bicycling, swimming…you get the idea. In the chance that your busy schedule will not permit a solid 30 minutes, splitting up your exercise regimen in half or increments of 10 minutes is better than nothing.

Weight management is the knowledge of healthful options, setting healthful goals, and achieving them through healthful means. You are unique and the path to your balanced life is lit by your discipline and perseverance.

Ayurveda Taste and Elements Key ~ Vital energies that make up our constitution

Ayurveda translates from Sanskrit as the knowledge for long life. The Ayurveda key zeros in on the three doshas (vital energies) that give identity and connection to the healing properties and natures of food and how they affect our bodies.

PITTA: Taste = sour, salty, pungent
     Elements = earth, fire, water, air

VATA: Taste = pungent, bitter, astringent
     Elements = air, fire, earth

KAPHA: Taste = sweet, sour, salty
     Elements = earth, water, fire

Relationships of the 5 Elements Theory

There are two main relationships which you must be familiar with to understand the application of the 5 Elements Theory. First is the Mother–Son relationship (also known as the sheng, generation, production, or creation cycle) and the Grandparent–Grandchild relationship (also known as the ke, ko, or control cycle).

These are presented below:

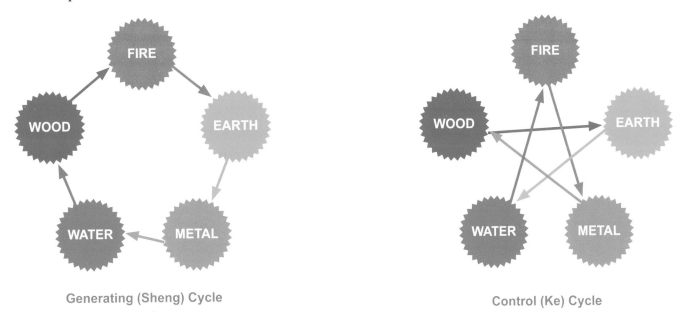

Generating (Sheng) Cycle   Control (Ke) Cycle

The Generating Cycle shows that Fire, for example, helps support Earth and the Control Cycle shows that Fire controls the growth of Metal. To understand how this might be applied, take a person experiencing problems with asthma. Asthma is a Metal (lung) condition sometimes with an underlying psychological component of grief or sadness. From a TCM perspective, asthma may present as a phlegm/damp condition. Following the five elements theory, then, we see that the Earth (spleen) may be weak (phlegm/damp coming from poor digestion, etc.) and not supporting Metal (lung) resulting in an asthmatic condition.

5 Elements

The 5 Elements are an approach to the etiology of disease and to associate symptoms or signs to particular organ pathologies.

- 5 Zang Organs [heart (including pericardium), lungs, spleen, liver, and kidney] Mainly manufacture and store essence: qi, blood, and bodily fluids

- 6 Fu Organs [gallbladder, stomach, large intestine, small intestine, urinary bladder, and "san jiao" a.k.a. triple burner — which are the three areas of the body cavity] Receive and digest food, absorb nutrient substances, transmit and excrete wastes

FIVE ELEMENTS	Wood	Fire	Earth	Metal	Water
Seasons	Spring	Summer	Late Summer	Autumn	Winter
Environment	Wind	Heat	Damp	Dry	Cold
• Zang	Liver	Heart	Spleen	Lung	Kidney
• Fu	Gallbladder	Small Intestine	Stomach	Large Intestine	Bladder
Directions	East	South	Middle	West	North
Tastes	Sour	Bitter	Sweet	Pungent	Salty
Sense Organs	Eye	Tongue	Mouth	Nose	Ear
Tissues	Tendon	Vessel	Muscle	Skin and Hair	Bone
Emotions	Anger	Joy	Worry *	Grief	Fear

5 Tastes

BITTER
[Effects heart and small intestine] Clears heat, dries dampness, stimulates appetite, and promotes urination and bowel movements

SWEET
[Effects stomach and spleen organs] Builds blood and energy, slows down acute reactions, and neutralizes the toxic effects of other foods; also lubricates and nourishes the body

PUNGENT
[Effects lungs and large intestine] Stimulates appetite, and promotes distribution of nutrients and circulation

SALTY
[Effects kidney and bladder] Softens hardness, nourishes blood, lubricates intestines to induce bowel movements, and helps get rid of accumulations

SOUR
[Effects liver and gallbladder] Astringent — which helps calm or stop abnormal discharges, fluids, and other substances such as diarrhea and heavy sweating

Traditional Chinese Medicine 5 Elements Food Chart

	FIRE (bitter)	EARTH (sweet)	METAL (pungent)	WATER (salty)	WOOD (sour)
Grains	Amaranth Corn	Millet Barley	Rice	Buckwheat	Oats Wheat Rye
Legumes	Red Lentil	Garbanzo Peas	Navy Soy	Aduki Black Kidney Pinto	Green Lentil Mung Lima
Nuts/Seeds	Sunflower Pistachio	Pine Nut Pumpkin	Almonds	Black Sesame Walnut	Brazil Cashew
Vegetables	Beet Dandelion Root Okra Red Bell Pepper Scallion Tomato	Cabbage Carrot Parsnip Rutabaga Spinach Squash	Asparagus Broccoli Celery Cucumber Mustard Green Onion Radish	Kale Mushrooms Seaweeds Water Chestnut	Green Bell Pepper Green Pea Lettuce String Bean Zucchini
Fruits	Cherry Persimmon	Fig Orange Papaya Pineapple Strawberry	Apricot Banana Pear	Mulberry Pomegranate Raspberry Watermelon	Avocado Grape Lemon Lime Plum
Cautions	Chocolate Sugar	Meat	Eggs	Cheese	Soft Dairy

Dr. Ken Grey and Carol Maglio

J & E Wine Time

Our version of a time signature is a loose and fun interpretation.
If you cook with wine like we do, then like most inebriated activities,
it will fly by and your fun and laughter will lead the way to an
exciting, tasty creation.

1 glass   *J&E Time Signature*   = ½ hour to 1 hour

½ bottle   *J&E Time Signature*   = 1 hour to 2 hours

1 bottle   *J&E Time Signature*   = 2 to 3 hours

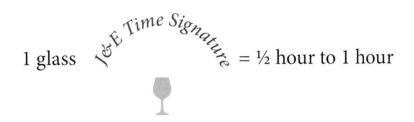

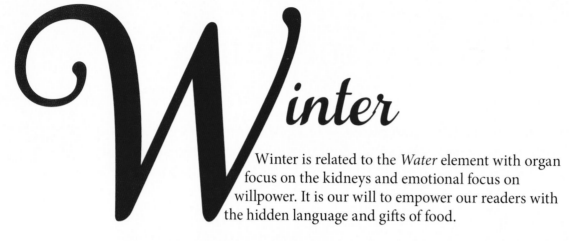

Winter

Winter is related to the *Water* element with organ focus on the kidneys and emotional focus on willpower. It is our will to empower our readers with the hidden language and gifts of food.

Moving into winter, we adjust our diet to accommodate the cold weather. It is important to make food choices that produce more heat. Packing on the pounds can be avoided by simply lessening the portions of these richer foods.

Vegetables can be eaten daily — some as salad but most in cooked form, either steamed or baked. Vegetable soups, especially on a cold or wet day, are nutritious, warming, and easy to digest. Some fried or sautéed foods fit more with the winter diet than in other seasons. Although too much heated oil is hard on the liver.

The energy of nature's plants is now focused in the roots below ground. So root vegetables like carrots, turnips, onions, and potatoes are the way to go. Garlic and ginger root will heat you up and adding cayenne to your dishes will warm you to your toes by warming your blood and increasing circulation.

Cooked whole grains make an excellent staple in winter. Complex carbohydrates burn well in the body as fuel and are good for the intestines for elimination. Millet and buckwheat are good body heaters and less starchy than other grains like brown rice, wheat, barley, or oats. If grains are cooked and eaten with beans such as red aduki beans, mung beans, black beans, or lentils, you will have a complete protein. Beans like the aduki are good for the kidneys, while black beans assist with virility.

Since Winter is related to the Water element, seafood such as fish and seaweed are highly beneficial, low fat sources of protein, minerals, and vitamins. Fish oils are known for their cancer preventing properties. Seaweed is known for the ability to remove accumulated radiation and other heavy metals and toxins.

Winter Superfoods

SWEET POTATOES are full of fiber, potassium, and vitamins A and C. Bake, roast, steam, or mash for an easy weeknight side dish. They are a year-round superfood.

POMEGRANATES and their juice have been credited with everything from lowering cholesterol to managing Type 2 diabetes and helping to fight prostate cancer. The tasty red seeds called arils are a good source of fiber, vitamins B and C, potassium, and polyphenols (antioxidants). They are loaded with antioxidants and compounds called tannins that may help keep the heart healthy.

KALE is praised for its anti-inflammatory properties and high levels of vitamins A and C, lutein, zeaxanthin, iron, and calcium.

GRAPEFRUIT with its red and pink varieties is also high in lycopene, the same antioxidant that's in cooked tomatoes and which may help prevent cancer, heart disease and macular degeneration.

CRANBERRIES AND CRANBERRY JUICE contain antioxidants that may protect against certain types of cancer and heart disease.

KIDNEY BEANS are high in soluble fiber that helps regulate blood sugar levels.

COCOA is high in phenols and flavonoids. Cocoa has twice as many antioxidants as red wine and almost three times as many as green tea.

Winter Appetizers

Chapter 1
Winter Appetizers

Fine as a stand-alone meal or as a precursor to Juice & Essence entrées. Our appetizers add an exploratory jolt to the most scrutinizing culinary adventurer!

Ginger Carrot Passion Soup

Birth & Balance

Serves 20

Combining these two outstanding roots (ginger and carrots), for the purposes of strengthening immunity and libido, is an ancient multicultural treatment. We were asked to come up with a cold soup, a main course, and a dessert for an "Arts in After School" committee fundraising luncheon. This important invitation allowed us to share healthful concepts of inventive cuisine for a new approach in school dietary education. This soup is easy to make, a dependable hit, and very user friendly.

Juice & Essence

The ginger and carrots benefit the kidneys, liver, and spleen in this immune system and vitality boosting soup. The combination of the ingredients creates an effect for improved circulation thanks to the ginger. The carrots offer more energy, better eyes, and increased metabolism and libido.

COMPLEMENT – A nice full-bodied Chardonnay will stand up nicely to the sweetness and richness of this soup. Something wood-aged from California's Napa Valley or Bordeaux. Look for butter, oak, and balanced fruit/crispness.

Ingredients

- 3 tablespoons clarified butter
- 4 tablespoons olive oil
- 1½ cups chopped sweet onion
- 1 teaspoon ground caraway seed
- ¼ teaspoon cayenne pepper
- ½ teaspoon ground turmeric
- ¼ teaspoon ground allspice
- ¼ teaspoon ground cardamom
- ¾ teaspoon ground anise seed
- 1 teaspoon ground white pepper
- 1 small head of garlic, cloves peeled and chopped
- ¾ cup grated fresh ginger
- 5 lbs. peeled, sliced carrots
- 1 medium Red Garnet sweet potato, peeled and chopped
- 12 cups chicken stock
- 3 cups water
- 2 cups sherry
- 4 teaspoons sea salt

Directions

1. Add butter and oil to a stockpot set over medium-high heat.
2. When hot, add the onion and sauté for 5 minutes.
3. Add the caraway seeds, cayenne pepper, turmeric, allspice, cardamom, anise seeds, white pepper and stir to combine.
4. Now add the garlic and ginger and sauté for 3 minutes.
5. Add the carrots and sweet potato and continue to sauté for 5 minutes more.
6. Stir in the chicken stock and water.
7. Cover and bring the mixture to a boil.
8. Lower the heat and continue to cook until the vegetables are tender; approximately 20 minutes.
9. Remove the pot from the heat.
10. Using an immersion blender, puree the soup until it is a smooth consistency.
11. Return the soup to the stove over medium-high heat and stir in the sherry and sea salt.
12. Cover and bring to a boil.
13. Reduce heat to low and continue to cook for 30 minutes.
14. Remove from heat and let cool down before placing in the refrigerator overnight. This allows the flavors to really blend together.

Lime Zest Fried Oysters & Calamari

J&E Time Signature

Birth & Balance

Serves 4

Originally invented as a topping for our **Super Cool Curry** (page 60), we decided that this could easily stand on its own. Perfect flavor, crunch, and balance. We "healthified" this dish by using whole wheat panko and garbanzo/fava bean flour. The lime zest gives this a real kick in the fresh ass! We dare you to turn your nose up at this one!

Juice & Essence

Oysters and calamari offer liver and kidney benefits that translate to assistance with insomnia, sexual dysfunction, restlessness, and irritability. Garbanzo beans work to help build blood and are the highest in iron of legumes with lots of protein which will also aid in reducing symptoms of nervousness, indecision, and internal and external dryness.

Complement or Contrast

CONTRAST – *Look for a dry, super-crisp white with pear/apple finish to contrast the fried seafood. Examples would be a central Napa Sauvignon Blanc, Albarino, or Italian.*

Ingredients

- 1 cup whole wheat panko
- 1 cup garbanzo/fava bean flour
- 2 teaspoons sea salt
- 2 teaspoons freshly ground black pepper
- Zest of 1 lime
- 1 dozen shucked oysters from Apalachicola, Florida
- 2 cups cleaned calamari, bodies sliced into ½"-rings, tentacles reserved
- 2 cups peanut oil

Directions

1 In a shallow baking dish, combine the panko, garbanzo/fava bean flour, salt, pepper, and the lime zest.

2 Add the peanut oil to a stockpot or deep fryer and heat the oil to a temperature of 375°F.

3 Dredge the oysters in the panko mixture and add in batches to the hot oil.

4 Fry until the breading is golden brown, approximately 5 minutes.

5 Transfer to paper towels to drain.

6 Maintain the oil at 375°F.

7 Now dredge the calamari slices and tentacles in the panko mixture and add in batches to the hot oil.

8 Fry just until browned, approximately 3 minutes. *(Do not overcook!)*

9 Transfer to paper towels to drain. Serve immediately.

*We serve them on top of the **Super Cool Curry.***

Bubble, Bubble, Shrimp Boil & Trouble!

Birth & Balance

Serves 4

Shrimp boils are easy-peasy and are great for family gatherings and fun sports events. This was one of our contributions to the 2011 Super Bowl fare. Guaranteed you will not find a comparable seasoning for shrimp. Hence the title!!!

Juice & Essence

Shrimp is nourishing to the liver and invigorating to the kidneys. It is also warming and energizing. Since it is rich in iodine, it will assist with low back pain, male virility, and fatigue. Cayenne is a natural cure for ulcers, aids with improving circulation, warms the body, and supports heart health.

CONTRAST – The peppery finish of this shrimp would do great with a little fruit. I would go with a domestic Riesling to bring in a little sweetness.

Ingredients

- 1 cup water
- 1 cup chicken stock
- Juice of 1 lemon
- Juice of 1 clementine
- ¾ cup chopped white onion
- 1 tablespoon minced garlic
- 1½ teaspoons ground mustard seed
- 1 teaspoon ground cayenne pepper
- 1 teaspoon ground ancho chile
- 1 teaspoon paprika
- 5 teaspoons sea salt
- ¼ cup olive oil
- 1 fresh rosemary sprig
- 2 lbs. large shrimp in shells
- 1 teaspoon sea salt
- 1 teaspoon ground cayenne pepper
- 1 teaspoon paprika
- 1 teaspoon white pepper

Directions

1 Add the water, chicken stock, lemon juice, clementine juice, onion, garlic, ground mustard seed, teaspoon cayenne pepper, ancho chile, 1 teaspoon paprika, 5 teaspoons sea salt, olive oil, and rosemary sprig to a large stockpot. Bring to a boil over high heat. Turn heat to medium, cover and simmer for 30 minutes.

2 Meanwhile, add the 1 teaspoon each of the sea salt, cayenne pepper, paprika, and white pepper to a large bowl. Set aside.

3 Remove the cover from the stockpot and add the shrimp.

4 Cook the shrimp until they turn pink and are just cooked, about 3 minutes.

5 Remove from heat and drain the shrimp out of the cooking liquid.

6 Place the shrimp in the bowl with the spice mixture and mix well to coat each shrimp.

7 Peel and eat! Enjoy!

Swordfish & Conch Fritters

Birth & Balance

Serves 4 to 6

We love conch fritters. Swordfish is an autumn/winter fish and during their run we wanted to capitalize on their meaty goodness and paired it with the chewy sweetness of the conch. Melding into the gorgeous structure we added beautiful peppers, Old Bay, herbs, and panko....mmmmmmmm!

Juice & Essence

Swordfish and conch are great sources of omega-3 fatty acids containing both EPA and DHA. Swordfish is also a great resource for the antioxidant selenium offering 58 mcg of selenium per serving or 83% of the daily value. It is a high protein fish that supports bone health because each serving supplies 14mcg of vitamin D. Conch is generally a good source of protein, iron, selenium, B12, folate, and vitamin E. Bell peppers improve appetite and help move stagnant food in the intestines, especially in cancer cases where digestion is very poor. They also reduce swelling, promote circulation, and are rich in vitamin C. Fresh thyme helps treat cough, common cold, headache, body aches, sore throat, nausea, indigestion, and abdominal distention (bloating).

Complement or Contrast

COMPLEMENT – Northern Italian oaky Chardonnay comes to mind or the balanced fruit and minerality of a Falanghina (Central Italy). Falanghina is originally a Greek varietal that is the first vine to be grown vertically versus horizontally. To contrast the flavors, quality Champagne would be your choice for this dish. The existing oak and small bubbles of a quality Champagne will neutralize the richness of the swordfish and conch.

Ingredients

- ½ lb. swordfish, minced
- ½ lb. conch, pounded to ¼"-thickness then minced
- ⅓ cup minced green bell pepper
- 4 teaspoons minced red bell pepper
- 1 teaspoon minced fresh jalapeño pepper
- ¼ cup minced celery
- ⅓ cup minced sweet onion
- 1¼ teaspoons minced fresh thyme
- 1½ tablespoons Old Bay Seasoning™
- ½ cup mayonnaise
- 1 cup whole wheat panko
- Safflower Oil for frying
- *Avocado Dipping Sauce* (page 136)

Directions

1. In a large bowl, combine the swordfish, conch, peppers, celery, onion, thyme, Old Bay Seasoning, mayonnaise, and panko.

2. Mix well.

3. Form into 2" patties and set aside.

4. Put enough safflower oil in a cast iron pan to measure ½" in depth and place over medium-high heat until hot.

5. Place the fritters into the hot oil and cook on both sides until golden brown.

6. Remove from the oil when cooked through and place on a paper towel-lined pan to drain.

7. Serve while hot with our *Avocado Dipping Sauce.*

J&E Curry Chicken Wings

Birth & Balance

Serves 4

Really, really tasty chicken wings! That's what we wanted. Nothing profound, just damn good! Going with curry allowed us to check the versatility of our *J&E Curry* blend while indulging in an appetizer dish that is frequently craved. Very delicious as is…there is no additional dip required!

Juice & Essence

Curry is blood moving, energizing, and warming. It also contains immune boosting qualities due to the circulation enhancing spices. Additional benefits to the spleen, stomach, and kidney channels. Secondary benefits from chicken include the treatment of poor appetite, edema, frequent urination, and fatigue. Honey works to balance liver functions, relieve pain, and assist with detoxification, stomach ulcers, canker sores, high blood pressure, and constipation. Vinegar helps with food poisoning, food stagnation, bad moods, and poor circulation; rectifies bleeding and helps remove parasites.

CONTRAST – A bold and spicy red such as a Malbec, Zinfandel, or Syrah is perfect here. The use of a fruit-forward, dry, powerful wine is needed to stand up to this spicy, intense, herbaceous dish. The combination will urge you to take another bite….and another sip!

Ingredients

- ½ cup cider vinegar
- ½ cup water
- ⅔ cup bourbon whiskey
- 4 tablespoons honey
- ½ teaspoon ground cayenne pepper
- 2 teaspoons sea salt
- 2 tablespoons *J&E Curry* (page 134)
- ⅓ cup olive oil
- 1 tablespoon sea salt
- 2 teaspoons onion powder
- 1½ teaspoons garlic powder
- 2 teaspoons smoked paprika
- Juice of 1 lemon
- 3 lbs. chicken wings, separated at joint
- ½ cup cold water
- 1 tablespoon cornstarch

Directions

1   Place the cider vinegar, ½ cup water, bourbon whiskey, honey, cayenne pepper, salt, and *J&E Curry* in a small saucepan and bring to a boil over high heat.

2   Turn the heat down to low and simmer for 1 hour.

3   Meanwhile, in a large bowl, mix together the olive oil, salt, onion powder, garlic powder, smoked paprika, and lemon juice.

4   Add the chicken wings and stir to coat with the marinade.

5   Cover and set aside at room temperature for 30 minutes.

6   Heat a gas grill to medium.

7   Coat grill with cooking spray.

8   Remove the chicken wings from the marinade and grill for 15 to 20 minutes until cooked through. Continue to turn wings as they are cooking

9   Move the cooked wings to the top grate for added dryness if desired.

10   Place the wings into a large bowl.

11   Once the sauce has simmered for 1 hour, mix together the ½ cup cold water and cornstarch and add the mixture to the sauce.

12   Bring back to a boil over medium-high heat and cook for a couple of minutes until the sauce is thickened.

13   Remove from heat and pour over the chicken wings in the bowl.

14   Toss to coat the wings with the sauce and serve immediately

Parmesan Stuffed Sausage Meatballs with Grapefruit, Fennel & Mint Marmalade

Birth & Balance

Serves 4

Creating a fun, simple appetizer made from spicy ground pork sausage and freshly grated Parmesan seemed right. A sweet, bitter, cool marmalade to go with it set it over the top. We felt the tastes together would be outstanding and we were right. You are sure to enjoy, as we did, the way the sweet-tangy bitterness melds with the heat and intense flavor of the meatballs.

Juice & Essence

Pork moistens and nourishes organs, tonifies qi, strengthens digestion, and aids in conditions of internal dryness. Health concerns related to pork are balanced with cholesterol lowering, cleansing, and antiparasite benefits of grapefruit. Additional benefits to the nervous system, respiratory functions, and liver are also achieved with this balanced combination. The combination of herbs support digestion and add enjoyable complexity.

CONTRAST – A nice Chianti would break through this dish nicely. Remember to choose a Chianti Classico Riserva such as Marchese Antinori.

Prepare the Sausage Meatballs

Ingredients

- 1½ lbs. hot Italian sausage, removed from casings
- ¼ cup fresh Parmesan chunks (approximately ¼"-pieces)
- 1 tablespoon fresh flat leaf parsley, finely chopped
- 2 tablespoons olive oil
- *Grapefruit, Fennel & Mint Marmalade* (page 138)

Directions

1 Take sausage meat and form into patties about 2" in diameter.

2 Place a few pieces of Parmesan chunks and some parsley into center of patty.

3 Enclose the sausage around the cheese and parsley to make a meatball.

4 Continue with remaining sausage, cheese, and parsley. You should have about 20 meatballs.

5 Heat olive oil in a nonstick sauté pan until shimmering.

6 Add meatballs and sauté, turning to brown on all sides.

7 Place on paper towel covered rack to drain.

8 Serve with *Grapefruit, Fennel & Mint Marmalade.*

Akra (Trinidadian Salt-Fish Cakes)

Birth & Balance

Serves 4 to 6

A fun Trinidadian finger food using salted cod, most likely originating from a time when salting was used to preserve food. The West Indies are known for incorporating many cultures into their culinary landscape. Dr. Ken's mom, Yvonne, is known for making the best Akra ever…but we are biased! This is based on her recipe.

Juice & Essence

Akra is strengthening to the spleen/pancreas, energizing and tonifying to the thyroid due to high iodine content of salt cod. It also offers some circulatory benefits, digestion assistance, and immune enhancement to be found in the herb and spice content.

CONTRAST – The salty, spicy fish cakes need a crisp, cold rosé with some festive fruit. French of course…maybe from Provence.

Ingredients

- 1 lb. boneless salted codfish
- 2 teaspoons white vinegar
- 1 tablespoon olive oil
- 1 tablespoon minced jalapeño, seeds and membrane removed
- ¼ cup minced onion
- 2 tablespoons chopped scallions, white and light green parts only
- 2 cups whole wheat pastry flour
- ½ teaspoon baking powder
- 1 tablespoon chopped fresh thyme
- 1 tablespoon freshly ground black pepper
- 1½ cups water
- Vegetable oil for frying

Directions

1 Place the codfish into a large bowl and add enough water to just cover the fish.

2 Stir in the vinegar and let the fish soak for 20 minutes.

3 Drain the water/vinegar mixture from the codfish and place the codfish into a large pot.

4 Add enough water to cover the codfish and bring to a boil.

5 Boil the codfish for 20 minutes and then drain out the water from the pot.

6 At this point, taste to be sure the salt level is to your liking. The soul of the Akra is in the codfish, so be careful not to diminish the taste of the fish too much. If it is still too salty: drain, add fresh water to cover, and bring to a boil for another 5 to 10 minutes.

7 Crumble the drained codfish into a large bowl, being sure to remove any bones you may find, and then set aside.

8 Heat the olive oil in a small sauté pan over medium-high heat.

9 Add the jalapeño, onion, and scallions and sauté for 2 to 3 minutes to soften.

10 Remove from heat and cool to room temperature.

11 Add enough vegetable oil to a large cast iron skillet to a depth of ¼" and heat to 350°F.

12 While oil is heating, add the flour, baking powder, thyme, pepper and jalapeño mixture to the codfish.

13 Add the water and mix the batter well.

14 Once the oil is to temperature, drop the batter by heaping tablespoons into the hot oil.

15 Fry on each side until golden brown.

16 Test with a fork to be sure the batter is cooked through. Serve immediately.

Beef Carpaccio with Garbanzo~Lemongrass Sauce

Birth & Balance

Serves 4

This is a traditional Italian dish that holds weight in our hearts. Our version specifies grass-fed beef as an important health and taste item. We made a garbanzo bean, fresh jalapeño, and lemongrass infused oil topping that we've never seen before. Clearly the simple nature of this dish warrants the investigation of any palate with a love for pure flavors.

Juice & Essence

Beef wins big in the enrichment of qi (energy) and in the blood department. While strengthening joints and connective tissue, beef will help treat edema, certain types of low back pain, knee pain, and weakness. Garbanzo beans help to heal the pancreas, stomach, and heart (interesting that they are shaped somewhat like a heart). Garbanzo beans contain more iron than other legumes and are also a good source of unsaturated fat. Lemongrass can be easily used for treating digestive tract spasms, stomachaches, high blood pressure, vomiting, cough, achy joints (rheumatism), fever, the common cold, and exhaustion. It is also used to kill germs and as a mild astringent. Capers are useful in assisting with the treatment of diabetes, fungal infections, chest congestion, intestinal worms, and skin diseases caused by parasites called "leishmaniasis." Capers are also good tonifiers of energy (qi) and blood. Cilantro is warming and beneficial to the lungs and large intestine. Cilantro is a breath freshener, balances the cold effects of clams and crabs, and assists with loss of appetite, hernia, nausea, diarrhea, measles, hemorrhoids, joint pain, and infections caused by bacteria or fungus.

CONTRAST – Okay, the richness of the meat and saltiness of the cheese needs a dry wine with nice tannins and a little fruit. Tempranillo! Spain! Ribera del Duero or Rioja.

Prepare the Garbanzo~Lemongrass Sauce

Ingredients

- ⅓ cup canned, drained garbanzo beans
- ½ cup *J&E Lemongrass Infused Oil* (page 132)
- 1 large clove garlic, pressed
- ¼ teaspoon fresh ground white pepper
- ¼ teaspoon sea salt
- 1 teaspoon Spanish capers
- 1 tablespoon minced fresh cilantro

Directions

1 Place the garbanzo beans, *J&E Lemongrass Infused Oil,* garlic, white pepper, sea salt, capers, and cilantro into a blender.

2 Blend on high until all of the ingredients are processed to a smooth consistency and set aside.

Prepare the Beef

Ingredients

- ¾ lb. grass-fed organic beef filet (freeze for about 2 hours to help with ease of thinly slicing)
- 1 small fresh jalapeño, thinly sliced
- 2 teaspoons small capers
- Provolone cheese
- Kale micro greens

Directions

1 Thinly slice the beef to ⅛"-thickness.

2 Place on plastic wrap and cover with another piece of plastic wrap.

3 Pound lightly to make thinner slices.

4 Place the pounded beef onto a chilled serving platter in a single layer.

5 Scatter the jalapeño and capers over the top of the beef.

6 Shave thin slices of provolone cheese over the beef to taste.

7 Place a mound of the kale micro greens in the center of the serving platter on top of the beef.

8 Drizzle the sauce to taste over the beef and serve immediately.

Winter Entrées

Chapter 2
Winter Entrées

We took the best the world has to offer and refined each contribution with respect to cultural ideals. We used our palates, taste experience, and history of chef interactions to lovingly create our entrées.

Shepherds Rabbit Stew Surprise

J&E Time Signature

Birth & Balance

Serves 6

Via text message:

KEN: Rabbit stew? In a pot pie? Leeks, roots and wabbit, root purée? When are we doing goose?

CAROL: We have rabbit!!!

KEN: Don't tell Elmer Fudd.

CAROL: Ha Ha!!

KEN: Shhhhhh! Be vewy vewy quiet!

CAROL: Might want to think about veggies in with the rabbit since we are taking out the turnip, rutabagas and potato. I have Swiss chard, Brussels sprouts, onion, garlic, celery and herbs. Did we want more in with the rabbit? For the topping should we add sweet potato? Think about it. Can't wait for Wednesday!!!

KEN: Sweet potato sounds delightful. And what's in with the wabbit sounds complete at the moment except add carrot. Wabbit season! Duck season! Wabbit season!

CAROL: Can't wait. Love wabbit season!!!

KEN: Our Elmer dialogue alone makes it on this page ;)))

Juice & Essence

Rabbit is very high in protein and low in cholesterol and fat. It is energizing and blood building with benefits to the stomach, spleen, and kidneys. Honey and hawthorn strengthen the heart. Elderberries ward off colds and boost the immune system. Parsnips, rutabaga, and turmeric are beneficial to the lungs, spleen, stomach, and liver thereby reducing and helping to expel mucus, clearing chest congestion, relieving inflammation, pain, and swelling as well as poor circulation.

Complement *or* Contrast

COMPLEMENT – A spicy red would be great! Our choices would be Malbec, Zinfandel, or a great South African blend such as Rustenberg.

Prepare Beer/Berry Reduction

Ingredients

- 3 cups Dogfish Head™ Chateau Jiahu Beer (honey & hawthorn fruit fermented with grape concentrate)
- ¼ cup dried hawthorn berries
- ¼ cup dried elderberries

Directions

Put all of the above ingredients into a saucepan and reduce over medium-high heat for 20 minutes and set aside.

Prepare Millet

Ingredients

- 1 teaspoon olive oil
- ¼ cup whole millet
- 1 cup boiling water

Directions

1. Heat the oil in a saucepan over high heat until shimmering.
2. Add the millet and stir until it has browned slightly.
3. Add the boiling water, cover and cook for 25 to 30 minutes until the millet is cooked through and all of the water has been absorbed; this way we do not lose the nutrients of the millet.
4. Set aside.

Shepherds Rabbit Stew Surprise ~ *continued*

Prepare Topping

Ingredients

- 1½ cups diced rutabaga
- ¾ cup diced turnip
- 2½ cups chopped peeled red potato
- 3 cups diced sweet potato
- 2 teaspoons sea salt
- 7 tablespoons unsalted butter
- 1 teaspoon freshly ground black pepper

Directions

1   Place the vegetables in a large stockpot.

2   Add enough water to cover 1" above the vegetables and stir in the salt.

3   Bring to a boil then reduce the heat and simmer for 20 minutes, or until everything is cooked through.

4   Drain the water from the pot.

5   Rice the vegetables into a large bowl using a potato ricer.

6   Stir in the butter, black pepper, and the reserved millet.

7   Cover and set aside.

Prepare Rabbit

Ingredients

- 1 whole rabbit (2½ to 3 lbs.), trimmed and cut into 6 pieces (include the kidney)
- 2 tablespoons red wine vinegar
- 1 tablespoon olive oil
- 2 teaspoons sea salt
- 1 teaspoon paprika
- 2 cups cold water
- ¼ cup olive oil
- 1 tablespoon freshly grated turmeric root
- 1 cup chopped onion
- 4 large garlic cloves, pressed
- 1½ cups chopped leek
- 1 cup diced carrots
- 1 cup diced celery (include some of the leaves)
- 1 cup diced parsnips
- 1½ cups chicken broth
- 1½ cups water
- 1 cup shredded Brussels sprouts
- 2 cups shredded Swiss chard
- 1 teaspoon minced habanero pepper
- 2½ teaspoons minced fresh marjoram
- 2½ teaspoons minced fresh thyme
- 2½ teaspoons minced fresh sage

Directions

1 Preheat oven to 400°F.

2 Mix together the rabbit, vinegar, 1 tablespoon olive oil, 2 teaspoons salt, 1 teaspoon paprika, and 2 cups cold water in a bowl and let sit for 15 minutes.

3 Add the ¼ cup of olive oil to a large stockpot.

4 Place over high heat until the oil is shimmering.

5 Remove the rabbit from the soaking liquid, discarding the liquid.

6 Sear the rabbit pieces and the kidney until nicely browned.

7 Remove from the pot and set aside.

8 To the stockpot, add the turmeric root, onion, garlic, leeks, carrots, celery, and parsnips.

9 Sauté the vegetables until just starting to soften.

10 Add the rabbit back into the pot.

11 Strain the beer/berry reduction into the pot.

12 Add the chicken broth and 1½ cups water.

13 Bring just to a boil.

14 Cover and reduce heat to low and cook for 20 minutes and remove the rabbit. Add the Brussels sprouts, Swiss chard, habanero pepper, marjoram, thyme, and sage.

15 Continue to cook uncovered over low heat.

16 Remove the rabbit meat from the bones (we recommend using your hands to do this). Gently shred the meat into small pieces and add back to the stockpot. Stir to combine and remove from the heat.

17 Place the rabbit stew mixture into a 2-quart casserole dish.

18 Gently spoon the topping mixture over the stew to cover completely.

19 Place in the oven and cook for 30 to 35 minutes until topping is lightly browned and the stew is bubbling.

20 Remove from oven and let rest for 10 minutes before serving.

Herbed Grilled Cheese

Birth & Balance

Serves 4

We did not know that more poetry could be made from a grilled cheese sandwich…but we did it. Delicious! An amazing Juice & Essence meal with no meat involved! The fun in this was making the perfectly balanced herb butter to slather onto our sprouted multigrain bread and adding paper thin slices of pear just to stun your taste buds while adding to the nutritional benefits.

Juice & Essence

The magic of this dish is in the bread and herb complex. Herbs like marjoram benefit the spleen, lungs, and stomach which will assist with clearing summer heat, water retention, lack of appetite, bad breath (halitosis), bloating, and food accumulation. The wheat found in most multigrain breads helps to tonify the kidneys, builds yin, and calms palpitations. It also helps with insomnia, irritability, menopausal difficulty, and emotional instability. Grains in their whole state are generally beneficial in the treatment of cancer and other serious degenerations. We chose to use sprouted multigrain bread due to the very special digestible nature. When wheat or any other seed is sprouted, it seldom produces an allergic reaction. Depending on how far a seed is allowed to sprout, it develops from a protein or starch to a leafy green or low-starch vegetable. Sprouted grains also have a cooling and cleansing nature. Cheese is a kidney yin enhancer by rectifying kidney yin deficiency, and based on this function cheese may aid in correcting complaints of dizziness, ringing in the ears, dry throat, dry mouth, fever, low backaches, weak legs, and spontaneous sweating.

Complement or Contrast

CONTRAST – This cheesy, soul warming, and sturdy dish will be best enjoyed with a medium finish, dry, light red such as a young Bordeaux, Chianti, or California Merlot. This type of wine will lift the dish and create a lighter dining experience.

Ingredients

- ¼ cup salted butter, melted
- 2 tablespoons Dijon mustard
- ¾ teaspoon minced fresh marjoram
- ½ teaspoon minced fresh rosemary
- ¾ teaspoon minced fresh thyme
- 1 cup shredded Irish aged cheddar cheese
- 1 cup shredded Swiss raclette cheese
- 1 cup shredded Irish Blarney Castle cheese (Gouda style)
- 1 D'Anjou red pear, sliced paper thin
- 8 slices sprouted multigrain bread

Directions

1 In a small bowl, combine the butter, mustard, marjoram, rosemary, and thyme.

2 Heat a grill pan over medium-high heat.

3 Spread one side of each piece of bread with the herb butter.

4 Place four slices, buttered side down, in the heated grill pan.

5 Top with a mixture of the three cheeses, using half of the cheese.

6 Place some of the pear slices on top of the cheese and put the remaining cheese on top of the pear.

7 Top with the remaining bread slices, buttered side up, pushing down lightly.

8 Grill for about 5 minutes on each side, or until nicely toasted and all of the cheese has melted.

9 Remove from the pan and let rest for a few minutes before slicing and serving.

Yogurt Marinated Chicken Breasts

Birth & Balance

Serves 4

Dr. Ken was treating a patient and trying to explain the process of how we create a recipe. In doing so, the patient explained the flavors and the foods she enjoys eating. This recipe encompasses all the flavors and textures she likes.

Juice & Essence

The star of this dish — chicken — is a tonic to the kidneys and spleen and warming to the core. Both energizing and blood building with overall yin nourishing elements increased by the use of a yogurt marinade. This adds moistness to the chicken and via digestion the lungs and large intestine therefore helping to resolve dry cough, relieve thirst, and constipation due to dryness.

CONTRAST – This is a unique instance whereas the food component is the acid. The contrasting elements of this dish stem from the acidic and slightly sour aspects of the yogurt. The warmer notes of Pinot Noir are elegant and dry with good fruit that temper the yogurt. Burgundy for elegance; Russian River for fruit.

Ingredients

- 3 cups Greek-style yogurt
- 1 teaspoon ground cardamom
- 2 teaspoons sea salt
- ½ teaspoon freshly ground black pepper
- 1 teaspoon ground mustard
- 2 teaspoons pressed garlic
- 1 tablespoon chopped fresh cilantro
- 2 lbs. boneless, skinless organic chicken breasts

Directions

1 In a large bowl, mix together the yogurt, cardamom, salt, pepper, ground mustard, garlic, and cilantro.

2 Add the chicken to the bowl and stir to coat the chicken with the yogurt mixture.

3 Pierce the chicken all over several times with a fork.

4 Cover and let marinate overnight or for at least 30 minutes.

5 Heat a grill to high heat.

6 Coat the grates with grilling/cooking spray.

7 Remove the chicken from the yogurt marinade letting the excess drip off.

8 Place the chicken on the grill.

9 Turn the heat down to medium.

10 Continue to cook for 15 minutes total, turning over halfway through, until chicken is cooked thoroughly. Serve immediately.

Super Cool Curry

Birth & Balance

Serves 4

We were thinking of adding a vegetable dish and came up with this. Later we added a modification of **Lime Zest Fried Oysters & Calamari** (page 36) as a topping…mmmm! For awhile we craved making a curry dish influenced by our experiences with Thai cuisine. This is a proper veggie Thai curry with a J&E twist!

Juice & Essence

This dish has an energizing, detoxifying, strengthening, and immune boosting blend of spices and herbs which are beneficial to the kidneys, liver, spleen/pancreas, and stomach. A very warming and circulatory invigorating seasoning blend with cancer fighting anti-inflammatory and arthritic pain reducing qualities. Turmeric is very beneficial for circulation, gets rid of dampness, and assists with regulating menses and menses pain. Coconut milk benefits the spleen, stomach, large intestine and is warming with properties that treat diabetic wasting thirst, edema, difficulty urinating, and worms. Carrot adds to the spleen and lung benefits while treating indigestion and cough. Basil benefits the lung, spleen, stomach, and large intestines while helping to detox, restore digestion, relieve gas complaints, and warm the body.

Complement or Contrast

CONTRAST – A spicy, complex dish rich in herbs and spices calls for a slightly dry, fruity white wine. I would pour a nice, semi-dry Riesling from Northern Italy, Austria, or the United States.

Prepare Curry

Ingredients

- 2 teaspoons celery salt
- 4 teaspoons ground cumin
- ¼ teaspoon ground ginger
- 2 teaspoons paprika
- ½ teaspoon ground mustard
- 3 teaspoons ground turmeric
- 2 teaspoons onion powder
- 1 tablespoon Sambal chili paste
- 1 tablespoon peanut oil

Directions

1 Combine all of the above ingredients together in a small bowl.

2 Set aside.

Prepare Vegetables

Ingredients

- ¼ cup peanut oil
- 4 garlic cloves, pressed
- 1 tablespoon grated fresh ginger
- 3 scallions, diced
- 1, 3"-piece lemon grass, trimmed and quartered lengthwise
- 5 small dried Thai chili peppers, broken in half (for less heat, discard some seeds)
- ¾ cup chopped red bell pepper
- 1½ cups sliced carrots
- 2 cups chicken broth
- 1, 13.5-ounce can coconut milk
- 1½ cups chopped plum tomato
- 1 cup broccoli florets
- 1 cup snow peas, trimmed
- 3 baby bok choy, chopped
- ¼ cup bamboo shoots
- ¼ cup fresh basil, sliced

Directions

1 Heat the peanut oil in a stockpot set over medium heat.

2 When hot, add the garlic, ginger, scallions, lemongrass, Thai chili peppers and the curry mixture.

3 Sauté for 5 minutes and then add the red bell pepper and carrots.

4 Continue to sauté for 8 minutes and add the chicken broth.

5 Cover the pot and bring to a boil.

6 Once boiling, add the coconut milk and tomatoes.

7 Cover and reduce heat to low.

8 Continue to cook for 10 minutes.

9 Now add the broccoli, snow peas, bok choy, bamboo shoots and basil.

10 Cook for 5 to 8 minutes, or until vegetables are just cooked through.

11 Serve topped with the *Lime Zest Fried Oysters & Calamari.*

Savory Chicken~Shiitake Strudel

Birth & Balance
Serves 20

This parcel of goodness begs to be ravaged; however, you must savor it! We were bold in this creation of a main course for the "Arts in After School" fundraising committee luncheon by skirting the two worlds of seasonal health and decadent flavor. As you can imagine, we set out to complement the depth and meatiness of the chicken and mushrooms with the light flakiness found in a strudel. All plates were licked clean!

Juice & Essence

This strudel is strengthening and warming. The chicken foundation delivers blood and muscle building elements. Shiitake mushrooms take this dish to curative heights in the area of immune system deficiencies. An additional benefit to be had from including shiitake mushrooms is in the area of colon cancer prevention. The herb and spice combination in this dish benefit the kidneys, liver, and spleen/pancreas by increasing their qi and general circulation of blood. Fresh fennel benefits the liver, kidney, spleen, and stomach channels. Fennel also harmonizes the stomach, treats gas, bloating, reduced appetite, vomiting, and menstrual cramps. Spinach nourishes blood and stops bleeding as well as diabetic thirst.

COMPLEMENT – A medium-body red that responds to the fennel and mushrooms... Pinot Noir (Central Coast or Sonoma) or a nice blend heavy with Syrah.

Prepare the Chicken

Ingredients

- 5 lbs. boneless, skinless organic chicken breasts
- Juice of 4 lemons
- 5 garlic cloves, pressed
- 1½ teaspoons minced fresh thyme
- 1 teaspoon minced fresh rosemary
- 1½ teaspoons minced fresh sage
- 1 teaspoon minced fresh fennel fronds
- 2 teaspoons salt
- ½ cup olive oil

Directions

1. Pierce the chicken breasts all over with a fork.
2. Combine all of the remaining ingredients in a large bowl.
3. Add the chicken and stir to coat with the marinade.
4. Cover and set aside to marinate for 1 hour in a cool place.
5. Remove the chicken from the marinade.
6. Reserve the marinade and place it in a smaller bowl so you can use it to baste the chicken while grilling.
7. Heat the grill to medium-high.

Note: To oil the grill, we cut an onion in half, dipped the cut side in olive oil, and rubbed it on the grill to distribute the oil and add extra flavor.

8. Grill the chicken breasts until firm on one side.
9. Baste with the marinade and flip over to other side.
10. Continue to cook until the grill marks are apparent and the chicken is cooked through, about 5 minutes more.
11. Remove from the grill and chop into 1" pieces.
12. Set aside while preparing the vegetables.

Prepare the Vegetables

Ingredients

- ½ cup unsalted organic butter
- ½ cup olive oil
- 1½ cups diced fresh fennel
- 3 leeks (white part only), thinly sliced
- ¾ cup minced shallots
- ½ cup sliced oyster mushrooms
- 1½ cups sliced crimini mushrooms
- 2 cups sliced, stemmed shiitake mushrooms
- 2 teaspoons minced fresh thyme
- 1½ teaspoons minced fresh sage
- 3 tablespoons all-purpose flour
- 3 cups chicken broth
- 1½ lbs. fresh spinach, cooked and excess liquid squeezed out
- 12 ounces crumbled queso blanco cheese

Directions

1. Heat a large sauté pan over high heat.
2. Add the butter and olive oil to the pan.
3. Combine the fennel, leeks and shallots and add to the hot pan.
4. Sauté until the vegetables are just softened.
5. Add the mushrooms and herbs and continue to sauté until the mushrooms have given off their liquid and are almost cooked through.
6. Lower the heat to medium.
7. Sprinkle the flour over the vegetables and stir to combine.
8. Continue to sauté the flour for 1 minute, add the chicken broth and stir to combine.
9. Continue to cook until the mixture is slightly thickened.
10. Remove from the heat and add the chopped chicken, spinach, and queso blanco cheese.
11. Stir well to combine and adjust the seasoning if necessary.
12. Cover and refrigerate overnight, or until chilled through.

Prepare the Phyllo Dough Oil

Ingredients

- 3 teaspoons minced fresh basil
- 1 teaspoon minced fresh sage
- 1 teaspoon minced fresh thyme
- ½ teaspoon minced fresh fennel fronds
- 2 cups grapeseed oil
- 3 tablespoons white truffle oil
- 1 teaspoon sea salt
- 1 teaspoon freshly ground black pepper

Directions

Combine all of the ingredients in a bowl and mix well to combine.

Assembly

Ingredients

2, 16-ounce packages phyllo dough

Directions

1 Preheat oven to 400°F.
2 Take 1 phyllo leaf and place on a work surface (be sure to cover remaining dough so it will not dry out).
3 Quickly brush it lightly with some of the herb oil mixture.
4 Repeat procedure two more times. You will have used 3 pieces of phyllo dough.
5 Cut the dough in half crosswise and, using a slotted spoon, place ½ to ⅔ cup of the chicken mixture closest to the longer side of each section of dough.
6 Fold the longest end over the filling and bring in the left and right sides of the dough to the center.
7 Then wrap the top end of dough around to completely enclose the chicken.
8 Place on a parchment-lined, rimmed baking sheet (leaving enough room for the other strudels), seam side down, and brush the top with a little more herb oil mixture to coat.
9 Lightly cover the pan with plastic wrap so the dough does not dry out while you prepare the remaining strudels.
10 Repeat this procedure with the remaining dough and chicken mixture. (You will get two strudels out of each of the 3 stacked phyllo sheets.)
11 Bake the strudels in the center of the preheated oven for about 30 minutes, or until deep golden brown.
12 Let rest for 10 minutes before serving.

We served the Savory Chicken~Shiitake Strudel with our **Mead Marinated Golden Beets** (page 94) and garnished with fresh seasonal berries and chives.

Brown Down Short Ribs

Birth & Balance

Serves 6

The holiday spirit still lingering in the air made the desire for comfort food plain and clear. Why should the festivities come to an end when short ribs and brown rice pasta make such good friends? As the old year came to a close and the new one opened, rubbing, searing, and slow cooking seemed perfectly spoken. We diced and chopped, boiled then ate, filled with the spices we did create. As we sat around feeling our full tummies, while the rest of the country snowing and Florida sunny, paying tribute to warmth and fire and light, because these ribs are sure to make anyone's night.

Juice & Essence

Beef is an energizer, a blood builder, bone and connective tissue strengthener. Beef also assists with low back pain and weak knee issues. It is also the champ contributor in this dish with benefits to the spleen, liver, kidneys, and large intestine. The vegetable component in the sauce offers immune system enhancement and detox benefits via the use of carrots and celery leaves. Carrots benefit the spleen and lungs thereby helping with cough and digestion. Celery benefits the stomach and liver channels assisting with dizziness and high blood pressure. The tomato along with spices increases circulation, aids digestion, and relieves certain types of dizziness. Sugar cane is a great resource for glucose, a source of immediate energy without as many calories as refined sugar. It aids in digestion and, due to high potassium content, can act as a mild laxative. Sugar cane is high in magnesium, calcium, and riboflavin (B2).

Complement or Contrast

COMPLEMENT – B.O.C.C. (Big Olé California Cab!) When you have a rich dish with undertones of sweetness and spice, you bring in a wine that carries those notes. The combination is explosive!

Ingredients

- 4 large garlic cloves, pressed
- ½ cup olive oil
- 2 tablespoons organic honey
- 1 teaspoon onion powder
- 1 teaspoon garlic powder
- 1 teaspoon paprika
- ¼ teaspoon ground allspice
- ⅛ teaspoon ground cinnamon
- ¼ teaspoon ground cloves
- ½ teaspoon dried mustard
- ½ teaspoon fresh ground black pepper
- 1 teaspoon freshly ground Himalayan salt
- 3 lbs. short ribs, trimmed of all visible fat
- 1 cup chopped celery leaves and some tender stems
- 1 cup chopped white onion
- 2 cups chopped carrots
- 2 teaspoons minced garlic
- 1, 6-ounce can organic tomato paste
- 1 cup Pinot Noir
- 1½ teaspoons minced fresh sage
- 1 teaspoon minced fresh oregano
- ½ teaspoon minced fresh thyme
- 3 sugar cane swizzle sticks
- ¼ cup chopped pimento
- 1, 28-ounce can San Marzano whole tomatoes
- 1 cup water
- 1 lb. brown rice pasta fusilli

Directions

1 Preheat the oven to 350°F.

2 In a small bowl, mix together the garlic, olive oil, honey, onion powder, garlic powder, paprika, allspice, cinnamon, cloves, dried mustard, pepper, and salt.

3 Using a sharp knife, cut some ½" slits randomly into the flesh of the meat.

4 Rub the garlic mixture evenly into the short ribs, being sure to get the rub into the slits also.

5 Let the meat sit for 30 minutes.

6 Coat the bottom of a large Dutch oven with olive oil and place over high heat.

7 Once the oil is hot and shimmering, add the meat and brown well on each side.

8 Remove the meat to a platter and set aside.

9 Lower the temperature to medium-low and add the celery, onions, carrots, and garlic and sauté for 5 minutes.

10 Add the tomato paste and stir to combine.

11 Now add the Pinot Noir, sage, oregano, thyme, sugar cane swizzle sticks, pimento, and San Marzano tomatoes.

12 Stir the mixture to combine well.

13 Cook for 5 minutes and then break up the tomatoes with the back of a spoon to your desired texture preference.

14 Add the meat and any accumulated juices back to the pot.

15 Place the cover on and put in the oven for 2½ to 3 hours total. Be sure to stir the mixture every 25 minutes.

16 After 1½ hours of cooking, add 1 cup water and continue to cook for another hour or so. The ribs should be very tender when done.

17 Remove from the oven and set aside while cooking the pasta.

18 Cook the brown rice pasta according to the package directions.

19 Drain and serve with the short ribs.

Salt Encrusted Pompano with Black Bean Sauce

Birth & Balance

Serves 4 to 6

Since May we had spoken of encrusting a fish with salt and how fun it would be to try it! We chose Pompano due to the seasonal availability. The use of black bean sauce would contrast in color while properly elevating the unique flavors of the Pompano, stemming in part from our application of black tea leaves.

Juice & Essence

This recipe is nourishing to the kidneys, heart, and liver due to the black beans. Additional benefits to kidney and reproductive functions assisting with low back ache and knee pain, hoarseness, laryngitis, kidney stones, bed wetting, urinary difficulty, and hot flashes due to menopause. Fish with omega-3 fatty acids help us in the areas of heart disease, immune deficiency, brain development, and malnutrition. Tea brightens the eyes, clears the voice, assists with gas, cools the body, and acts as a diuretic and astringent. Tea is also a good digestive aid and cuts the fats and oils from a rich meal. Tamarind offers benefits to the heart and digestion by lowering cholesterol and softening stool. It is high in vitamin C, reduces fever, and protects against colds.

COMPLEMENT – A wine is needed that will complement the fish and properly contrast the black beans. We need a well-balanced, dry, long-finish with a solid minerality. A wine that can stand on its own, such as Terre di Tufi or Greco di Tufi (Central Italy).

Prepare Black Bean Sauce

Ingredients

- 1, 15-ounce can black beans, undrained
- ¾ cup mirin
- 1 tablespoon chili sauce with garlic
- 2 tablespoons Asian fish sauce
- 1 tablespoon soy sauce
- ½ teaspoon hot chili oil
- 2 dried Thai chili peppers
- ½ cup espresso flavored vodka
- 1 tablespoon grated fresh ginger
- 1 tablespoon pressed garlic
- ½ teaspoon onion powder
- 1 tablespoon tamarind concentrate
- ¼ teaspoon freshly ground
  Himalayan salt
- ½ teaspoon freshly ground
  black pepper

Directions

1 Combine all of the ingredients in a medium saucepan set over medium heat.

2 Cover and cook for 1 hour, stirring occasionally.

3 Lightly mash some of the beans with the back of a spoon.

4 Cover and keep warm.

Salt Encrusted Pompano
with Black Bean Sauce ~ *continued*

Prepare Fish

Ingredients

- ½ teaspoon dried black tea leaves
- ½ cup lukewarm water
- ¼ cup olive oil
- 1 tablespoon chopped fresh culantro
- 1 tablespoon chopped fresh tarragon
- ¼ teaspoon chopped fresh sage
- 1½ teaspoons chopped fresh thyme
- ½ teaspoon freshly ground Himalayan salt
- 1, 3½-lb. whole pompano, cleaned, scaled, and gutted (head and tail left on)
- 6 egg whites
- 4½ lbs. kosher salt

Directions

1 Preheat the oven to 400°F.

2 In a small bowl, combine the black tea leaves and lukewarm water.

3 Let the tea steep for 30 minutes.

4 Strain out the water and put the tea leaves into a small bowl.

5 Add the olive oil, all of the fresh herbs, and the Himalayan salt.

6 Fill the fish cavity with the mixture and set aside.

7 Lightly beat the egg whites in a large bowl.

8 Add the kosher salt and stir to combine. (The mixture will have the texture of wet sand.)

9 Line a roasting pan that is large enough to fit the fish with parchment paper.

10 Put a 1" layer of the salt mixture onto the parchment paper, being sure the salt layer is slightly larger than the fish.

11 Place the fish on top of the salt layer, being sure that the abdominal incision is covered so that none of the salt leaks into the cavity.

12 Gently pack the rest of the salt mixture over and around the fish to completely enclose it.

13 Bake the fish in the center of the preheated oven for 50 minutes.

14 Remove from oven and let rest for 10 to 15 minutes.

15 Crack the salt shell and remove the chunks of shell to expose the fish.

16 Fillet the fish and serve with the black bean sauce.

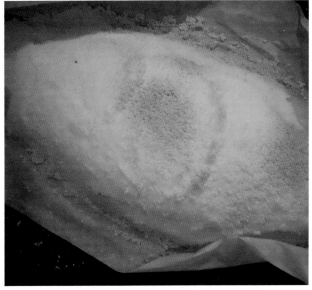

Tuna & White Bean Salad

Birth & Balance

Serves 4

We were just looking for something to munch on while we were cooking when we came up with this salad. The Spanish tuna fillets in olive oil were perfect! Add some beans, vegetables, and some crusty bread and we have a healthy, satisfying meal.

Juice & Essence

Tuna, filled with omega-3 fatty acids, is also very beneficial to the liver, kidneys-adrenals, and lungs. Blood building qualities with yin tonifying attributes of fish nicely balanced by the drying attributes of the beans. Helpful aspects of beans include beautiful skin, sharper short term memory, improved circulation, and strengthening of low back and knees. Celery benefits the stomach, spleen/pancreas, liver, improves digestion, purifies blood, and assists with vertigo and nervousness. Sunflower seeds are energizing, used to treat constipation due to dryness, and also beneficial to the spleen/pancreas.

CONTRAST – A dry and crispy Pinot Grigio such as Jermann or Villa Russiz Albarino, Muller Turgau, Northern Italian Sauvignon, Bordeaux Sauvignon, or California Pinot Gris. The world of Pinot Grigio is untapped. There are some producers that create some wonderful wines with quite a developed finish. A few extra dollars here will go quite a long way.

Ingredients

- 2, 6.7-ounce jars tuna fillets in olive oil, drained
- 1, 15-ounce can white beans, drained and rinsed
- ½ cup chopped pickled Peppadew peppers
- 2 tablespoons capers
- ¼ cup minced shallot
- ½ cup sliced celery, leaves and heart
- ⅔ cup chopped tomato
- ½ teaspoon minced fresh oregano
- ¼ teaspoon minced fresh rosemary
- ⅓ cup fresh lemon juice
- ¼ cup extra-virgin olive oil
- ¼ cup toasted sunflower seeds
- Salt and pepper to taste

Directions

1 Place the drained tuna in a large bowl.
2 Break the tuna into bite-size pieces.
3 Add the remaining ingredients and gently stir to combine.
4 Serve with toasted bread or crackers.

Wahoo Fish Stew

Birth & Balance   Serves 4

Nothing like a fish stew for restoring the soul, energizing the body, and tantalizing the taste buds! Wahoo holds its texture and taste. Stews are a great way of administering medicinal herbals such as thyme, cilantro, and oregano. It is a winter-warmer and immunity pick-me-up. This is a thoroughly satisfying and healthy stew.

Juice & Essence

Wahoo is beneficial to the kidneys, liver, and spleen. The chopped onions, tomatillo, tomato, cayenne, jalapeño, and kale help make this a detoxifying stew with blood building, strengthening, and energizing qualities. Immune system boosters like thyme and oregano, super micronutrients and antioxidant veggies such as kale, and the circulation enhancing spices cayenne and black pepper make this an extremely well rounded healthful stew. Red quinoa is very high in protein. It is a pure protein as it contains essential amino acids.

CONTRAST – Velvety with solid fruits and a flowery finish from one of my favorite places in the world — Sardinian Vermentino — or a steel fermented Chardonnay from Calabria.

Ingredients

- 2 tablespoons olive oil
- 1 cup chopped onions
- 3 cups fish stock
- 2 cups water
- ½ cup white wine
- 1 tablespoon sea salt
- ½ teaspoon freshly ground black pepper
- ¼ teaspoon ground cayenne pepper
- ½ teaspoon paprika
- ¼ teaspoon ground mustard
- ½ teaspoon celery salt
- 1 small tomatillo, chopped
- 1 whole red fresh jalapeño pepper, seeded and sliced into 3 pieces
- Juice of 1 lemon
- 2 teaspoons scallion greens, chopped
- 1 large yellow tomato, chopped
- 1 large red tomato, chopped
- 2 teaspoons fresh cilantro (leaves only)
- ½ teaspoon chopped fresh thyme
- ½ teaspoon chopped fresh oregano
- 1 cup thinly sliced green kale
- 3 tablespoons butter
- 2 lbs. Wahoo fillets
- 2 teaspoons extra-virgin olive oil
- Salt and pepper
- 2 tablespoons fresh lime juice
- 2 cups cooked red quinoa

Directions

1. Place a large stockpot over medium-high heat.
2. Add the olive oil to the hot pot and sauté the onions just until softened, about 5 minutes.
3. Add the fish stock, water, white wine, sea salt, black pepper, cayenne pepper, paprika, ground mustard, celery salt, tomatillo, jalapeño, lemon juice, scallions, and tomatoes.
4. Cover and simmer for 1 hour.
5. Now add the cilantro, thyme, and oregano.
6. Cover and cook for another 10 minutes.
7. Add the sliced kale and the butter to the stockpot.
8. Cover and turn off the heat. The kale will cook from the residual heat.
9. Meanwhile, coat the Wahoo fillets with the 2 teaspoons of olive oil and add salt and pepper to taste.
10. Heat a grill to high. (We used an infrared grill.)
11. Once the grill has come to temperature, reduce the heat to medium.
12. Grill the Wahoo for about 3½ minutes per side.
13. Remove from the grill and cut into large cubes. Add fish and the lime juice to the stock.
14. Stir to mix the fish into the stock.
15. Serve immediately in bowls over the red quinoa.

Juice & Essence Sushi

Birth & Balance

Serves 4

Creating our own sushi roll was an inspiration found on Palm Beach island at a world renowned Italian restaurant. Our bartender made us a traditional Italian aperitif while we reflected on our first paid, educating luncheon. We began with Carol's favorite fish, salmon, and went from there. The use of red quinoa and sake-infused black currants are a brilliant addition. Enjoy!

Juice & Essence

Omega-3 fatty acids in the salmon enhances brain function and mood balancing (GLAs in black currant), benefits the central nervous system. Anti-inflammatory attributes, high fiber, and protein are found in quinoa, which is also great for vegetarians who crave higher concentrated energy foods. Seaweed offers intestinal cleansing and tonifies the kidneys, making this a blood building dish that helps prevent tumors and softens masses and benefits the pericardium and therefore the heart.

COMPLEMENT – The sweet aspects and richness of salmon needs a crisp, fruity passenger in a New Zealand Sauvignon Blanc. Sweet, melon, apple, grass . . . . yum!!!

Prepare the Quinoa

Ingredients

- 1 cup red quinoa, rinsed well
- 1 cup fish stock
- ½ cup mirin

Directions

1. Combine all ingredients in a small saucepan.
2. Cover and bring to a boil over high heat.
3. Reduce heat to low and simmer for 20 minutes, or until tender and all of the liquid has been absorbed.
4. Uncover and set aside to cool.

Soak the Currants

Ingredients

- ½ cup sake
- ¼ cup dried currants

Directions

1. Pour the sake into a small sauce pan.
2. Bring just to a boil over high heat.
3. Remove from heat and add the currants.
4. Set aside to steep for 30 minutes.
5. Drain the currants from the sake, reserving the currants only.

Prepare the Salmon

Ingredients

- ½ lb. wild salmon fillets with skin
- 2 tablespoons Asian chili oil
- 1 cedar plank, soaked in water for at least 2 hours

Directions

1. Coat the salmon with the Asian chili oil.
2. Heat a grill to medium.
3. Place the cedar plank on the grate and close the lid.
4. When the plank starts smoking, it is ready.
5. Place the salmon fillets, skin side down onto the plank.
6. Close the lid and cook for 7 minutes.
7. Remove from the grill and set aside to cool.

Juice & Essence Sushi ~ *continued*

Prepare the Jerusalem Artichokes

Ingredients

- ¼ lb. Jerusalem artichokes, peeled and sliced ¼" thick
- 1 teaspoon extra-virgin olive oil

Directions

1. Heat a small sauté pan over medium heat.
2. Add the olive oil and the sliced Jerusalem artichokes.
3. Sauté the artichokes for about 8 to 10 minutes or until tender.
4. Remove from pan and set aside to cool.
5. Once they are cool, slice into strips.

Prepare the Sauce

Ingredients

- 1 tablespoon minced scallions (white part only)
- ¼ teaspoon minced garlic
- ½ teaspoon minced ginger
- 1 teaspoon chili oil
- 1 teaspoon tamarind concentrate
- ⅓ cup soy sauce
- 1 tablespoon fresh lime juice

Directions

Combine all of the ingredients into a bowl and set aside to allow the flavors to blend.

Assembly

Ingredients

- 4 sheets nori (seaweed sheets)
- 8 chives
- Bamboo mat and paddle for rolling sushi

Directions

1 Place one nori sheet on the bamboo mat.

2 Put a thin layer of quinoa over the nori.

3 Sprinkle all over with some of the currants.

4 Then add some slivers of the Jerusalem artichokes.

5 Place two chives and some of the salmon in the center of the nori.

6 Using the bamboo mat as a guide, tightly roll the layers together to make a sushi roll.

7 Continue in the same manner with the remaining nori sheets and the rest of the ingredients to make three more rolls.

8 Slice and serve with the sauce.

Bodacious Beautiful Turkey Burgers with Spicy Avocado Sauce

Birth & Balance

Serves 4

Friends inspired this creation. It is the type of meal that you can't help but love and do over and over again. We hand ground the turkey to ensure quality and then chopped and diced to our hearts content. Seasoned perfectly and grilled under a crisp, clear Florida night sky. Hope you do the same!

Juice & Essence

Turkey is blood building, strengthening, calming, circulation enhancing, and warming. It is also beneficial for the kidneys, liver, lungs, stomach, and spleen. The use of avocado as a sauce brilliantly lubricates the lungs and intestines and is a natural source of lecithin, a brain food. Additional benefits include the increase of red blood cells, remedy for ulcers, and beautification for skin. The jalapeño and chipotle aid in digestion, warmth, and circulation. The micro greens and cilantro add a higher octane energy source rich in blood building, antioxidant-rich chlorophyll.

CONTRAST – This choice is not about the individual components but the sandwich as a whole. We recommend a light, medium-body red. Think Merlot, Central Coast blends, or Barbera . . . even a Pinot Noir, Burgundy for elegance, and Russian River for fruit.

Prepare the Spicy Avocado Sauce

Ingredients

- 1 avocado
- ½ teaspoon minced chipotle chili in adobo sauce
- ½ teaspoon adobo sauce
- ¼ teaspoon jalapeño green pepper sauce
- Juice from ½ lime
- ½ teaspoon minced fresh cilantro
- ¼ teaspoon sea salt
- ¼ teaspoon freshly ground black pepper

Directions

1 Remove the peel and seed from the avocado and place in a medium size bowl.

2 Mash with a fork.

3 Add the remaining ingredients and mix well.

4 Set aside and prepare the turkey burgers.

Prepare Turkey Burgers

Ingredients

- 1.75 lbs. turkey tenderloins, trimmed of all skin and fat
- 1 tablespoon minced green jalapeño pepper (seeds & ribs removed)
- ½ teaspoon ground white pepper
- ¾ teaspoon sea salt
- ½ teaspoon onion powder
- ½ teaspoon garlic powder
- 1 teaspoon paprika
- ¼ teaspoon ground cumin
- ½ teaspoon ground ancho chili pepper
- 1 teaspoon chopped fresh cilantro
- ½ teaspoon chopped fresh oregano
- 1 tablespoon olive oil
- 1 large egg
- 8 whole wheat naan flatbreads, cut into rounds to fit burgers
- 1 cup micro greens
- 1 medium tomato, cut into slices

Directions

1 Put the turkey tenderloins through a meat grinder or you can have your butcher grind them for you. (We grind our own so that we know what is in the meat. We do not want any added fats or skin in our ground turkey.)

2 Place the meat in a large bowl.

3 Add the jalapeño, white pepper, salt, onion powder, garlic powder, paprika, cumin, ancho chili pepper, cilantro, oregano, olive oil, and egg.

4 Mix together gently.

5 Form the mixture into 4 burgers.

6 Heat the grill to high.

7 Place the burgers on the grill and close the lid for 5 minutes.

8 Reduce the heat to medium and grill for 8 to 10 minutes more, or until cooked through.

9 Place the naan rounds on the grill for a few minutes until lightly toasted.

10 Top with a turkey burger, spicy avocado sauce, micro greens, tomato, and another naan round.

11 Serve with *Lentil & Black Soy Bean Fritters* (page 104).

Drunken Turkey Legs

Birth & Balance

Serves 6

This was our salute dish to St. Patrick's Day. In place of corned beef, we chose to "wing it" and grabbed two clay pots and brined some turkey legs. Kiss the Blarney Stone then set sail on a unique culinary adventure!

Juice & Essence

Turkey benefits the spleen, stomach, and kidneys. A simple blood building, kidney strengthening, body warming dish due to the parsnips, juniper berries, caraway seeds, cayenne pepper, ground mustard, and white vinegar. The spices offer warmth for sluggish circulation, the immune system, and appetite. Celery root benefits the stomach, spleen/pancreas, and liver. It improves digestion and purifies blood, promotes sweating, and helps with vertigo. Potato is mildly diuretic and also tonifies the spleen/pancreas while energizing the body, lubricating the intestines, and fortifying the kidneys.

Complement *or* Contrast

COMPLEMENT – Rich root vegetables and turkey in this dish calls for fragrant, fruity, dry wines such as Pinot Noir (California or Burgundy), Syrah, Malbec, Zinfandel, or even an Australian Shiraz would work as well.

Prepare the Brine

Ingredients

- 2 tablespoons sea salt
- 2 tablespoons olive oil
- 2 tablespoons white vinegar
- 2 teaspoons paprika
- 2 teaspoons ground mustard
- 2 teaspoons garlic powder
- 2 teaspoons onion powder
- 1 teaspoon cayenne pepper
- 1 cup water
- 6 turkey legs (approximately 4 lbs.)

Directions

1 Combine all of the ingredients in a large bowl.

2 Cover and refrigerate overnight.

Prepare the Vegetables

Ingredients

- 1½ cups celery root, chopped into 1"-pieces
- 2 large russet potatoes, cut into 2"-pieces
- 2½ cups carrots, cut into 2"-pieces
- 1½ cups parsnips, cut into 2"-pieces
- 2½ cups rutabaga, cut into 2"-pieces
- ½ cup extra-virgin olive oil
- 2 teaspoons ground mustard
- ½ teaspoon ground cloves
- 1 teaspoon caraway seeds
- ½ teaspoon whole allspice
- 1 teaspoon whole juniper berries
- 1 teaspoon ground white pepper
- 1 teaspoon minced fresh rosemary
- 1 teaspoon minced fresh thyme
- 1 teaspoon minced fresh sage
- 1 tablespoon minced fresh parsley
- 2 lemons, sliced
- 3 clementines, sliced
- 3 cups "The Bruery–Orchard White Belgian Style Ale"

Special Equipment
2 clay roasting pots

Directions

1 Completely submerge the clay pots in cold water and let soak for 15 minutes.

2 Combine the celery root, potatoes, carrots, parsnips, rutabagas, olive oil, ground mustard, cloves, caraway, allspice, juniper berries, white pepper, rosemary, thyme, sage, and parsley in a large bowl.

3 Mix everything together well and set aside.

4 After 15 minutes of soaking (can soak longer), remove the pots from the water.

5 Divide the vegetable mixture evenly into the bottoms of the clay pots.

6 Evenly divide the citrus slices and place on top of the vegetables.

7 Remove the turkey legs from the brine and reserve the brine.

8 Place the turkey legs on top of the citrus slices (three in each clay pot).

9 Pour the reserved brine over the turkey legs, dividing evenly, into the clay pots.

10 Now pour 1½ cups of the ale into each clay pot.

11 Place the covers on the pots and put them into a cold oven.

12 Turn the oven to 450°F.

13 Roast the turkey legs and vegetables for 80 minutes.

14 Remove the pots from the oven and let them rest for 10 to 15 minutes before serving.

Jumbamacalobstalaya!!!

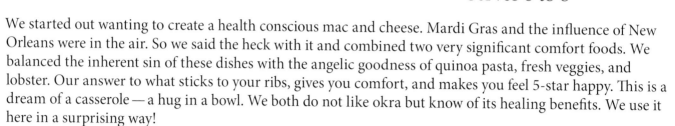

Birth & Balance

Serves 6 to 8

We started out wanting to create a health conscious mac and cheese. Mardi Gras and the influence of New Orleans were in the air. So we said the heck with it and combined two very significant comfort foods. We balanced the inherent sin of these dishes with the angelic goodness of quinoa pasta, fresh veggies, and lobster. Our answer to what sticks to your ribs, gives you comfort, and makes you feel 5-star happy. This is a dream of a casserole — a hug in a bowl. We both do not like okra but know of its healing benefits. We use it here in a surprising way!

Juice & Essence

Andouille sausage and milk are beneficial to the kidneys and liver, lubricating to the intestines, and blood building. The use of jalapeño and cubanelle peppers offer a circulatory benefit with warming, immune system boosting attributes. The attractive and welcoming way we added okra in the process added benefits in the areas of lowering cholesterol, lubrication of the throat and lungs, balancing blood sugars, healing ulcers, and keeping joints limber. Lobster offers iodine and other great nutrients such as a healthy dose of essential fatty acids.

COMPLEMENT – Where to begin? This rich and creamy dish needs a bold, big, fruity, dry wine with a looooong finish. We need big, buttery, oaky, fruity Chardonnay…Bordeaux or California. The bigger the better!

Prepare the Topping

Ingredients

- 2 Andouille sausages
- 12 fresh okra
- 2 tablespoons minced fresh jalapeño (ribs and seeds removed)
- 1½ cups panko
- 2 tablespoons extra-virgin olive oil

Directions

1 Preheat oven to 425°F.

2 Remove the casings from the Andouille sausages

3 Finely chop the meat.

4 Transfer to a sauté pan and cook over medium heat for 8 to 10 minutes until lightly browned.

5 Set aside to cool.

6 Cut the okra in half.

7 Remove the insides and place them in a bowl and set aside to be used in the sauce later.

8 Mince the green flesh of the okra and put into a large bowl.

9 Add the jalapeño, panko, cooked sausage and olive oil.

10 Mix well and then spread out into a thin layer on a large rimmed baking sheet.

11 Place on the center rack of the preheated oven and bake for 5 minutes being sure to stir often so that the mixture dries out evenly. Do not brown!

12 Set aside to cool.

13 Lower the oven temperature to 350°F.

Jumbamacalobstalaya ~ *continued*

Prepare the Vegetables

Ingredients

- 2 teaspoons olive oil
- ⅓ cup minced cubanelle peppers
- ⅓ cup minced shallots
- ⅓ cup sundried tomatoes
- 1 medium garlic clove, chopped
- ½ cup dry sherry
- Reserved insides from the okra
- ¾ cup low-fat milk

Directions

1. Heat a small sauté pan over medium heat with the 2 teaspoons of olive oil.

2. When the oil is hot, add the peppers and shallots.

3. Sauté for 5 minutes, or until softened and set aside.

4. Place the sundried tomatoes, garlic, sherry, and the okra insides into a small saucepan.

5. Bring to a boil and cook for 10 minutes.

6. Transfer the mixture to a food processor fitted with the chopping blade.

7. Add the milk and process until the mixture is smooth.

8. Set aside.

Assembly

Ingredients

- 16 ounces quinoa pasta shells
- 1½ cups shredded Fontina cheese
- 1½ cups shredded Kerry Gold aged cheddar
- 1½ cups shredded smoked Gouda cheese
- 1 cup low-fat milk
- ½ teaspoon ground cayenne pepper
- ½ lb. cooked lobster meat, cut into 1½"-chunks

Directions

1 Bring a large pot of water to a boil over high heat.

2 Once boiling, add the quinoa pasta shells and cook until just al dente (still slightly firm), about 5 minutes.

3 Drain the pasta well and transfer to a large bowl.

4 Add the cheeses, milk, cayenne pepper, sautéed peppers and shallots, the sundried tomato mixture, and the lobster.

5 Stir to combine well and pour into a 2-quart casserole dish.

6 Sprinkle the topping in an even layer over the pasta.

7 Bake in a preheated 350°F. oven for 20 to 30 minutes or until heated through.

Seafood Chowder

J&E Time Signature

Birth & Balance

Serves 4

Amazingly perfect! We needed to share a soup or chowder for winter. As it turned out, a meal was planned for us by Carol that fit the bill. We went with it. As usual, we sat with the available ingredients and put them together for the splendid concoction you see here.

Juice & Essence

Mussels nourish the kidneys and liver, increases yang energy, and strengthens the joints and connective tissues. Mussels help with dizziness, vertigo, night sweats, impotence, and low back pain. Shrimp also nourishes the liver and energizes the kidneys. Use shrimp to help with impotence and low breast milk. Scallops are low in fat and high in protein and omega-3 fatty acids. Scallops strengthen kidney energy; help with urinary incontinence, fatigue, shortness of breath, poor appetite, dry throat, and constipation. Kale with its sweet and slightly bitter-pungent flavor eases lung congestion, benefits the stomach, and treats duodenal ulcers. Kale is an exceptional source of chlorophyll, calcium, iron, and vitamin A. Turnips help to improve circulation of qi energy; builds blood, promotes sweating, rids the body of mucus and other damp conditions, relieves coughing, helps with sluggish digestion, and improves appetite. Turnip is alkalizing in nature and helps detoxify the body. Parsnips benefit the spleen/pancreas and stomach; help clear liver and gallbladder blockages, is a mild diuretic, and assists with constipation. Carrots benefit the lungs, strengthen the spleen/pancreas; improves liver function, stimulates the elimination of waste, acts as a diuretic, dissolves accumulations such as stones and tumors, treats indigestion, reduces stomach acid and heartburn. Carrots contain an essential oil that destroys pinworms and roundworms. They are also alkaline-forming and clear acidic blood conditions including acne, tonsillitis, and rheumatism. Celery benefits the stomach and spleen/pancreas, calms the liver, improves digestion, cleanses the blood, and reduces vertigo, nervousness, eye inflammation, burning urine, and headaches. Onions promote warmth and more energy in the body. They reduce clotting and help purify the body. Onions retard the growth of viruses and help clean the arteries.

Complement *or* Contrast

CONTRAST – Classic California Chardonnay would be wonderful with this rich, deep and tomato-based seafood chowder. Imagine if you will (close your eyes if you like) an ice bucket with a bottle of dry, buttery, oaky Napa Chardonnay with a little fruit and citrus…. Yummo! I recommend Cakebread or Grgich Cellars. The result you are looking for is a showdown between two contrasting flavors that result in an embrace that makes you want to do it again…and again…and again.

Prepare the Mussel Stock

Ingredients

- 1 cup white wine
- 1 cup water
- 3 lbs. mussels, cleaned

Directions

1 Put the wine and water into a large saucepan and bring to a boil over high heat.

2 Add the mussels to the saucepan and cover.

3 Reduce the heat to medium and cook for about 8 to 10 minutes and remove from heat.

4 Uncover and let cool until the mussels can be handled, about 5 minutes.

5 Remove the mussels from the shells and place in a small bowl.

6 Strain the broth through a cheesecloth-lined strainer into a separate bowl.

7 Cover and chill the mussels and broth separately until ready to use in the chowder.

Prepare the Chowder

Ingredients

- 3 tablespoons extra-virgin olive oil
- ½ cup diced pancetta
- ¾ cup diced fresh fennel
- ⅓ cup diced turnips
- ⅓ cup diced parsnips
- ½ cup diced carrots
- ⅓ cup diced yellow bell pepper
- 1 tablespoon minced and seeded Serrano pepper
- ⅔ cup thinly sliced celery
- 1 cup chopped yellow onions
- 1 tablespoon minced garlic
- 2 fresh bay leaves
- 1½ teaspoons minced fresh thyme
- 1½ teaspoons minced fresh basil
- 2 teaspoons sea salt
- 1 teaspoon ground black pepper
- ½ teaspoon paprika
- 1, 28-ounce can San Marzano tomatoes
- ½ large lemon
- 3 cups chopped green kale
- ⅓ lb. squid-bodies (tubes) only, cut into ¼"- to ½"-slices
- ½ lb. bay scallops
- ¾ lb. rock shrimp

Directions

1 In a large stockpot, heat the oil over medium-high heat.

2 Add the pancetta and sauté until browned.

3 Add the fennel, turnips, parsnips, carrots, yellow bell peppers, Serrano pepper, celery, onion, and garlic.

4 Sauté for about 8 minutes until the vegetables soften, stirring occasionally.

5 Add the bay leaves, thyme, basil, salt, pepper, and paprika and stir to combine with the vegetables.

6 Crush each tomato with your hands and add to the pot along with the remaining tomato liquid.

7 Squeeze the juice from the lemon half into the pot and add the mussel broth.

8 Stir to combine, reduce heat, and bring to a simmer with the pot partially covered for 10 minutes.

9 Increase heat to medium and add the scallops, shrimp, and squid.

10 Cover and cook for 5 minutes then stir in the mussels and kale.

11 Cover again and continue to cook for 5 minutes.

12 Remove from heat and let rest, covered, for 5 minutes more and serve.

Mix-Masterful Meat Loaf

J&E Time Signature

Birth & Balance

Serves 8

Putting our stamp on a meatloaf was a joyful experience. We had to do it right which meant grass-fed beef, buffalo and veal, homemade sauce for the topping, and fresh herbs for seasoning. We added a few unique touches of love for added comfort. This is a warm hug from the inside. Enjoy!

Juice & Essence

Hemp oil offers the anti-inflammatory benefits of omega-3, -6, and -9 fatty acids which aid in brain health and prevention or retardation of neurodegenerative diseases. The onset of conditions such as Alzheimer's and Parkinson's diseases may be delayed by consuming a diet rich in hemp. Similarly, hemp can cause the symptoms of these diseases to be reduced or their progression slowed. Buffalo is blood building, energizing and strengthening to joints and tendons as is veal and eggs. Pine nuts offer benefits to the liver, lungs, and large intestine while helping to treat dizziness, dry cough, and constipation. Cayenne can be a healing aid to ulcers while fortifying the stomach, increasing blood circulation and bodily warmth. Shiitake mushrooms help fight intestinal and cervical cancer and are beneficial to digestion by strengthening the stomach. Use shiitake in the aid against viral diseases and the lowering of cholesterol and fat in the blood. Tomatoes help balance the liver while assisting with dizziness and poor circulation.

Complement or Contrast

CONTRAST – With this light meat and a rich complex seasoning blend many choices come to mind. Rosso di Montalcino is a dry, light fruit, light finish with a little dirt. A Cabernet or Super Tuscan (Sangiovese/Cabernet blend) work as well.

Prepare Sauce

Ingredients

- 2 teaspoons hemp oil
- 1 teaspoon pressed garlic
- ⅓ cup chopped shallots
- 1, 14.5-ounce can organic diced tomatoes
- 1, 14.5-ounce can organic fire-roasted tomatoes
- 1 tablespoon bottled horseradish
- 2 teaspoons apple cider vinegar
- 1 tablespoon Worcestershire sauce
- 2 teaspoons cayenne pepper
- 1½ teaspoons sea salt
- 1 teaspoon black pepper

Directions

1 Heat the oil in a saucepan over medium-high heat.

2 Add the garlic and shallots.

3 Sauté for 1 minute and add the tomatoes, horseradish, vinegar, Worcestershire, cayenne, salt, and pepper.

4 Bring the mixture to a boil and reduce heat to a simmer.

5 Simmer uncovered for 30 minutes.

6 Remove from heat.

7 Process the sauce to a smooth consistency using an immersion blender.

8 Set aside to cool to room temperature.

Prepare Meatloaf

Ingredients

- 2 tablespoons hemp oil
- ½ cup minced yellow onion
- ¼ cup minced green bell pepper
- ¼ cup minced celery
- 1 tablespoon pressed garlic
- 2 tablespoons finely grated carrots
- 1, 3.5-ounce package shiitake mushrooms, minced
- 2 tablespoons minced pimento
- 1 teaspoon minced fresh thyme
- 1 tablespoon minced fresh parsley
- 1 teaspoon sea salt
- 1 teaspoon freshly ground white pepper
- 1 lb. grass-fed organic ground beef
- 12 ounces organic ground buffalo
- ½ lb. organic grass-fed ground veal
- 3 large organic eggs
- 3 tablespoons pine nuts, toasted
- 1 teaspoon ground mustard
- ½ cup whole wheat panko

Directions

1 Preheat the oven to 375°F.

2 Heat the oil in a large sauté pan over medium-high heat.

3 Add the onion, bell pepper, and celery and sauté for 3 minutes.

4 Add the garlic, carrots, mushrooms, pimento, thyme, parsley, salt, and pepper.

5 Continue to sauté the vegetables for another 3 minutes then set aside to cool to room temperature.

6 Put the beef, buffalo and veal into a large mixing bowl.

7 Add the cooled vegetables, eggs, pine nuts, ground mustard, and panko.

8 Mix together with your hands to completely incorporate all of the ingredients.

9 Divide the mixture in half and form into two equal size loaves.

10 Place the loaves in a roasting pan and pour some of the cooled sauce over the top of each loaf to cover.

11 Roast in the center of the oven for 60 minutes until the loaves are cooked through.

12 Slice and serve with the remaining sauce.

Winter Accompaniments

Chapter 3
Winter Accompaniments

These accompaniments are gorgeous mates to the flavor notes and visual canvases of Juice & Essence entrées. These accompaniments are a fresh take on vegetable combinations that, as is customary with Juice & Essence, have an unpredictably delicious twist!

Mead Marinated Golden Beets

Birth & Balance

Makes approximately 5 cups

This recipe was also a part of our "Arts in After School" committee luncheon. Mead offered us a sweet way to marinate beets as a side while creatively paying tribute to a classic winter-warming beverage. The honey base of mead brightened the flavor. Pre-making this side came in handy for us because we were transporting our creation and would be required to educate and entertain within a limited time frame. Surprisingly this simple however harmonious endeavor was extremely well received!

Juice & Essence

Beets are helpful to the heart and liver. They are also blood building, energizing, vascular circulation enhancing, and hormone balancing while offering menopause and menstrual regulating qualities. A sweet detoxifier to the liver and moistening to the intestines to assist with constipation due to intestinal dryness. Mead is a wine made from honey and thereby easier on the liver/gallbladder offering less chance of hangover. Honey supports the beets in its endeavor to detox, treat intestinal dryness, and offers additional benefits to the lungs, spleen, and large intestine.

Ingredients

- 12 medium size golden beets
- 2 bottles of mead (honey wine)
- 1 teaspoon dried tarragon

Directions

1 Preheat oven to 425°F.

2 Wash and trim the beets.

3 Cut out 2 pieces of heavy-duty foil measuring 18"×28".

4 Divide the beets and place them in the center of each piece of foil.

5 Enclose the beets in the foil making sure there are no openings.

6 Place the packets on a rimmed baking sheet.

7 Roast them in the oven for 1 to 1¼ hours, or until the beets are cooked through.

8 Meanwhile, combine the mead and the tarragon in a medium saucepan over medium-high heat.

9 Bring to a boil and cook for 5 to 10 minutes just to blend the flavors.

10 Remove from heat and set aside until the beets are ready.

11 Remove the beets from the foil packets.

12 Carefully rub off the skins from the beets.

13 Cut them into ¼"-slices and place in a 9"×13" glass baking dish.

14 Pour the mead mixture over the beets. They should be covered by the liquid.

15 Cover and refrigerate overnight before serving.

Gorgonzola Stuffed Shells

Birth & Balance   Serves 4

Stuffed shells for us had to be interesting. We chose Gorgonzola for a punch of flavor and because we had not yet worked with it in our recipes. Gorgonzola is a cheese-lovers cheese. Additional impact from pancetta and bell peppers assure satisfaction as a stand-alone or side dish.

Juice & Essence

A mild benefit to the spleen, stomach, and kidneys due to qi nourishing properties in these areas from the pork, which also nourishes blood, enriches yin, and moistens dryness. Cheese offers additional strengthening properties. The herbs assist in reduction of bloating, hiccups, and indigestion. Bell peppers improve the appetite, reduce swelling, promote circulation, and are rich in vitamin C.

Ingredients

- 16 jumbo pasta shells
- 1 teaspoon grapeseed oil
- ¼ cup diced pancetta
- ¼ cup minced orange bell pepper
- ¼ cup minced yellow bell pepper
- ¼ cup minced sweet onion
- 1 tablespoon minced fresh tarragon
- 2 cups part-skim ricotta cheese
- ¼ cup Gorgonzola cheese
- 2 cloves garlic, pressed
- Salt and pepper to taste
- 2 teaspoons olive oil
- ½ cup chicken stock
- ½ cup freshly grated Parmesan cheese

Directions

1. Preheat oven to 350°F.
2. Cook the pasta shells in a large pot of boiling salted water until just beginning to soften.
3. Do not overcook since they will cook again in the oven!
4. Drain well and toss with the grapeseed oil.
5. Set aside.
6. Heat a small sauté pan over medium-high heat.
7. Add the pancetta and cook until crispy.
8. Remove from pan to a paper towel to drain.
9. To the same sauté pan, add the peppers and onion.
10. Sauté for 5 minutes until softened and set aside.
11. In a large bowl, combine the tarragon, ricotta cheese, Gorgonzola cheese, garlic, crispy Pancetta, and the cooked peppers and onion.
12. Season the cheese to taste with salt and pepper.
13. Coat the bottom of a glass 8"×8" baking dish with olive oil.
14. Fill the shells with the cheese mixture and place in the baking dish.
15. Add the chicken stock to the bottom of the baking dish and sprinkle the Parmesan cheese on top of the shells.
16. Bake the shells for 35 to 40 minutes until the shells are heated through. Serve immediately.

Pickled Veggies

Birth & Balance

Serves 4

Seasonally colder climates will offer limited access to fresh vegetables and fruits in the winter. One of the healthier methods for storing veggies is pickling. We created a mildly spicy, extremely interesting medley of pickled goodness that you will find great for afternoon or evening snacking.

Juice & Essence

Green beans are beneficial to the spleen/pancreas and kidneys. Carrots are beneficial to the liver, lungs, spleen/pancreas, are rich in the antioxidant vitamin A, and protect against cancer. Juniper berries ward off the common cold while mustard and fennel seeds warm the stomach and aid indigestion. Vinegar assists with food poisoning, assists in improving circulation, stops bleeding, removes parasites, and relieves edema. A simple preparation for helping with diabetic thirst, frequent urination, excessive abdominal bloating and gas, hernias, and dry conditions such as thirst and constipation due to dryness and dry cough.

Ingredients

- 1 large red bell pepper, sliced into ¼"-strips
- 2 medium fennel bulbs, trimmed and cut into ¼"-sticks
- 6 fresh thyme sprigs
- 2 fresh fennel fronds
- 2 cups green beans, trimmed
- 3 large carrots, cut in half crosswise and then into ¼"-sticks
- 2 cups white vinegar
- 1 cup cider vinegar
- 1½ cups water
- 3 tablespoons light brown sugar
- 5 whole garlic cloves, peeled
- 2 teaspoons sea salt
- 8 juniper berries
- 1 teaspoon whole mustard seeds
- ¼ teaspoons caraway seeds
- ¼ teaspoon fennel seeds
- ½ teaspoon crushed red pepper
- ½ teaspoon whole white peppercorns
- ½ teaspoon whole pink peppercorns

Directions

1 Decoratively place the red bell pepper, fennel, thyme sprigs, and fennel fronds in a large glass jar with a lid. (Make sure it is large enough to hold all of the vegetables and liquid. You can use more than one jar if necessary.)

2 Set aside the carrots and green beans since they will be cooked in the pickling liquid.

3 To a large saucepan, add the vinegars, water, brown sugar, garlic, salt, juniper berries, mustard seeds, caraway seeds, fennel seeds, crushed red pepper, and peppercorns.

4 Cook the mixture over medium heat until the sugar dissolves.

5 Bring to a boil.

6 Add the carrots and green beans and cook for 1 minute.

7 Remove the pan from the stove.

8 Remove the carrots and green beans from the pickling liquid and add them to the glass jar with the peppers and fennel.

9 Pour the pickling liquid into the jar to cover the vegetables.

10 Let the pickled vegetables cool at room temperature for 1 hour.

11 Place the lid on the jar and refrigerate for 1 day before serving.

They will keep for 2 weeks in the refrigerator.

Clay-Pot Roasted Zucchini

Birth & Balance   Serves 4

When we brought out the clay pot again, we used one that was glazed inside to create this dish. Only the bottom of the pot is glazed to help keep the delicate vegetables from sticking. The tremendous aromas from the fennel pollen, herbs, and lemon zest all come together in a delicately tender symphony. We wanted a vegetable side that could bend to our whim of flavors without too much personality resistance. Zucchini was the perfect chameleon of vegetables for this mission!

Juice & Essence

Zucchini, also known as summer squash, benefits the spleen, stomach, and large intestine. Zucchini are also a resolver of toxins and helpful in dispersing inflammation. Supplemental gifts of this dish are found in rectification of indigestion, bloating, edema, difficulties urinating, irritability, and constant thirst due to the tomato content. Fennel pollen relieves indigestion by easing gas and bloating.

Ingredients

- ½ cup chopped sweet onion
- 2 teaspoons grapeseed oil
- 1 teaspoon lemon zest
- 1 teaspoon minced fresh thyme
- 1 lb. zucchini, sliced on the diagonal
- 2 medium tomatoes, sliced
- ¼ teaspoon fennel pollen
- Salt and pepper to taste
- ¼ cup chicken stock

Directions

1 Soak the clay pot in water for 15 minutes.

2 Meanwhile, sauté the onion in grapeseed oil over medium-high heat until the onion is softened and lightly browned.

3 Remove the clay pot from the water.

4 Add the onions to the bottom of the pot.

5 In a large bowl, mix together the lemon zest, thyme, and zucchini.

6 Add salt and pepper to taste.

7 Place zucchini over the onions in the clay pot.

8 Top with the tomato slices, more salt and pepper, and the fennel pollen.

9 Pour the chicken stock over the vegetables.

10 Cover and place in a cold oven.

11 Turn the oven to 425°F.

12 Bake the vegetables for 30 to 35 minutes, or until they are cooked through.

Sautéed Chinese Broccoli

Birth & Balance   Serves 4

This is a popular vegetable with our blend of sauces and seasonings taken from our experiences with Asian cuisine. We wanted a quick sauté full of flavor and health benefits. We got it!

Juice & Essence

Chinese broccoli is beneficial to the spleen, stomach, and bladder while offering diuretic assistance. This dish is helpful in brightening the eyes and can be used when there is an occurrence of eye inflammation and nearsightedness. Chinese broccoli includes abundant pantothenic acid and vitamin A, which benefit rough skin and has more vitamin C than citrus. Sesame seeds strengthen the liver and kidneys, lubricates the intestines and the five yin organs (heart, liver, kidney, spleen/pancreas, and lungs). As a general tonic, sesame seeds are energizing and help with low backache, weak knees, and stiff joints. Additional benefits are in the areas of rheumatism, headache, dizziness, numbness, and paralysis caused by deficient blood or yin.

Ingredients

- 2 teaspoons olive oil
- 1 tablespoon pressed fresh garlic
- 1½ lbs. Chinese broccoli, chopped into 2"-pieces
- 1 tablespoon ponzu sauce
- 1 tablespoon soy sauce
- 3 teaspoons sesame oil
- 1 tablespoon toasted sesame seeds

Directions

1 Heat a large sauté pan over medium-high heat.

2 Add the olive oil and garlic.

3 Sauté for 1 minute then add the Chinese broccoli.

4 Sauté for 3 to 4 minutes and add the ponzu, soy sauce, and sesame oil.

5 Continue to cook for another 2 minutes until the Chinese broccoli is cooked through.

6 Stir in the toasted sesame seeds and serve immediately.

Lentil & Black Soy Bean Fritters

Birth & Balance   Serves 4

This is an instead of…instead of French fries…instead of corn fritters…instead of bread or any starch. We chose high protein…high taste…high nutrition…high flavor. Dare to be different…dare to share…dare to enjoy the lentils and black soy! Enjoy!!!

Juice & Essence

Lentils and black soy beans benefits the heart, spleen, and large intestine. This is a stimulating dish for the adrenals, circulation, and vitality via tonifying the kidney essence. A tasty detoxifier also treating rheumatism, kidney disease, and kidney-related problems such as low back pain and weak knees. Additionally this is a great combination to include in treatment of distention, water swelling, jaundice, body tightness, and tendon contractions. Garbanzo and fava beans are a high-iron, gluten-free substitute for a binder.

Ingredients

- 1, 15-ounce can organic black soy beans
- 1, 15-ounce can organic red lentils
- ½ cup chicken broth
- ½ cup Jose Cuervo Especial tequila
- 1 tablespoon chopped shallot
- 3 large garlic cloves, pressed
- ¼ cup chopped tomato
- 1 teaspoon chopped fresh oregano
- 1 teaspoon chopped fresh cilantro
- ½ teaspoon sea salt
- ½ teaspoon freshly ground black pepper
- ¼ teaspoon paprika
- ¼ teaspoon cayenne pepper
- 1 teaspoon olive oil
- 3 tablespoons garbanzo bean-fava flour
- 1 cup cornmeal
- 1 quart canola oil for frying

Directions

1. To a medium-size saucepan, add the black soy beans, lentils, chicken broth, tequila, shallot, garlic, and tomato.
2. Bring to a rapid boil and cook for 10 minutes.
3. After the 10 minutes, use an immersion blender and puree the mixture fully.
4. Now add the oregano, cilantro, salt, pepper, paprika, cayenne pepper, and olive oil.
5. Mix together well and transfer the mixture to a bowl.
6. Cover and place in the refrigerator to cool.
7. Once the bean mixture has cooled, stir in the garbanzo bean-fava flour.
8. Place the cornmeal in a shallow dish.
9. Form the bean mixture into 3" balls and roll the balls in the cornmeal to coat them.
10. Place on a baking sheet.
11. Continue this process with the rest of the mixture.
12. Meanwhile, heat the canola oil in a large, deep pot.
13. Bring the oil temperature to 350°F.
14. Add the balls to the hot oil and fry until light golden brown.
15. Remove from the oil and place on a paper towel-lined baking sheet to drain.
16. Serve while still hot.

Savory Cabbage

Birth & Balance

Serves 4 to 6

We had to try our hand at cabbage as it would best suit our **Drunken Turkey Legs** (page 82). Cabbage and St. Patrick's Day seem to go hand-in-hand. This was one staple side we would not be without!

Juice & Essence

Cabbage is beneficial to the spleen, stomach, and large intestine channels. A slightly warming, thermal-natured vegetable warmed by the savory spices and herbs. A detoxifier, cleans the blood, strengthens digestion, unblocks intestines, and resolves alcoholic thirst. Additional uses include aid for treatment of the common cold, whooping cough, frostbite, mental depression and irritability, ulcers, and beautifying the skin. Onion lowers blood pressure and cholesterol, decreases phlegm as well as inflammation of the nose and throat. The herbs, horseradish, and mustard are immune boosting, circulation enhancing, and detoxing with additional cleansing benefits to the lungs found in the horseradish, thyme, and sage.

Ingredients

- 4 tablespoons olive oil
- 1 medium sweet onion, chopped
- 1 medium head of green cabbage, thinly sliced
- 1 teaspoon salt
- ½ teaspoon freshly ground black pepper
- ½ teaspoon minced fresh rosemary
- ½ teaspoon minced fresh thyme
- ½ teaspoon minced fresh sage
- 1 teaspoon minced fresh parsley
- 1 tablespoon Dijon mustard
- 1 tablespoon prepared "hot" horseradish

Directions

1 Place a large frying pan over medium-high heat.

2 Add the olive oil and onions and sauté for 5 minutes.

3 Add the cabbage, salt, pepper, and herbs.

4 Cover and cook for 15 minutes stirring often.

5 Uncover and add the mustard and horseradish stirring to combine.

6 Place the cover back on and remove from the heat.

7 Let the cabbage sit for 5 minutes before serving to allow the flavors to blend.

Herb & Root-Buttered Roasted Roots

Birth & Balance

Serves 4

An enlightening moment was derived from this winter warmer. We created something special here. A side dish that is much more than a side dish. We crammed a good amount of roasted roots into this recipe and hid a few in the butter that will delight you with bursts of exquisite flavors.

Juice & Essence

Squash is a warming way to reduce inflammation, improves energy and circulation. Rutabaga reduces the risk of cardiovascular disease by lowering cholesterol and keeping blood sugar better balanced by slowing down the absorption of digested food. Rutabaga is also a great source of daily potassium providing 16 percent of the daily value and is an excellent source of vitamin C. Turnips improve circulation of qi energy and blood; promotes sweating and helps to rid the body of mucus. Turnips are alkalizing and help to detoxify the body. Chestnuts benefit the spleen and stomach; strengthen the kidneys and connective tissue of the body. Chestnuts improve circulation of blood and help to stop bleeding. Use chestnuts to assist with low back soreness and lower leg weakness. Sage and thyme help with common cold, headache, cough, bodily aches and pains, sore throat, nausea, vomiting, indigestion and abdominal distention.

Prepare the Garlic

Ingredients

- 1 large head of garlic
- 1 tablespoon extra-virgin olive oil

Directions

1 Preheat the oven to 425°F.

2 Cut ¼" from the top of the head of garlic and discard.

3 Place the head of garlic (cut side up) on the center of a sheet of aluminum foil large enough to totally enclose the garlic.

4 Drizzle the cut side with the olive oil and wrap the foil around to totally enclose the garlic.

5 Place the foil packet in the center of the preheated oven for 45 minutes, or until the garlic is soft.

6 Remove from the oven and open the foil to let the garlic cool.

7 Keep the oven heated to 425°F.

8 When cool enough to handle, squeeze out the garlic cloves and set aside.

Herb & Root-Buttered Roasted Roots ~ *continued*

Prepare the Parsnip-Chestnut Butter

Ingredients

- 1 medium size parsnip, cut into 1"-chunks
- 7 roasted and peeled chestnuts from a jar
- 1 tablespoon minced fresh sage
- 1 teaspoon minced fresh thyme
- 2 tablespoon extra-virgin olive oil, divided
- ½ teaspoon sea salt
- ½ teaspoon freshly ground black pepper
- 1 tablespoon Frangelico
- 2 tablespoons water

Directions

1 Cover a rimmed baking sheet with foil.

2 Place the parsnips, chestnuts, sage, thyme, and 1 tablespoon of the extra-virgin olive oil into the pan and mix together well.

3 Spread them out in a single layer and roast in the middle of the preheated 425°F. oven for 15 to 20 minutes, or until the parsnips are cooked through.

4 Put the roasted parsnip and chestnut mixture into a food processor fitted with the chopping blade.

5 Add the remaining 1 tablespoon of extra-virgin olive oil, salt, pepper, Frangelico, water, and the roasted garlic cloves to the food processor.

6 Process until the mixture is a fine puree and set aside.

Prepare the Root Vegetables

Ingredients

- 3 lbs. butternut squash, peeled, seeded and cut into 2"-chunks
- 1¼ lbs. rutabaga, peeled and cut into 2"-pieces
- 1 small turnip, cut in half and cut into ¼"-slices
- 2 small shallots, cut in half and thinly sliced
- 3 tablespoons extra-virgin olive oil
- 1 teaspoon sea salt
- ½ teaspoon freshly ground black pepper

Directions

1 Cover a rimmed baking sheet with foil.

2 Place the squash, rutabaga, turnips, shallots, olive oil, salt and pepper together on the baking sheet.

3 Mix together well and spread the vegetables out on the pan in a single layer.

4 Place the pan in the center of the preheated 425°F. oven and roast for 40 minutes, or until vegetables are cooked through.

5 Transfer the vegetables to a large bowl.

6 Carefully mix in the parsnip-chestnut butter and stir to combine well.

7 Transfer the vegetable mixture into a buttered 9"×9" casserole dish.

8 Preheat the broiler with the oven rack set at the top third of the oven.

9 When the broiler is heated, place the casserole dish on the rack and broil for 5 to 10 minutes, or until the top is golden brown. Serve while hot.

Smashed Cauliflower & Rosemary

Birth & Balance

Serves 4

This was created as a side for our *Mix–Masterful Meat Loaf* (page 90). With dreams of making a flavorful, low starch mash we formed a columbine of goodness. We succeeded in creating a really tasty floral dish with beautiful texture and consistency.

Juice & Essence

Cauliflower benefits the spleen and stomach by fortifying them. Count on cauliflower to treat indigestion and help stop cold type stomach pain. Potato can be used to help digestive issues as well since it is beneficial to the spleen and stomach. Use potato to assist with toxins, breast abscesses, acute hepatitis, tonsillitis, mumps, and stomach and duodenal ulcers. Rosemary benefits the lung and stomach. Its warming nature moves energy and helps diminish cold. Use rosemary to aid with common cold, headache, abdominal pain, digestion, and menstrual pain. Garlic benefits the spleen, stomach, and lungs. Use garlic to reduce toxins and parasites, improve immune system, and assist with malaria-like diseases, whooping cough, and flu symptoms.

Ingredients

- 1 large head of cauliflower, chopped into small pieces
- 1 medium russet potato, peeled and diced
- 4 cups organic chicken broth
- 4 medium cloves of garlic, peeled and smashed
- ½ teaspoon freshly ground white pepper
- 1 teaspoon sea salt
- 3 small fresh rosemary sprigs

Directions

1 Place the cauliflower, potato, chicken broth, garlic, pepper, salt, and rosemary sprigs into a large saucepan.

2 Cover and cook over medium heat for 20 to 25 minutes, or until the vegetables are cooked through.

3 Remove rosemary sprigs.

4 Strain the cauliflower mixture in a fine sieve. (You can reserve the broth for another use — it is very tasty!)

5 Put the cauliflower mixture back into the saucepan.

6 Use a potato masher to smash the mixture into a smooth puree. Serve immediately.

Winter Desserts

Chapter 4
Winter Desserts

The surprisingly astounding Juice & Essence dessert world is an amazing place! We feature satisfying and creative inventions with nutritionally balanced and in most cases gluten-free ingredients. Enjoy!

Winter Sensations

Birth & Balance

Makes about 3½ dozen

Our Winter Sensation cookies are a creative and delicious way of working the warming immune system boosting benefits of ginger into a winter dessert/snack. We found inspiration in the Trinidadian Friendship Cookie, spliced it with the popular ginger snap, and adorned them with the Juice & Essence special touch. Don't forget to share!

Juice & Essence

Using almond meal flour adds healing benefits to the lungs and intestines while using coconut flour adds a strengthening element to the heart. Ginger benefits the spleen, stomach, and lungs while warming the body, treating common cold, vomiting, and cough with excess phlegm. Cinnamon and cardamom are warming, circulating, and helpful with nausea, vomiting, bloating, loss of appetite, threatened miscarriage, and diarrhea. Walnuts benefit the kidneys, fortify kidney essence, warm the lungs, assist with wheezing and coughing, low back pain, frequent urination, and constipation caused by dryness.

Ingredients

- ¼ cup organic coconut sugar
- ¼ cup organic turbinado sugar
- 1 cup almond meal flour
- 1¼ cups coconut flour
- 2¼ teaspoons baking soda
- 1 teaspoon ground ginger
- ½ teaspoon ground cinnamon
- ½ teaspoon ground cardamom
- ½ teaspoon coarse sea salt
- ½ teaspoon grated fresh ginger
- ¼ cup molasses
- ¼ cup pure maple syrup
- ½ teaspoon vanilla
- ¾ cup walnut oil
- 1 large organic egg
- ¼ cup turbinado sugar (for rolling the cookies in before baking)

Directions

1 Preheat oven to 350°F.

2 Put the coconut sugar, ¼ cup turbinado sugar, almond meal, coconut flour, baking soda, ground ginger, cinnamon, cardamom, salt, fresh ginger, molasses, maple syrup, vanilla, walnut oil, and egg into a large mixing bowl.

3 Blend the mixture together with an electric hand mixer until all of the ingredients are combined. Refrigerate for 30 minutes to let the dough become firmer.

4 Put the remaining ¼ cup turbinado sugar into a small bowl.

5 Roll the dough into 1" balls.

6 Swirl them around in the turbinado sugar to coat the outside of each ball.

7 Place the balls on a parchment-lined baking sheet keeping them about 1" apart.

8 Bake in the middle of the preheated oven for 10 to 12 minutes.

9 Remove from the baking sheet to a rack to cool completely.

Trinidadian Holiday Black Cake
Juice & Essence Style

Birth & Balance

Makes about 48 cupcakes or four 9"×5" loaves

Calypso, soca, roti, parang, pastels, wining, lyming, tomato choka and black cake represent the Trinidadian holidays. It's always a party in Trinidad, the home of one of the most enjoyed carnivals in the world. One taste of this cake and celebration of the West Indies will flood your veins and enliven your smile. Special gratitude to Dr. Ken's mom for sharing her dear generational secrets of love and authentic flavor.

Juice & Essence

Prunes offer benefits to the liver and aid in healing liver diseases while assisting with constipation. Use prunes to help with the wasting thirsting symptoms of diabetes. Cherries are qi tonifying and beneficial to the spleen/pancreas. Use cherries in the cases of involuntary semen emission, gout, arthritis, and rheumatism. Currants and raisins help build strong blood and benefit the liver and kidneys. Walnuts strengthen kidneys, warm the lungs, and moisten the intestines thereby assisting with low back pain, lower leg weakness, and impotence, frequent urination, wheezing, and coughing. Nutmeg, allspice, clove, and ginger tonify yang energy thereby warming the body, rectifying sluggish circulation, treating common cold, weak knees, and low back pain along with sluggish lymph and immune systems. Ghee has a unique benefit to the body of balancing hormones and tonifying the essence that governs the connective tissue. Ghee promotes resistance against disease, fast healing from injuries and intestinal inflammations such as ulcers and colitis. Eggs help build blood and yin qualities.

Prepare the Fruit

Note: This step needs to be done at least 7 to 14 days in advance.

Ingredients

- 2 cups dried prunes
- 2 cups dried cherries
- ½ cup dried currants
- 1 cup golden raisins
- ½ cup raisins
- one 750-ml. bottle of Black Forest Cherry Brandy
- one 750-ml. bottle Myers Dark Rum©
- 2 tablespoons Angostura Aromatic Bitters
- ½ cup Cointreau

Directions

1 Combine all of the ingredients together into a large airtight container and set aside at room temperature for 7 to 14 days.

2 After the 7 to 14 days, strain the fruit from the alcohol (reserving the alcohol) and place into the bowl of a food processor fitted with the chopping blade.

3 Process the fruit until it is coarsely chopped and put it back into the container with the alcohol and set aside.

Prepare "Browning"

Ingredients

- 1 lb. light brown sugar
- ½ cup boiling water

Directions

1 Put the light brown sugar into a large sauté pan and place over medium heat.

2 Stir the sugar constantly until it is melted and turning dark brown.

3 Slowly add the ½ cup of boiling water while constantly stirring until the mixture is combined.

4 Remove from heat and let cool just a little. *Do not let it get hard or it will not mix into the cake batter. If this happens, just gently reheat the "browning" until it is liquid again.*

5 Preheat oven to 250°F.

Trinidadian Holiday Black Cake
Juice & Essence Style ~ *continued*

Assembly

Ingredients

- 1 cup coarsely chopped walnuts
- 1 teaspoon cinnamon
- ½ teaspoon ground allspice
- ⅛ teaspoon ground cloves
- ¼ teaspoon ground ginger
- ⅛ teaspoon freshly grated nutmeg
- 2 cups all-purpose flour
- 4 teaspoons baking powder
- 2 cups organic coconut sugar
- 1 cup organic turbinado sugar
- 2, 7.5-ounce jars ghee (clarified butter)
- 8 organic eggs
- 1 teaspoon orange zest
- 1 teaspoon grapefruit zest
- 1 teaspoon lemon extract
- 2 teaspoons almond extract
- 2 teaspoons vanilla extract

Directions

1 Prepare the desired pans for baking; place 48 liners into cupcake pans or line the 9"×5" baking pans with parchment paper.

2 Mix the walnuts, cinnamon, allspice, cloves, ginger, nutmeg, flour and baking powder into a mixing bowl and set aside.

3 Cream together the coconut sugar, turbinado sugar and ghee with an electric hand mixer in a large mixing bowl.

4 Add the chopped fruit and alcohol mixture as well as the "browning" and stir to combine.

5 Add the eggs one at a time and beat well after each addition.

6 Now add the orange zest, grapefruit zest, lemon, vanilla, and almond extracts until combined.

7 Gradually add the flour mixture beating well after each addition.

8 Put the batter into the desired baking pans filling the cupcake pans to the top and the baking pans ¾ of the way full.

9 Bake the cupcakes for about 1½ hours and the baking pans for 2 to 2¼ hours.

To Finish

Ingredients

one 750-ml. bottle Myers Dark Rum©

Directions

1 Immediately upon removing the pans from the oven, pour some more rum over each cake: 1 teaspoon of rum poured over each cupcake, 3 tablespoons of rum poured over each 9"×5" baking pan.

2 Let the cakes cool completely before serving.

3 Store covered at room temperature.

Cranberry~Ginger Walnut Bread

Birth & Balance

Makes one 9"×5"×3" loaf

Warm, fresh baked bread goes well with our *Grapefruit~Fennel & Mint Marmalade* (page 138)...or is it vice versa? Well they both go well with our *Parmesan Stuffed Sausage Meatballs* (page 44)...or is it vice versa? We chose the combination of cranberry, ginger, and walnut for the tart taste, digestive aid, and strengthening qualities respectively.

Juice & Essence

Walnuts are highly beneficial to the kidneys, bladder, and urinary tract. They are also beneficial to the lungs in cases of asthma. Walnuts assist with kidney yang which warms the body and encourages circulation. Healthy kidneys benefit the brain, bone marrow, and emotionally your willpower. Cranberries aid in the treatment of kidney stones.

Ingredients

- 2 cups all-purpose flour
- 2 teaspoons baking powder
- ½ teaspoon salt
- 1 teaspoon ground cinnamon
- ¼ teaspoon ground allspice
- 6 tablespoons unsalted butter, softened
- ¾ cup sugar
- 2 large eggs
- ¾ cup milk
- 1 cup walnuts, toasted and coarsely chopped
- ½ cup dried cranberries
- ¼ cup crystallized ginger, coarsely chopped

Directions

1 Preheat the oven to 375°F. with the rack in the middle position.

2 Butter and flour a 9"×5"×3" loaf pan and set aside.

3 Combine flour, baking powder, salt, cinnamon, and allspice in a medium-size bowl, mix well.

4 In a small bowl, mix the toasted walnuts, dried cranberries, and crystallized ginger.

5 Add 1 teaspoon of the flour mixture to the nut mixture and stir to coat the nuts and fruit with the flour. This will prevent the nuts and fruit from sinking to the bottom during baking.

6 Set aside.

7 In a large bowl, cream the butter and sugar together until combined well.

8 Beat in the eggs and milk.

9 Add the flour mixture and nut mixture.

10 Blend until just combined. *Do not over mix!*

11 Pour into prepared pan.

12 Bake for 45 minutes, or until a tester inserted in the middle comes out clean.

13 Cool on a rack for 10 minutes.

14 Remove from pan and finish cooling on the rack.

*We served this delicious bread with our **Grapefruit~ Fennel & Mint Marmalade.***

Joy to the World Winter Warmer Bread Pudding

Birth & Balance

Serves 6 to 8

Reminiscent of the classic candy bar this bread pudding includes the three magical ingredients that have made it timeless — almonds, chocolate, and coconut. Pure pleasure!

Juice & Essence

Raisins help increase energy and can be used as a blood tonic as grapes contain valuable cell salts known to build and purify the blood and improve the cleansing function of the glands. Raisins or grapes benefit the liver and kidneys thus their corresponding tissues, bones, joints, and tendons. Coconut milk is strengthening and tonifies the heart. It can be used as a good source of saturated fat for vegetarians but beware if you already have a lot of saturated fat in your diet. Coconut milk helps increase semen and overall yin fluids. It is also helpful in treating edema stemming from heart weakness and diabetes. Almond milk lubricates the intestines and is good for lung conditions including coughing and asthma. Cinnamon and nutmeg increase yang and the warming circulating energy of the body. Use them to help with chilled limbs, sluggish digestion, low back, knee, and cold type pains, diarrhea, and low blood pressure. Eggs nourish the blood and brighten the eyes. Use for dry cough, blurred vision, and hoarse voice.

Ingredients

- 1 teaspoon unsalted butter
- 2 lbs. Challah (egg bread) cut into 2"-slices and then torn into 1"- to 1½"-pieces
- 1 cup golden raisins, lightly chopped
- 1 pint coconut milk creamer
- 1, 13.66-ounce can of coconut milk
- 1 cup unsweetened almond milk
- ½ cup organic granulated coconut sugar
- ¼ cup organic granulated cane sugar
- ½ cup organic sweetened flaked coconut
- 7 organic eggs
- 2 teaspoons vanilla extract
- ¼ teaspoon white truffle oil (optional)
- ½ teaspoon cinnamon
- ⅛ teaspoon freshly grated nutmeg
- ½ cup sliced almonds, lightly chopped

Directions

1 Preheat oven to 375°F.

2 Spread the 1 teaspoon of butter evenly on the inside of a 3"-deep 13"×9" baking pan.

3 Combine the bread and raisins into an extra-large bowl and set aside.

4 In a medium size bowl, whisk together the coconut milk creamer, coconut milk, almond milk, coconut sugar, cane sugar, flaked coconut, eggs, vanilla extract, white truffle oil, cinnamon, and nutmeg until completely incorporated.

5 Pour the mixture over the bread and raisins and mix well.

6 Set aside for 30 minutes to let the bread soak up the liquid.

7 Pour the bread pudding into the buttered baking pan and top with the almonds.

8 Bake for 30 minutes until the pudding is set.

9 Remove from the oven and let sit for 10 to 20 minutes before slicing.

Sauce Options

We served the bread pudding on a puddle of Marie Brizard Chocolate Royal Liqueur.

For another delicious option, try this sauce:

Ingredients

- 1, 15-ounce can cream of coconut (such as Coco Lopez)
- 6 tablespoons unsweetened cocoa powder
- 1 teaspoon vanilla extract

Directions

1 Heat the cream of coconut and cocoa powder over low heat for 5 minutes while whisking constantly.

2 Remove from heat and whisk in the vanilla extract.

3 Serve warm with the bread pudding.

Orange~Carrot~Olive Oil Cake

Birth & Balance

Serves 8 to 10

On your quest for a divine cake you must stop here! We used fresh carrot juice in place of some of the liquid, thereby elevating the nutritional benefits and healthy sugar content. This however is an orange cake of tremendous proportions made unique to the core by the addition of olive oil and goat's milk.

Juice & Essence

Benefits from carrots include stimulation for the spleen, regulation for digestion, and an opening sensation to the diaphragm. The use of orange peel assists with ridding the body of phlegm, treatment of indigestion, abdominal distention, pain, nausea, vomiting, and some types of chest oppression. Using goat's milk adds lung and kidney benefits in the areas of fatigue, weakness, and dry cough. Extra-virgin olive oil is the most trusted vegetable oil and has been consumed with healthful results for thousands of years. Olive oil is beneficial to the heart and cleansing to the arteries.

Ingredients

- 2¼ cups organic granulated sugar
- 1¼ cups goat's milk
- ½ cup extra-virgin olive oil
- ¼ cup fresh carrot juice
- ¼ cup fresh orange juice
  (we used honeybell)
- 1 tablespoon orange zest
- 3 large eggs
- 2¼ cup + 1 tablespoon all-purpose flour
- 1 teaspoon baking powder
- 1 teaspoon sea salt
- ½ teaspoon baking soda
- 1 cup powdered sugar, sifted
- 1 teaspoon melted butter
- 1 to 2 tablespoons orange juice,
  as needed
- 1 teaspoon orange zest
- *Strawberry~Beet~Fennel Sauce* (page 130)

Directions

1 Preheat the oven to 350°F.

2 Grease and flour a 12-cup Bundt pan and set aside.

3 Combine the sugar, goat's milk, olive oil, carrot juice, and orange juice in a large bowl.

4 Whisk in the eggs and zest.

5 In another bowl, combine the flour, baking powder, salt, and baking soda.

6 Whisk the dry ingredients together well.

7 Add the flour mixture to the liquid mixture, gently whisking the ingredients together until smooth.

8 Pour into the prepared pan and bake for 55 to 60 minutes, or until golden brown and the cake starts to pull away from the sides of the pan.

9 Cool completely in the pan placed on a wire rack.

10 Loosen the edges of the cake from the pan and invert onto a serving plate.

11 Make the glaze by whisking the powdered sugar, melted butter, 1 tablespoon orange juice, and zest together.

12 Add more of the orange juice by the teaspoon until the glaze is a slightly loose consistency.

13 Drizzle all over the cooled cake.

14 Let the glaze set then slice and serve with *Strawberry~Beet~Fennel Sauce.*

Winter
Sauces & Spices

Chapter 5
Winter Sauces & Spices

Juice & Essence Sauces & Spices are meant to be the perfect complement to our Juice & Essence recipes. This chapter will guide you through this part of the creative cooking process.

Strawberry~Beet~Fennel Sauce

Birth & Balance

Makes about 3 cups

Great sauce to bathe in, wash your hair with, or use as lip gloss . . . just kidding! However it is that good!!! In this case, we created it as a beautifully delicious way to work the healing benefits of beets into a dessert sauce. We tested this sauce on a private dinner in Palm Beach with a table full of beet haters . . . they loved it!! The ground fennel seed with the strawberry and the beets are a winning combination.

Juice & Essence

Beet is a heart strengthener and circulation improver. This sauce will offer mental calmness and a sense of wellbeing. Extended benefits include nourishment for the spleen, lung, kidneys, and liver, relief from dizziness, indigestion, alcohol hangover, and constipation. Enjoy as a blood cleanser, intestine moistener, and hormone regulator. Fennel is great for harmonizing digestion and soothing reflux. Strawberries are rich in silicon and strengthen teeth and gums. They are also beneficial for arterial and connective tissue repairs, benefit the spleen/pancreas, improve appetite, and moisten the lungs.

Ingredients

- 4 cups fresh strawberries, washed and trimmed
- 1 teaspoon whole fennel seeds, finely ground in a spice mill
- 3 tablespoons Palmetto honey
- ¼ cup fresh beet juice
- ¼ cup fresh orange juice (we used honeybell)

Directions

1   Place the strawberries in the bowl of a food processor fitted with the chopping blade.

2   Add the remaining ingredients and process until completely pureed.

3   Serve with the *Orange~Carrot~Olive Oil Cake* (page 126).

J&E Lemongrass Infused Oil

Birth & Balance

Makes about 1 cup

We were stunned that lemongrass oil could not be found in the supermarket…so we created it. Later enjoying it drizzled over our *J&E Beef Carpaccio* (page 48) and in the *Avocado Dipping Sauce* (page 136) used for our *Swordfish & Conch Fritters* (page 40). The uses are endless.

Juice & Essence

Lemongrass is a fragrant way to reduce inflammation and hypertension. Lemongrass helps to cleanse the liver, kidneys, bladder, pancreas, and digestive tract. It is also beneficial to digestion and increases circulation, reduces cholesterol, uric acid, and excess fats in the body. Use lemongrass to reduce severity of indigestion and upset stomach. Grapeseed oil contains a high amount of omega-6 fatty acids as well as smaller amounts of omega-3 and omega-9 fatty acids. Omega-6 is an essential nutrient that you need to get from food as the body cannot make it. Omega-6 helps with diabetic neuropathy, rheumatoid arthritis, allergies, attention deficit hyperactivity disorder, breast cancer, eczema, high blood pressure, menopausal symptoms, mastalgia, multiple sclerosis, osteoporosis, and premenstrual syndrome.

Ingredients

- 2, 6"-pieces of lemongrass, smashed and cut into 1"-pieces
- 1 cup grapeseed oil

Directions

1 Put the lemongrass and grapeseed oil into a small saucepan and bring to a simmer.

2 Continue to simmer the mixture for 10 minutes.

3 Remove the pan from the heat and set aside for about 1 hour, or until cool.

4 Strain out the lemongrass pieces and discard.

5 Use the oil in our *Avocado Dipping Sauce,* salad dressings, or anywhere you use oil and want an extra special taste of lemongrass.

J&E Curry

Birth & Balance

Makes about ¼ cup

It was a joy to embrace our inner Indian and figuring out the signature *J&E Curry* recipe. We were like chemists in a lab of love! Surprisingly it only took us one night! The use of fenugreek was new to us and more than harnessing the heat was a successful sweet interplay of spice nature that for centuries has added healing benefits to a wide array of dishes. It was a joy to familiarize ourselves with each spice equaling the now very familiar combination called curry that could entertain any palate when used as a seasoning.

Juice & Essence

Curry made from turmeric, ginger, cayenne, and other amazing spices offer significant circulatory and warming benefits. Turmeric, the main spice, is considered to be the most important and sacred spice of Hindus. It is used in various religious and social rituals. In Ayurvedic medicine, turmeric is used as a whole body cleanser, digestive aid, a treatment for infections, arthritis, jaundice, and other liver problems. In Chinese medicine, turmeric is known as yellow ginger and used to treat liver and gallbladder problems such as lowering blood pressure, increasing appetite, alleviating pain, and reducing inflammation. Fenugreek, with estrogen-like properties, has been found to help increase libido and lessen the effect of hot flashes and mood fluctuations common with menopause and PMS. Other benefits include assistance with asthma, sore throat, acid reflux, and some cardiovascular benefits. Fennel and mustard seed bring wonderful antioxidant, anti-inflammatory, decongestant, and antispasmodic benefits to the table. Ginger and cumin are great for warding off common colds. Cayenne pepper is healing to the intestines and a cure for ulcers.

Ingredients

- 1 teaspoon black peppercorns
- ½ teaspoon mustard seeds
- 1 teaspoon fennel seeds
- ½ teaspoon celery salt
- 1 teaspoon cumin
- ½ teaspoon ground coriander
- 2 teaspoons fenugreek
- ½ teaspoon ground ginger
- ¼ teaspoon ground allspice
- ¼ teaspoon ground turmeric
- ¼ teaspoon paprika
- ¼ teaspoon cayenne pepper
- ⅛ teaspoon ground red pepper flakes

Directions

1 Place the black peppercorns, mustard seeds, and fennel seeds into a spice grinder.
2 Finely grind and place in a small bowl.
3 Add the remaining ingredients and mix well.
4 Store the curry in an airtight container.

Avocado Dipping Sauce

Birth & Balance

Makes about ¾ cup

Tart, clean, creamy, and tantalizing. We created this dipping sauce with our *Swordfish & Conch Fritters* (page 40) in mind. Please explore its many uses with other fish dishes, a dip for veggies, and as a healthy sandwich spread.

Juice & Essence

Avocado builds blood, harmonizes the liver, and lubricates the lungs and intestines. They are a natural source of lecithin; a brain food rich in copper which aids in red blood cell formation and is a nutritious protein source often recommended for nursing mothers. Avocado is also used as a remedy for ulcers and to beautify the skin. Dill adds to yang energy which helps the body to get rid of cold and increases circulation of blood. Dill assists the body in getting rid of fish and meat toxins, helps assist with abdominal bloating and pain, poor appetite, vomiting, and low back pain. Lime is one of the most valuable fruits therapeutically for people who have eaten high-fat/protein diets. Lime helps destroy bad breath by destroying putrefactive bacteria in both the intestines and mouth. Its antiseptic, anti-microbial, and mucus-resolving action make it useful during dysentery, colds, flu, hacking coughs, and parasite infestation. Lime benefits the liver and encourages the formation of bile, promotes weight loss, cleanses the blood, and treats high blood pressure. Tequila is helpful in treating ulcerative colitis, TBS, colon cancer, and Crohn's disease.

Ingredients

- 1 ripe Haas avocado, peeled and cut into cubes
- 1 teaspoon lime zest
- ¼ cup lime juice
- 2 tablespoons tequila
- 2 tablespoons water
- 1 teaspoon fresh dill
- 1 tablespoon fresh garlic chives
- ¼ teaspoon cayenne pepper
- ¼ cup *J&E Lemongrass Infused Oil* (page 132)

Directions

1 Put the avocado, zest, lime juice, tequila, water, dill, chives, cayenne, and *J&E Lemongrass Infused Oil* into a blender.

2 Blend on high until all of the ingredients are a smooth consistency.

3 Add salt and pepper to taste if desired.

Grapefruit~Fennel & Mint Marmalade

Birth & Balance

Makes about 3 cups

The intent here was to sow something healthy and sweet for our *Parmesan Stuffed Sausage Meatballs* (page 44) with which to eat. When we looked at Parmesan stuffing, pink grapefruit with its acid comes jumping. In the annals of marmalade, it's fennel that balances. Can't forget the masterful mint for within this masterpiece it is the tint!

Juice & Essence

Grapefruit balances the flow of qi in the lung, spleen, and stomach meridians, helps treat dry cough, indigestion, burping, belching, and the ill effects of alcohol intoxication. Fennel benefits the liver, kidney, spleen, and stomach by balancing qi, assisting with excess gas, and abdominal distention, indigestion, reduced appetite, vomiting, and some types of menstrual pain. Lemon juice alkalizes and is a great detox aid via lymph assistance. Mint acts as a cooling digestive aid.

Ingredients

- 5½ cups water (use less if fruit is very juicy)
- 1 large pink grapefruit
- 3 cups sugar
- ¼ cup finely chopped fresh fennel
- 2 tablespoons lemon juice
- 1 tablespoon fresh mint leaves, torn into ¼"- to ½"-pieces

Directions

1 Bring the water to a boil in a stockpot.

2 Meanwhile, slice the whole grapefruit into very thin slices.

3 Then cut the slices into thin strips.

4 Next cut the strips into very small pieces.

5 Keep all of the juice that is given off while you are cutting the grapefruit.

6 Add the grapefruit pieces and juice to the boiling water.

7 Return to a boil and add the fennel and sugar.

8 Continue boiling for 45 to 60 minutes until it begins to thicken.

9 Place a porcelain dish in the refrigerator to get cold. You will be testing the marmalade mixture on this dish to see if you have the right consistency.

10 Once the mixture starts to thicken, remove the dish from the refrigerator and place a small dollop of the marmalade mixture onto it. If it congeals to your desired consistency, remove the marmalade from the heat.

11 You can transfer the mixture to a glass jar to cool.

The marmalade can be stored in the refrigerator for 2 weeks.

Spring

In the Chinese system of the Five Elements, the spring season is correlated with the element *Wood,* which governs the gallbladder and liver. The Wood element refers to the living, growing entities: trees, plants, and the human body.

The color associated with this element is the predominant one of spring — the green of young plants. The nature of spring and the Wood element is described as beginning or birth. Mentally, this corresponds to the "idea." The Wood element creates our mental clarity and our ability to focus, plan, and make decisions.

The eyes and the nails, especially the toenails, are the Wood element's indicator. So you may check both the eye tissue and nails for the state of health of the liver and Wood element in the body. The liver craves the sour flavor including vinegary foods.

The emotion of the liver is anger. Suppressed anger or communication may injure the liver and gallbladder. The liver has the function of a military leader who excels in his strategic planning; the gallbladder occupies the position of an important and upright official who excels through his decisions and judgments. Essentially, it stores and distributes nourishment for the entire body, is involved in the formation and breakdown of blood, and filters toxins (unusable materials) from the blood. The liver can deactivate hormones like thyroid and sex hormones, thus influencing the metabolism. It also governs the joints and tendons.

Moderate intake of naturally sweet foods such as apples, carrots, pears, and some acrid spices such as ginger, cardamom, cinnamon, basil, chives, and garlic are recommended. No overeating, especially of heavy, hard-to-digest foods; concentrated sweets, such as sugar; overuse of warm hot spices; overuse of alcohol, tea, or coffee.

Spring Superfoods

SWEET POTATOES OR YAMS are full of fiber, potassium, and vitamins A and C. Bake, roast, steam, or mash for an easy weeknight side dish. They are a year-round superfood.

GLOBE ARTICHOKES are actually related to milk thistle and contain silymarin that is the same active ingredient that is used as a liver tonic. They also contain cynarin, a phytonutrient that also supports liver health.

GARLIC has so many health benefits it's hard to list them all, but it is among Traditional Chinese Medicine's list of liver rejuvenating foods. Garlic is a strong antioxidant and excellent for cardiovascular health. It has been shown to suppress the growth of tumors and is a natural blood thinning agent as well as a natural antibiotic.

CHERRIES are another spring food that Traditional Chinese Medicine says helps relieve liver chi (subtle energy) stagnation. Tart cherries help with gout, osteoarthritis, and provide cardiovascular benefits.

ASPARAGUS is high in B vitamins, folate, potassium, rutin, selenium, and vitamin K. Asparagus helps regulate blood pressure and strengthen kidney function.

LEEKS are high in sulphides that protect against heart disease and lower high blood pressure. Those compounds are also protective against colon and prostate cancers. Leeks are eye health-boosters with their lutein and zeaxanthin content, and they are high in vitamin K and key minerals.

FAVA BEANS are another nutrient-dense food that's normally harvested in the spring. They are high fiber and low calorie, ideal for using in a weight loss diet after those winter food indulgences. Fava beans contribute to heart health and stabilize blood sugar.

Spring Appetizers

Chapter 1
Spring Appetizers

Fine as a stand-alone meal or as a precursor to Juice & Essence entrées. Our appetizers add an exploratory jolt to the most scrutinizing culinary adventurer!

Lager Braised Mussels & Clams

J&E Time Signature

Birth & Balance

Serves 4

"Beer is proof that God loves us and wants us to be happy." ~Benjamin Franklin
We thought we wanted to get our friends drunk so why not get some mussels and clams drunk and then eat them! You'll want to have annatto seeds for this…yes, it is in the ingredients already but it really added a unique perfume. You will enjoy the smell as we did when they simmer in the mixture of coriander, mustard seeds and lemon while letting off their cleansing scent.

Juice & Essence

With the focus of spring being the liver, mussels are the star that nourish the liver and strengthen connective tissue and joints. They also treat dizziness, vertigo, night sweats, low back pain and increase libido. Clams, like mussels, benefit the liver and kidneys. Clams also help the spleen and stomach. They treat edema, extra phlegm, goiters, dry cough and night sweats. Annatto, mustard and coriander seeds are used to help tone, balance and strengthen the liver and reduce inflammation. Their uses include lowering of cholesterol, blood pressure and excess mucus. They help with indigestion, bloating, and heartburn and relieve constipation. Lemon, onion and garlic are very beneficial for the immune system and help heal liver damage and also protect the liver from further deterioration. Lemon is also great for the lymph system and is a natural diuretic. Lager beer is a natural source of vitamins B6, E, and C as well as several essential oils.

Complement or Contrast

CONTRAST – *Sancerre is the quintessential seafood wine. The dry, crisp, medium acid and mellow fruits of this style go wonderfully with this dish to contrast with the briny, pungent mussels and the mustard, coriander, and annatto seeds.*

Ingredients

- 1 small yellow onion, chopped
- 1 tablespoon minced garlic
- 1, 12-ounce bottle lager beer
- ½ teaspoon mustard seeds
- ¼ teaspoon coriander seeds
- ¼ teaspoon annatto seeds
- 1 large lemon, sliced
- 2 cups no salt added chicken broth
- 1 teaspoon sea salt
- 1½ lbs. PEI mussels
- 2-dozen little neck clams
- 2 tablespoons chopped fresh parsley

Directions

1 In a large sauté pan, put the onion, garlic, beer, mustard seeds, coriander seeds, annatto seeds, lemon slices, chicken broth, and salt.

2 Bring to a boil over high heat.

3 Reduce the heat to medium and add the mussels.

4 Cover and cook for 5 minutes, or until the shells have opened.

5 Discard any of the mussels that did not open.

6 Remove the rest of the mussels from the broth and put into a bowl; cover to keep warm.

7 Add the clams to the simmering broth, cover and cook for 5 minutes, or until the clams have opened.

8 Discard any of the clams that did not open.

9 Add the mussels back to the pot with the clams and stir to combine.

10 Top with parsley and serve hot along with some crusty bread if desired.

Shrimp & Lobster Pesto Kabobs!

J&E Time Signature

Birth & Balance

Serves 4

In the quest to offer simple, tasty, yet eloquent selections for spring, we took shrimp and lobster and good old high-quality store bought pesto (or you can do even better…homemade) and voila!!!!

Juice & Essence

Lobster and shrimp are a low-fat, high-protein resource for liver-nourishing food. They also tonify the kidneys and therefore treat low back pain. Kidney yang-enhancing qualities warm the body and increase energy. Pesto adds to the spring focus on liver health. Basil benefits the lungs, spleen, stomach, and large intestine. Basil also helps to eliminate dampness, get rid of toxins, and assist with headaches, menstrual irregularity, bloating, and gas. Pine nuts assist the liver, lung, and large intestine and help with dizziness, dry cough, and constipation. Bell peppers contain lycopene, which attacks free radicals and is beneficial in helping protect your heart from cardiovascular disease.

Complement or Contrast

CONTRAST – My recommendation is a citrusy, steel-fermented Italian Chardonnay to contrast the rich lobster and herbaceous pesto.

Ingredients

- 3 tablespoons homemade or good quality store-bought basil pesto
- ½ lb. extra large shrimp, cleaned
- 2, 8-ounce Florida lobster tails (meat cut out of shell and cut into medallions)
- 1 large red bell pepper, cut into 1"×1"-chunks
- Metal or bamboo skewers (soak the bamboo skewers in water for 10 minutes before using)

Directions

1 In a large bowl, mix together the pesto, shrimp, and lobster medallions. Set aside to marinate for 20 minutes.

2 Spray the grill grates with cooking spray and preheat the grill to high heat.

3 Alternate putting the shrimp, lobster, and bell pepper onto the skewers.

4 Place the skewers on the grill and turn to cook all sides of the shellfish for a total of 10 minutes or to desired doneness.

5 Remove from the skewers and serve while still hot.

Sweet Plantain & Corn Fritters

Birth & Balance

Makes about 2 dozen

We already know that, texture-wise, sweet plantain and corn make a wonderful couple. Our job became finding a way to complement the juicy kernels of golden corn and the straightforward succulence of the sweet plantain. We accomplished this by adding Bailey's Irish Cream, fresh mint, coconut, star anise, and a meld of wonderful ingredients.

Juice & Essence

Plantains offer heart-healthy fiber, lubricate the lungs and large intestines, treat constipation, and ulcers and are good for reducing edema. Use plantains for assisting with colitis and hemorrhoids. They help detoxify the body and are useful in the treatment of drug addiction, especially alcoholism, marked by heat symptoms and sugar cravings. Rich in potassium, plantains are used universally for hypertension because they can reduce blood pressure. Corn benefits the heart, lung, spleen, liver, stomach, and gallbladder. Its functions are the tonification of lungs while helping to calm the heart. It is also great for assisting with difficult urination, gallstones, jaundice, hypertension, and the symptoms of hepatitis. Coconut benefits the spleen, stomach, and large intestine. It also assists with difficult urination, edema, and additionally will help with severe dehydration and diarrhea. Goat's milk, besides being high in calcium, is also rich in conjugated linoleic acid, a substance that reduces blood sugar. It benefits the lung, kidney, stomach channels, and increases energy. Goat's milk treats fatigue, hiccups, mouth sores, and chronic thirst. Beer is a natural source of vitamins B6, E, and C as well as several essential oils. Mint aids the digestion of fats, soothes the stomach, and stimulates bile production and flow. Mint can also be used to assist with Irritable Bowel Syndrome.

CONTRAST – The light bubbles of Prosecco elevate and enlighten this comforting appetizer.

Ingredients

- 1 large sweet, yellow plantain
- 1 ear of sweet corn-on-the-cob
- 1 tablespoon minced red onion
- ½ teaspoon olive oil
- ½ cup coconut flour
- ¼ cup all-purpose flour
- ⅛ teaspoon ground star anise
- ⅛ teaspoon ground cayenne pepper
- ½ teaspoon baking powder
- ½ teaspoon sea salt
- 6 ounces beer, at room temperature
- 6 ounces evaporated goat's milk
- 1 tablespoon pure maple syrup
- ¼ cup Bailey's Irish Cream Liquor
- 1 tablespoon Garden of Life Living Foods Extra-Virgin Coconut Oil, liquefied
- 1 large organic egg
- ⅛ cup organic unsweetened coconut flakes
- 1½ teaspoons minced fresh parsley
- 1 teaspoon minced fresh mint
- ¼ cup Garden of Life Living Foods Extra-Virgin Coconut Oil

Directions

1 Cut a slice lengthwise down the center of the plantain being sure to go through the skin only. Then cut it in half crosswise.

2 Bring a pot of water to boil that is large enough to hold the plantain halves.

3 Boil them for 15 minutes.

4 Remove from the water and, when cool enough to handle, remove the peel.

5 Chop the plantain into small pieces about the same size as the corn kernels and place into a bowl.

6 Remove the corn kernels from the cob and add them to the bowl with the plantains.

7 Set aside.

8 Put the onion and ½ teaspoon olive oil into a small frying pan set over medium-high heat.

9 Cook the onion until it is just translucent.

10 Remove from heat and set aside to cool.

11 In a large mixing bowl, whisk together the coconut flour, all-purpose flour, star anise, cayenne pepper, baking powder, and salt.

12 Add the beer, evaporated goat's milk, maple syrup, Bailey's, the 1 tablespoon liquefied coconut oil, and egg.

13 Whisk the ingredients together to combine.

14 Stir in the coconut flakes, parsley, mint, plantain, corn, and onion.

15 Heat a cast iron skillet over medium-high heat and add the ¼ cup coconut oil.

16 Once the oil is hot, drop the batter by the tablespoon into the hot oil.

17 Cook until golden brown on each side.

18 When the edges are browned, that is a good indication that it is time to flip the fritters over.

19 Serve hot drizzled lightly with a well-aged, good quality balsamic syrup or Sriracha sauce.

Dandelion Greens, Beet, & Bean Rolls

Birth & Balance   Serves 6

Fresh dandelion leaves are very nutritious. The challenge for us was to make them attractive to eat. The accompaniments we chose all skyrocket this dish into a highly beneficial powerhouse. The concept of softening the dandelion greens by blanching gave the subtle assistance needed to release nutrients and curb bitterness. Raw grated yellow beets touched each roll with a middle note of sweet earthy texture. Our bean puree allowed us to work in some salt along with softness and binding qualities.

Juice & Essence

This dish is rich in blood cleansing properties offered both by dandelion greens and beets. Beets also detox the liver, cool the body and help rid the body of dampness. Dandelion greens are useful for damp heat complaints such as psoriasis and eczema. Beets fortify the liver functions by treating liver stagnation and sluggishness, purifying the blood, and when used with carrots, promote hormone regulation. Additionally this dish is a blood builder and heart strengthener due to the beet and garbanzo bean content. Garbanzo beans are the highest in iron of the legume family and benefit the spleen/pancreas, heart and lungs.

Complement or Contrast

CONTRAST – New Zealand Sauvignon Blanc's bright melon and pear qualities will temper the slightly bitter dandelion greens.

Directions

1 In a large pot of boiling water, blanch the dandelion greens for 2 minutes, or until softened but still bright green.

2 Transfer the greens to a bowl of ice water to stop the cooking.

3 Carefully remove the leaves from the water and drain on a rack.

4 Heat the safflower oil in a sauté pan over medium heat.

5 Add the shallots and garlic and sauté for 2 minutes.

6 Add the garbanzo beans and continue to cook for 3 minutes more.

7 Remove from heat and add the rosemary, sherry, and salt.

8 Stir to combine.

9 Let cool for 5 minutes.

10 Place the beans into a food processor fitted with the chopping blade.

11 Process the mixture until very smooth.

12 Lay a dandelion leaf flat on a work surface.

13 Place 1 teaspoon of the bean puree on the center of the leaf.

14 Top with some of the grated beet and roll up the leaf to cover the beans and beets.

15 Continue with the rest of the leaves, beans, and beets.

16 They may be served cold or at room temperature.

17 Drizzle the rolls with a little of the walnut oil before serving.

Ingredients

- 20 dandelion greens, tough stems removed
- 2 tablespoons safflower oil
- 2½ tablespoons minced shallots
- ½ teaspoon minced garlic
- 1, 15.5-ounce can garbanzo beans, rinsed and drained
- ¼ teaspoon minced fresh rosemary
- ¼ cup sherry
- ½ teaspoon salt
- 1 cup grated fresh yellow beets
- Walnut oil

Rock Shrimp~Heirloom Tomato Pasta Salad

Birth & Balance

Serves 6

Our first time using rock shrimp worked out very well in this toss. We used simple ingredients with the focus on flavor and healthful purpose, bolstered by plays on texture that were guided by the star ingredient. The heirloom tomatoes were gifts and opened us to a beautiful play on the senses. We were given ones that tasted like wine and some like chocolate…who knew??!!!

Juice & Essence

Shrimp is a stomach, liver and kidney tonifier with benefits for male virility, liver balance, thirst, blood circulation and stomach opening. The high antioxidant containing tomatoes assist with cancer prevention, dizziness, mouth sores, wasting thirst, red eyes and indigestion. The significant quantity of supportive spices and herbs boosts the immune system and provides energy. Cayenne pepper, in significant measure, strengthens the stomach, invigorates circulation and helps heal intestinal ulcers. Celery balances liver functions, clears heat, assists with lowering high blood pressure and helps with dizziness, vertigo, headache and red eyes. Onions treat the common cold, diarrhea and worms.

CONTRAST – Central Napa steel fermented or very lightly aged (one year or less) Chardonnay to accompany the shrimp, tomato and pasta. The inherent crisp nature of this wine can handle the ingredient combination. Example: Gringich Hills.

Ingredients

- 1, 12-ounce box whole wheat penne pasta (we used Hodgson Mill Whole Wheat Gourmet Pasta with Flax Seed)
- 2 teaspoons sea salt
- 1 teaspoon cayenne pepper
- 1 teaspoon paprika
- 1 teaspoon onion powder
- 1 teaspoon garlic powder
- 1 teaspoon ground New Mexican chili pepper
- 3 tablespoons extra-virgin olive oil
- 1½ lbs. shelled and cleaned rock shrimp
- 2 tablespoons olive oil
- 3½ cups chopped fresh heirloom tomatoes
- 2 tablespoons minced whole scallions
- ⅔ cup diced celery
- 1 cup diced sweet onion
- ⅛ teaspoon minced seeded fresh habanero pepper
- ½ cup diced fresh fennel
- 1 teaspoon chopped fresh fennel fronds
- ¼ cup chopped fresh basil
- 1 cup fresh basil oil (mix 1 cup olive oil, 35 fresh basil leaves, pinch of salt in blender until combined)
- Juice of 1 lemon
- 1½ teaspoons ground smoked black pepper
- Salt to taste

Directions

1 Cook the pasta according to the package directions.

2 Drain, rinse, and set the pasta aside to cool.

3 Combine the salt, cayenne pepper, paprika, onion powder, garlic powder, ground New Mexican chili pepper, and 3 tablespoons of olive oil in a large bowl.

4 Add the rock shrimp and stir to coat well with the rub.

5 Heat a large sauté pan over medium-high heat.

6 Add the olive oil and the shrimp when the pan is hot.

7 Sauté until the shrimp is cooked through about 5 minutes.

8 Remove from heat and put the shrimp into a large bowl.

9 Place the pasta, tomatoes, scallions, celery, sweet onion, habanero, fennel, fennel fronds, basil, basil oil, lemon juice, and smoked black pepper into the bowl with the shrimp and mix well.

10 Add more salt to taste.

11 Serve immediately or cover and chill up to 1 day.

Beer Battered Yellow Squash

J&E Time Signature

Birth & Balance

Serves 4

We heated up the cooling nature of squash and balanced it out with cayenne, black pepper, paprika, and a cast iron pan on high. Gel that together with a beer batter and you have yourself a spring treat worth trying. Enjoy!

Juice & Essence

Summer squash is cooling, helps with detoxing, and decreases inflammation. It is great for treating difficult urination and issues with edema as well as thirst. Eating squash helps the spleen, stomach, and large intestine. Beer is a natural source of vitamins B6, E, and C as well as several essential oils. Quinoa flour is gluten-free, high in protein, and contains all the amino acids necessary for our nutritional needs. It is also high in iron and calcium and a good source of manganese, magnesium, and heart healthy fiber.

Complement or Contrast

CONTRAST – Champagne or Prosecco are my favorite wines with fried appetizers. The effervescence and good acids work in contrast to the fried food and help to lighten the entire experience.

Ingredients

- 1 teaspoon fresh lemon zest
- 1, 12-ounce lager beer
- 1½ cups quinoa flour
- ½ teaspoon ground cayenne pepper
- ½ teaspoon paprika
- 2 teaspoons freshly ground black pepper
- 2 teaspoons sea salt
- 1 cup safflower oil
- 3 large yellow summer squash, thinly sliced (about ⅛"-thickness)

Directions

1 In a large bowl, whisk together the zest, beer, flour, cayenne pepper, paprika, black pepper, and salt.

2 Heat a cast iron pan over medium heat.

3 Add the safflower oil and heat the oil until it is shimmering or to 325°F.

4 Dip each squash slice into the batter shaking off the excess.

5 Drop into the oil and cook on each side for 1 to 2 minutes, or until lightly browned.

6 Remove from the oil when done and drain on paper towels.

7 Continue frying with the remaining squash.

8 Serve immediately while still warm.

Cauliflower~Ricotta~Rice Paper Ravioli with Carrot~Leek Sauce

J&E Time Signature

Birth & Balance

Serves 4

This is not your average ravioli but ravioli none the less. Choosing to roast the cauliflower was a home run that allowed for this cold appetizer to retain the warmth and comfort expected of this Italian tradition. The rice paper gives this dish wings and a delightful transparency. We chose to balance temperature and color by serving it on a warm palate of our *Carrot~Leek Sauce* (page 236).

Juice & Essence

The cauliflower in this combination nicely tonifies the spleen and stomach, with assistance in the areas of indigestion, pain, and tendency toward chill. Garlic warms the stomach and energizes the spleen, detoxes and kills worms, and helps with food accumulation and stagnation. Tarragon is also detoxing and relaxing. Tarragon promotes the production of bile by the liver which helps digestion and the process of eliminating toxic waste from the body. It also helps induce appetite. This sauce, due mainly to the leek content, is warming with benefits to the spleen, lungs, and stomach. This dish treats indigestion, cough, and difficulty swallowing. The carrot component helps dissolve accumulations such as stones and tumors. Carrots are alkaline forming and clear acidic blood conditions including acne, tonsillitis, and rheumatism. Tomatoes offer benefits to the stomach and cleanse the liver, purify the blood, and detoxify the body in general.

Complement or Contrast

COMPLEMENT – This thoughtful and complex appetizer commands a medium fruit, dry, low acid and low tannin wine. Example: Dolcetto Didogliani (the only region for Dolcetto) or, to make it easier, a central coast California Merlot or an easy drinking California table wine such as "Red Truck."

Prepare the Ravioli

Ingredients

- 5 cups chopped cauliflower
- ½ cup fresh tarragon leaves
- 1 medium garlic clove, minced
- 1 teaspoon freshly ground white pepper
- ¼ teaspoon freshly ground black pepper
- ½ teaspoon ground mustard
- 1 teaspoon sea salt
- 2 tablespoons extra-virgin olive oil
- 1 cup part-skim ricotta cheese
- 12 sheets of rice paper (spring roll wrappers)

Directions

1 Preheat the oven to 425°F.

2 Mix together the cauliflower, tarragon leaves, garlic, white and black pepper, ground mustard, salt, and olive oil.

3 Place on a rimmed baking sheet.

4 Roast the cauliflower in the pre-heated oven for 15 minutes, or until tender.

5 Put the cauliflower into a food processor fitted with the chopping blade.

6 Add the ricotta cheese and puree until very smooth.

7 Fill a large bowl with water.

8 Submerge one sheet of rice paper into the water for a few seconds until it has softened slightly. Drain and place on a cutting board.

9 Cut the rice paper into quarters.

10 Take one of the quarters, point side facing you, and place 1 rounded teaspoon of the cauliflower puree on the pointed edge.

11 Fold over and wrap in the sides to completely enclose the puree.

12 Place on a tray and cover with plastic wrap so the ravioli does not dry out.

13 Continue filling and wrapping the remaining ravioli.

14 Place the tray of ravioli into the refrigerator while preparing the sauce.

Prepare the Sauce

Ingredients

- 2 tablespoons extra-virgin olive oil
- 2 tablespoons clarified butter
- 3 cups diced carrots
- 1¼ cup cleaned, sliced leeks
- 4 cloves garlic, minced
- ½ cup sweet vermouth
- ½ cup dry sherry
- ½ cup hot water
- 1, 14.5-ounce can organic diced tomatoes
- Salt and pepper

Directions

1 Heat a large saucepan over medium heat.

2 Add the olive oil and butter to the pan.

3 Then add the carrots, leeks, and garlic and sauté for 2 minutes.

4 Cover and continue to cook for 20 minutes, stirring occasionally.

5 Remove cover and add the vermouth, sherry, water, and tomatoes.

6 Sauté the mixture for 10 minutes over medium heat while stirring occasionally.

7 Put the carrot mixture into a food processor fitted with the chopping blade and puree until smooth. Add salt and pepper to taste.

8 Put the mixture back into the saucepan and reheat the sauce until desired temperature.

9 Put the hot sauce on the bottom of the plate and top with the ravioli.

10 Garnish the plate with fresh tarragon sprigs if desired.

Spring Entrées

Chapter 2
Spring Entrées

We took the best the world has to offer and refined each contribution with respect to cultural ideals. We used our palates, taste experience, and history of chef interactions to lovingly create our entrées.

Himalayan Salt Plate
Grilled Pompano

Birth & Balance

Serves 4

Carol had a Himalayan crystal salt slab in her pantry that we couldn't wait to use. The opportunity finally presented itself when we chose the in-season pompano to christen it! Spectacular efforts were made in the area of sauce creation to complement this simple, fun and tasty fish preparation.

Juice & Essence

The key ingredient: mineral salt — benefits the stomach, kidney, large intestine, and small intestine channels. Pure forms of mineral salt offer assistance with clearing heat, cooling the blood, resolving toxins, phlegm and food accumulations in the upper venter (abdomen), bleeding gums, sore throat, toothache, toxins due to lime disease, and snake and insect bites. Pompano offers considerable amounts of omega-3 fatty acids which serve liver health and anti-inflammatory purposes. Goat's milk benefits the lungs, kidney and stomach channels, by energizing and detoxing. Goat's milk also treats with vomiting, thirst, and diarrhea.

CONTRAST – "New World" Riesling – Good fruit yet dry and crisp to play on the Himalayan salt and hearty nature of the Pompano used in this dish. Example: Trimbach.

Prepare the Fish

Ingredients

- 4 pompano fillets (8 ounces each)
- 2 tablespoons extra-virgin olive oil
- ¾ teaspoon Pensey Spices Florida Seasoned Pepper Mix
- Himalayan Crystal Salt Slab

Directions

1 Rub the pompano fillets with the oil and sprinkle both sides with the pepper mix.

2 Place the salt plate on a cold grill.

3 Turn the grill heat to high and close the cover.

4 Heat for about 15 minutes until the salt plate is hot.

5 Place the fillets on top of the salt plate and cook for 2 minutes.

6 Flip the fillets over and cook for another 2 minutes.

7 Remove to a dish and cover to keep warm while preparing the sauce.

Prepare the Sauce

Ingredients

- 1 tablespoon olive oil
- 1 tablespoon minced onion
- ½ teaspoon minced garlic
- ½ cup fresh squeezed Minneola orange juice
- ½ cup low-fat goat's milk
- ½ teaspoon sea salt
- ½ teaspoon minced fresh tarragon
- ¼ cup whole milk Greek-style yogurt (room temperature)

Directions

1 Heat the oil in a sauté pan over medium-high heat.

2 Add the onion and garlic and sauté for 2 minutes.

3 Add the orange juice and sauté for 2 more minutes.

4 Reduce heat to medium and whisk in the goat's milk, salt, and tarragon.

5 Cook the sauce for 2 minutes.

6 Remove the pan from the heat and whisk in the yogurt.

7 Stir the sauce until the yogurt is incorporated.

8 Pour the sauce over the fish and serve.

Juice & Essence Leg of Lamb

Birth & Balance

Serves 6

Inspired by the Easter season and the celebration of rebirth, we took a cut of meat customary to the Mediterranean and the Middle East and implemented some flavors from the Far East. The method of using the spicy, sweet paste of seasoned peanut butter to serve as the binding agent to the grape leaves and moisture sealant to the leg of lamb was ingenious. Besides being a take on stuffed grape leaves, we infused this holiday gift with a balanced and healthful array of festive essence.

Juice & Essence

Lamb is a very warm, nourishing, energizing, and blood building meat with the ability to help relieve low back and knee soreness, weakness, abdominal pain, and hiccups. The organs receiving health benefits from lamb are the spleen and kidneys. Adding peanuts to this dish not only creates a tasty version of it, the peanuts are also beneficial to the spleen and lungs, helpful in treating dry cough, nausea, and a weak stomach. The spices and herbs in this dish add to the energizing, immune boosting, and phlegm relieving benefits of this main course. Coriander benefits the lung and spleen channels, helps aid in sweating, assists with bloating, and treats measles.

CONTRAST – With so many elements in this dish we need a robust, dry red wine with good tannins and some fruit to envelope the amazing flavors. Example: South African such as Rustenberg or my personal suggestion is Sella Mosca's Marchese Villa Marina from Italy.

Ingredients

- 1, 16-ounce jar natural creamy peanut butter
- 1 tablespoon minced garlic
- 4 tablespoons Tupelo honey
- 2 tablespoons soy sauce
- 1 tablespoon ponzu sauce
- 3 tablespoons olive oil
- 1 teaspoon whole mustard seeds
- 1 teaspoon whole coriander seeds
- 1 teaspoon dried rosemary
- 1 tablespoon dark cocoa powder
- 1 teaspoon paprika
- ½ teaspoon cayenne
- ½ teaspoon ground New Mexican chile
- 1 teaspoon lemon zest
- Juice of 1 lemon
- 1 teaspoon sea salt
- 6 large garlic cloves, thinly sliced
- 1, 6- to 7-lb. leg of lamb, trimmed of fat
- 1, 16-ounce jar grape leaves

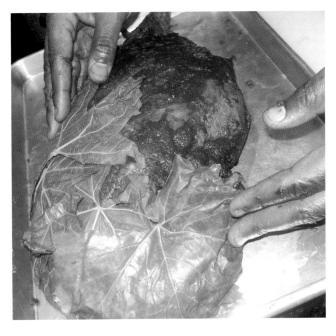

Directions

1 In a large bowl, combine the peanut butter, garlic, honey, soy sauce, ponzu sauce, and olive oil.

2 Finely grind the mustard seeds, coriander seeds, and dried rosemary in a spice mill and add to the peanut butter mixture.

3 Add the cocoa powder, paprika, cayenne, New Mexican chile, lemon zest, juice, and salt.

4 Mix together well and set aside.

5 Using a paring knife, cut random 1" slits all over the leg of lamb.

6 Completely insert the six thinly-sliced garlic cloves into the slits.

7 Remove the grape leaves from the brine.

8 Fully open each leaf and place on a rack to drain slightly.(Start out by draining about half of the leaves in the jar. You will not need the entire jar.)

9 Place the leg of lamb on a rimmed baking sheet.

10 Cover all sides of the lamb completely with the peanut butter mixture.

11 Now place the grape leaves on top of the peanut butter mixture.

12 Be sure to overlap the leaves so that the lamb is completely covered.

13 Cover and refrigerate overnight or up to 2 days.

14 Preheat the oven to 450°F.

15 Remove the lamb from the refrigerator for 30 minutes prior to roasting and transfer to a roasting pan.

16 Cover the pan with aluminum foil and place in the preheated oven for 1 hour.

17 Remove the foil from the pan and continue to roast for another 30 minutes.

18 Remove from the oven and let rest for 20 minutes.

19 Remove the grape leaves, carve and serve.

Cioppino with Pine Nut Crusted Seared Tuna & Fried Green Tomatoes

Birth & Balance

Serves 4

We started off wanting to make a seafood stew that was light and decided to top it with pine nut encrusted tuna and fried green tomatoes. As it turned out, our Cioppino was not light. It was chock full of seafood! It ended up hearty and beautifully cemented with the topping of tuna and fried green tomatoes.

Juice & Essence

Fish supplements qi, blood, liver, and kidneys, which help to invigorate yang, harmonize the stomach, and treat indigestion. Pine nuts enter lung channels and treat dry cough. Clams nourish the liver and moisten dryness. The herbs and spices, namely clove and orange peel, strengthen the spleen and digestion.

Complement or Contrast

CONTRAST – A Bordeaux Chardonnay with its normally buttery and oaky characteristics will help enhance this dish.

Prepare the Stock

Ingredients

- 1 fennel bulb, quartered
- 1 medium onion, quartered
- 2 large garlic cloves
- 3 tablespoons extra-virgin olive oil
- 1 teaspoon crushed red pepper flakes
- 1, 28-ounce can whole
  San Marzano tomatoes
- 1 cup red wine
- 2, 8-ounce bottles clam juice
- 1 cup chicken stock
- 2 bay leaves
- 2 teaspoons minced fresh thyme
- 2 tablespoons minced fresh oregano
- 2 tablespoons minced fresh basil
- 2 large strips of zest from a
  large orange
- 1 tablespoon balsamic vinegar
- Sea salt and pepper to taste

Directions

1. In a food processor fitted with the chopping blade, coarsely chop the fennel, onion, and garlic.
2. Heat the olive oil in a large stockpot over medium heat.
3. Add the fennel, onion, and garlic mixture along with the crushed red pepper flakes.
4. Sauté stirring occasionally until softened and onion is translucent about 8 minutes.
5. Add the tomatoes, red wine, clam juice, chicken stock, bay leaves, thyme, oregano, basil, zest, and balsamic vinegar.
6. Add salt and pepper to taste.
7. Bring the stock to a boil then reduce the heat and simmer for 20 minutes to blend flavors.
8. Remove the bay leaves and orange rind.
9. Keep the stock at a simmer while preparing the tomatoes and tuna.

Cioppino with Pine Nut Crusted Seared Tuna & Fried Green Tomatoes ~ *continued*

Fried Green Tomatoes

Ingredients

- 3 large green tomatoes
- 1 cup all-purpose flour
- ½ cup cornmeal
- ½ teaspoon garlic powder
- ½ teaspoon onion powder
- ½ teaspoon ground white pepper
- 1 teaspoon sea salt
- ½ teaspoon fresh ground black pepper
- ½ teaspoon smoked black pepper (optional)
- ½ teaspoon paprika
- 2 large eggs
- 1 cup buttermilk
- ½ teaspoon Sicilian sea salt
- ¼ teaspoon fresh ground pepper
- 1 large garlic clove, smashed
- 1 cup canola oil
- 7 tablespoons butter

Directions

1 Slice the green tomatoes into 1"-slices.

2 Set on a rack over a baking sheet.

3 Combine the flour, cornmeal, garlic powder, onion powder, white pepper, salt, black pepper, smoked black pepper, and paprika in a shallow dish.

4 Mix the egg, buttermilk, ½ teaspoon salt, ¼ teaspoon pepper, and smashed garlic clove in another shallow dish.

5 Dip each slice of tomato in the egg wash first and then coat evenly with the cornmeal mixture.

6 Place on rack to dry until ready to fry.

7 Meanwhile, heat the oil and butter in a large cast iron skillet until hot.

8 Fry the tomatoes in batches until browned and crisp about 5 to 8 minutes each side.

9 Drain on rack set over a baking sheet.

Tuna

Ingredients

- 1 lb. fresh tuna steaks divided into four servings
- ¼ cup pine nuts, finely ground
- 1 teaspoon Sicilian sea salt
- ½ teaspoon freshly ground Grains of Paradise
- Sprinkle of ground cayenne pepper
- 3 tablespoons canola oil

Directions

1. Combine the pine nuts, salt, and the Grains of Paradise in a small bowl.
2. Press this coating all over the tuna steaks.
3. Sprinkle the top with a little cayenne pepper to taste.
4. Add the canola oil to a medium size sauté pan over medium-high heat until the oil is shimmering. Add the tuna and sear for 1 to 2 minutes on each side to desired doneness.
5. Set aside.

Finish the Stock and Seafood Assembly

Ingredients

- 1½ lbs. little neck clams
- 1½ lbs. mussels
- ¼ lb. calamari, body sliced in two, legs left whole
- ½ lb. sea scallops cut in half horizontally
- Seared tuna
- Fried green tomatoes
- ¼ cup fresh parsley, chopped for garnish

Directions

1. Add the clams to the stock, cover and cook for about 5 minutes.
2. Add the mussels, calamari and scallops.
3. Cover and cook for about 5 minutes more until the shells are open and the seafood is just cooked through.
4. Spoon into large bowls and top with seared tuna and fried green tomatoes.
5. Sprinkle with parsley and serve.

Hog Snapper with Cocoa~Chili Rub & Strawberry~Lavender Sauce

J&E Time Signature

Birth & Balance

Serves 4

What better way to take a wonderful Florida fish and awaken it with the basis of most women's favorite food…chocolate! We did our best to create a sauce that would bring the multipurpose herb of lavender to the forefront. The sweet, red-colored sauce complements the brown tinge of our hog snapper.

Juice & Essence

This is a heart healthy dish due to the essential fatty acids found in the hog snapper. Unadulterated cocoa is also beneficial to the heart and circulation. Chili helps reduce phlegm in the lungs and aids in lung health. Additionally this dish improves the immune system, breathing, and aids as an anti-depressant and libido enhancer. Lavender offers detoxifying benefits. Strawberries are useful for arterial and connective tissue repairs due to their richness in silican and vitamin C.

Complement or Contrast

CONTRAST – A great dish that deserves the great Spanish seafood wine…Albarino. Enough said!!! Albarino is from northern Spain and is the essential food wine. It is light and dry with notes of citrus, melon, and pear that bring together the flaky white fish, sweet strawberries and earthy cocoa/chili rub. Example: Lagar de Cervera.

Strawberry~Lavender Sauce

Ingredients

- ¼ cup raspberry liquor
- 3 tablespoons dried lavender flowers
- 1 quart strawberries, hulled, divided

Directions

1 Mix the liquor and the lavender flowers in a small saucepan.

2 Heat to simmer and continue to cook for 10 minutes.

3 Set aside to cool.

4 Put half of the strawberries through a juice machine to make 1½ cups of juice.

5 Strain the juice through a fine mesh sieve into a small saucepan.

6 Cut the remaining strawberries into thin slices and set aside.

7 Strain the raspberry liquor and lavender mixture through a sieve into the saucepan with the strawberry juice.

8 Bring the mixture to a simmer and reduce down to ¼ cup.

9 Add the sliced strawberries and remove from heat.

10 Keep warm while preparing the fish.

Prepare the Fish

Ingredients

- 1½ lbs. hog snapper fillets
- 1 tablespoon cocoa powder
- ½ teaspoon ground New Mexican chili pepper
- ⅛ teaspoon cayenne pepper
- 1 teaspoon sea salt
- 1 tablespoon extra-virgin olive oil

Directions

1 Preheat broiler.

2 Mix together the cocoa powder, ground chili, cayenne pepper and salt in a mortar and pestle to combine.

3 Spread the olive oil on a baking sheet.

4 Place the fish on top and turn to coat with the oil.

5 Thoroughly rub the cocoa and chili mixture onto the top of each fillet.

6 Broil the fish for about 10 minutes, or until cooked through.

7 Serve with Strawberry~Lavender Sauce.

J&E Perfect Patty Melt

J&E Time Signature

Birth & Balance

Serves 4

Starting with a simple question: *Why don't we do our version of a patty melt?*
The answer: *A plethora of unique modifications to a classic hot sandwich.*

First we prepared the burger meat in an unorthodox fashion that yielded an extremely juicy patty. Second we selected pickled daikon radish for salt and sour and scallions instead of onions as a topping. Third the sprouted wheat bread, and finally Munster cheese was all part of our devious plan to raise the patty melt bar!

Juice & Essence

Beef benefits the spleen, liver, stomach, kidneys, and large intestine channels. Increases qi and blood, enriches yin/fluids, strengthens tendons, joints, and bones. Beef is also helpful with low back pain and knee weakness. Daikon radish benefits the lung and stomach, stimulates circulation, resolves toxins, and treats food accumulation, blocked qi, and blood. Scallions help expel toxins, treat cold symptoms, fever, chills, headache, abdominal pain, blocked urination and defecation. Sprouted wheat bread is predigested and therefore easier on individuals with gluten allergies. Wheat nourishes the heart and kidneys.

Complement or Contrast

CONTRAST – B.O.C.C.! (BIG OL' CALIFORNIA CAB) **It takes this beefy, cheesy, delicious concoction then flips it upside down and gives it a spanking. Example: Platinum series from Sterling or Heitz Cabernet.**

Prepare the Onions

Ingredients

- 1 teaspoon clarified butter
- 1 teaspoon extra-virgin olive oil
- 1¼ cup sliced scallions (white parts only)
- 1 tablespoon chopped pickled daikon radishes

Directions

1. Heat a small frying pan over medium-high heat.
2. When hot, add the clarified butter and oil.
3. Add the scallions and set the heat to low.
4. Continue to cook slowly for 15 to 20 minutes until the scallions are caramelized.
5. Add the pickled daikon radishes and mix together with the scallions.
6. Keep warm while preparing the patties.

Prepare the Patties

Ingredients

- 2 lbs. 80% organic grass-fed ground beef
- 1 teaspoon sea salt
- ½ teaspoon ground black pepper

Directions

1. Mix all of the ingredients together and divide the meat in to 4 even balls.
2. Heat the grill to high and place the meatballs on the grill.

3. Immediately lower the heat to medium-high and cook for 8 minutes.
4. Flip the meat over and using a metal spatula, squash the ball to flatten into a burger.
5. Continue to cook for 5 minutes for medium-well.

Assembly

Ingredients

- 8 slices sprouted wheat bread
- 8 slices Munster cheese
- 2 tablespoons butter-at room temperature

Directions

1. Spread butter on one side of each slice of bread.
2. Place a grill pan on the grill and heat until hot.
3. Put the buttered side of 4 slices of the bread in the pan.
4. Top each with one slice of the cheese, a burger, some of the onion/daikon radish mixture, another slice of cheese and top with another piece of bread, buttered side up.
5. Grill until the bread is toasted and crisp.
6. Carefully turn the sandwich over and grill on the other side until the bread is toasted and crisp. Serve immediately.

Parmesan~Mustard Baked Chicken

J&E Time Signature

Birth & Balance

Serves 4

This is a familiar dish to us, simple, straightforward, and full of flavor. We modified a few aspects from its original content for healthier purposes. The use of Parmesan in a sparing fashion adorned the breasts with a gluten-free, crisp and tasty crust. By substituting a combination of Parmesan, herbs and mustard for the usual flour we upped the ante on health benefits.

Juice & Essence

Mustard is warming, stimulating, pungent and useful as a diuretic. It strengthens digestion particularly in the case of loose, watery stools and assists with resolving a stagnant liver and sluggish spleen. Mustard is beneficial in drying up white or clear lung phlegm. Chicken is a general strengthening agent and energizer. Specific organs affected are the spleen- pancreas and stomach. Additionally, chicken can be used to help improve the condition of bone marrow, improve appetite, poor lactation and help diabetes. Basil balances qi and blood, warms the body, detoxifies, treats headaches, menstrual irregularities, diarrhea, burping and belching. Cayenne pepper warms and strengthens the stomach, invigorates circulation and helps heal the intestines.

CONTRAST – Light, crisp, flowery red with medium fruit to mellow the sharp, spiciness of this dish. Examples: Barbera, Dolcetto, Grgich Merlot.

Ingredients

- 4, 8-ounce boneless, skinless chicken breasts
- ½ teaspoon sea salt
- ½ teaspoon freshly ground black pepper
- 2 tablespoons delicatessen-style mustard
- 2 tablespoons extra-virgin olive oil
- 1 teaspoon minced fresh thyme
- 1 teaspoon minced fresh marjoram
- 2 teaspoons minced fresh basil
- ½ teaspoon cayenne pepper
- ¾ cup grated fresh Parmesan cheese

Directions

1 Place the oven rack at the top of the oven and preheat to 450°F.

2 Evenly salt and pepper the chicken breasts and set aside.

3 Combine the mustard, oil, herbs, and pepper in a small bowl.

4 Rub the mustard mixture onto both sides of the chicken breasts.

5 Coat each breast with 3 tablespoons of the grated cheese. Place on a rimmed baking sheet and bake for 15 to 20 minutes until the chicken is cooked through.

Clay-Pot Roasted Citrus Herb Chicken over Artichoke, Arugula & Tomato Salad with Crispy Potato Skin~Pancetta Croutons

Birth & Balance   Serves 4

The inspiration for this dish came from the quest for a light, airy dish that would bring spring to the table. The floral colors, herbs, even the use of potato skins as crispy, airy croutons replacing bread, create an effervescent feeling to lighten and fill any evening.

Juice & Essence

This is an immune system boosting dish with benefits to the liver, kidneys and spleen. It aids in digestion, anti-cancer, blood building, and circulation. Chicken is the star of this dish; it renews energy as well as being a blood builder. The rosemary, thyme, tarragon, and oregano aid digestion and boost the immune system. The organ systems benefited are primarily the kidneys and spleen by virtue of the chicken and the liver via the tomato.

Complement or Contrast

CONTRAST – For the combination of this herb-flavored chicken, citrus, and earthy artichoke creation, we need this wine to be dry, earthy, have fairly low tannins, and have a surprisingly long finish. When choosing Chianti, always choose one that is labeled Classico Riserva. It is well worth the additional investment.

Prepare the Chicken

Ingredients

- 1, 3- to 4-lb. whole organic roasting chicken
- 1 whole sprig plus 1½ teaspoons chopped fresh rosemary
- 1 whole sprig plus 1 teaspoon chopped fresh thyme
- 1 whole sprig plus 1 teaspoon chopped fresh tarragon
- 1 whole sprig plus ½ teaspoon chopped fresh oregano
- 1 lime, zested
- 1 Meyer lemon, zested
- 1 small orange, zested
- 2 tablespoons extra-virgin olive oil
- ¼ teaspoon freshly ground Grains of Paradise
- Salt and pepper to taste
- 1½ cups white wine
- Paprika

Directions

1 Prepare the clay roasting pot: submerge in cold water for 15 minutes.

2 Wash the chicken inside and out.

3 Dry and place all of the whole herb sprigs inside the cavity of the chicken and set aside.

4 In a small bowl, combine all of the chopped herbs, all of the citrus zests, olive oil, Grains of Paradise, and salt and pepper to taste.

5 Rub the mixture all over the chicken.

6 Remove the clay pot from the water.

7 Cut the zested Meyer lemon and zested orange in half (reserve the lime for another use) and place in the bottom of the clay pot.

8 Add the wine and then place the chicken on top of the citrus halves.

9 Sprinkle the top of the chicken with paprika and more salt and pepper.

10 Cover and place in a cold oven on the middle rack.

11 Turn the oven on to 450°F. and roast for 80 minutes.

12 While chicken is roasting, prepare the Potato Skin~Pancetta Croutons and Ghee Re-Smashed Potatoes. After 80 minutes, remove pot from oven.

13 Remove cover and let chicken rest and cool.

Clay-Pot Roasted Chicken ~ *continued*

Potato Skin~Pancetta Croutons

Ingredients

- 3 lbs. baby potatoes, divided
- ½ cup pancetta cut into ¼" dice
- ¼ teaspoon ground coriander
- ½ teaspoon sea salt
- ¼ teaspoon white pepper
- 2 tablespoons extra-virgin olive oil

Directions

1 Take 1½ pounds of the potatoes and cut in half.

2 Scoop out the insides leaving some flesh on the skin.

3 Cut potato skin halves into ½"-pieces. (Reserve the inside flesh as well as the remaining whole potatoes for the "Ghee Re-Smashed Potatoes".)

4 Combine the potato skin pieces, diced pancetta, ground coriander, salt, white pepper, and olive oil on a sheet pan and mix well.

5 Roast on the middle rack of a 500°F. oven for 15 minutes.

6 Flip the mixture to get crispy on the other side and roast for another 15 minutes, or until golden brown.

7 Set aside to cool

Ghee Re-Smashed Potatoes

Ingredients

- Reserved flesh from Potato Skin~Pancetta Croutons
- Remaining 1½ lbs. baby potatoes
- 1½ teaspoon ghee (clarified butter)
- ½ teaspoon sea salt
- ¼ teaspoon ground white pepper

Directions

1 Place the reserved potato flesh from the potato skin croutons into a small pot.

2 Peel the remaining 1½ pounds of potatoes and cut into quarters.

3 Fill the pot with water just to cover the potatoes.

4 Bring to a boil on medium heat and cook, uncovered, for 15 minutes, or until the potatoes can be pierced easily with a fork.

5 Drain well and place back in the hot pot.

6 Add ghee, salt, and pepper.

7 Mash together well.

8 Divide mixture into portion sizes and pack into small ramekins and place on a parchment-lined baking sheet.

9 Broil potatoes until they are browned and bubbling.

10 Lightly sprinkle the tops with paprika and serve hot.

Prepare the Dressing

Ingredients

- 1 teaspoon freshly ground mustard seed
- Dash of poultry seasoning
- Dash of dried Italian seasoning
- 1 tablespoon Champagne vinegar
- Pan juices from chicken, including juice from citrus halves
- ¼ cup white wine
- Salt and pepper to taste

Directions

1. Combine the mustard seed, poultry seasoning, Italian seasoning, Champagne vinegar, and pan juices including citrus juices to a sauté pan.
2. Boil over high heat for 5 minutes.
3. Add the white wine and reduce for another minute.
4. Remove pan from heat and add salt and pepper to taste.
5. Cool in the refrigerator for 20 minutes.

Assembly

Ingredients

- 2 lemons
- 6 to 8 baby artichokes
- 8 cups of arugula
- ¾ cup grape tomatoes
- Dressing
- Roasted Citrus Herb Chicken
- Potato Skin~Pancetta Croutons
- Ghee Re-Smashed Potatoes

Directions

1. Fill a medium size bowl with water.
2. Squeeze the juice of the two lemons into the water and add the lemon halves.
3. To prepare the artichokes: cut off the upper third with a sharp knife.
4. Peel off the outer leaves until you reach the light green, tender leaves.
5. Trim the stems and peel the outer layer.
6. Place in the lemon water.
7. Repeat with the remaining artichokes.
8. Place the arugula on a platter.
9. Cut grape tomatoes in half and place on top of arugula.
10. Slicing the artichokes needs to be done right before serving so they do not turn brown. Using a mandolin, thinly slice the whole baby artichokes.
11. Place in a small bowl and mix with a small amount of dressing to coat.
12. Scatter the artichokes on top of the salad.
13. Cut chicken into serving size pieces and place on top of salad.
14. Drizzle with dressing.
15. Scatter the Potato Skin~Pancetta Croutons over the salad and serve with the Ghee Re-Smashed Potatoes on the side.

Crab Cake Layered Lobster Medallions with Mango~Brandy Citrus Drizzle

J&E Time Signature

Birth & Balance

Serves 4 to 6

We wanted to stuff something! Originally it was going to be king crab legs and then…divine intervention brought us some fresh lobster tail from the Florida Keys, so we went with that. The circular feel of the medallions and the Florida mango being in season, inspired this dish for spring. The Mango~Brandy Citrus Drizzle is the icing on the cake!

Juice & Essence

Crab is a general bone builder used for bone fractures, dislocations, poison ivy, and burns. Crab is beneficial to the liver and stomach. The gallbladder, heart, and lungs receive healing from a combination of the herbal and vegetable ingredients. This dish is a great source of calcium. It is also great for blood circulation due to the use of fresh ginger, ground cumin, and coriander. This dish also assists with joint and lower back pain. The antibacterial and antiviral agents of the onion, lime zest, garlic, and spices add to the immune system boosting power and also aids in digestion. Mango treats coughing, wheezing, nausea, vomiting, and indigestion. Cardamom, ginger, and cayenne aid in the circulation of energy and blood, warm the body, treat bloating, poor appetite, and menstrual pain. They also benefit the liver, kidneys, and stomach.

Complement or Contrast

COMPLEMENT – *Medium, sweet Gewurztraminer celebrates the mango, and the orange and brings together the sweetness of the fruit in this medley of seafood.*

Prepare the Drizzle

Ingredients

- 1 cup fresh mango
- 2 tablespoons extra-virgin olive oil
- Juice of 1 small lime
- Juice of ½ orange
- ¼ cup brandy
- ¼ teaspoon pumpkin pie spice
- ¼ teaspoon caraway seeds
- ⅛ teaspoon ground ginger
- ⅛ teaspoon ground cardamom
- ⅛ teaspoon freshly ground Grains of Paradise
- ¼ cup heavy cream
- Pinch of ground cayenne pepper
- Salt

Directions

1 Puree the mango, olive oil, lime, and orange juices in a blender until smooth.

2 Place in a small saucepan and add the brandy, pumpkin pie spice, caraway seeds, ground ginger, cardamom, Grains of Paradise, and heavy cream.

3 Heat just to blend flavors. Do not boil!

4 Cool to room temperature.

5 Strain the mixture through a fine mesh sieve into a bowl so that the texture is very smooth.

6 Add a pinch of cayenne pepper and salt to taste.

Can be made 1 day in advance. Bring to room temperature before serving.

Crab Cake Layered Lobster ~ *continued*

Prepare the Crab and Lobster

Ingredients

- 1 tablespoon extra-virgin olive oil
- ½ cup Vidalia onion
- 1 teaspoon minced fresh ginger
- 1 small clove garlic, minced
- ½ cup finely diced red bell pepper
- ½ teaspoon ground cumin
- ¼ teaspoon ground coriander
- ½ teaspoon freshly ground Grains of Paradise
- 8 ounces fresh jumbo lump crabmeat
- ½ cup whole-wheat panko breadcrumbs
- ¼ cup chopped fresh cilantro
- 1 teaspoon lime zest
- 2 tablespoons mayonnaise
- 1 large egg
- Dash of hot sauce or to taste
- Salt and pepper to taste
- 4, 8-ounce Florida lobster tails
- 4 tablespoons extra-virgin olive oil

Directions

1 Heat the oil in a small sauté pan over medium heat.

2 Add the onion, ginger, garlic, and red bell pepper.

3 Sauté until vegetables begin to soften.

4 Add the cumin, coriander, and Grains of Paradise and continue to cook until vegetables are tender. Set aside to cool to room temperature.

5 Mix the cooled vegetable mixture in with the lump crab, panko, cilantro, lime zest, mayonnaise, egg, hot sauce, salt, and pepper.

6 Shape into small patties about 2" to 3" in diameter and place on parchment-lined baking sheet. Chill while preparing lobster tails.

7 Place lobster tails in a steamer pot and steam for 8 to 10 minutes, or until just cooked through.

8 Take out of shell and cut into medallions.

9 Then season the lobster lightly with salt and pepper.

10 Set aside while cooking crab cakes.

11 Heat 3 tablespoons olive oil in a large sauté pan over medium heat.

12 Place crab cakes in pan and cook on each side until golden brown.

13 Set aside and keep warm.

14 Meanwhile, heat the remaining tablespoon of olive oil in another large skillet over medium–high heat.

15 Sear the lobster medallions until lightly browned on the edges.

16 Place the lobster medallions on a platter and top each with a crab cake.

17 Drizzle the top with the Mango~Brandy Citrus Sauce.

*We served this delicious seafood combination with our **Florida Sweet Corn Salad** (page 210).*

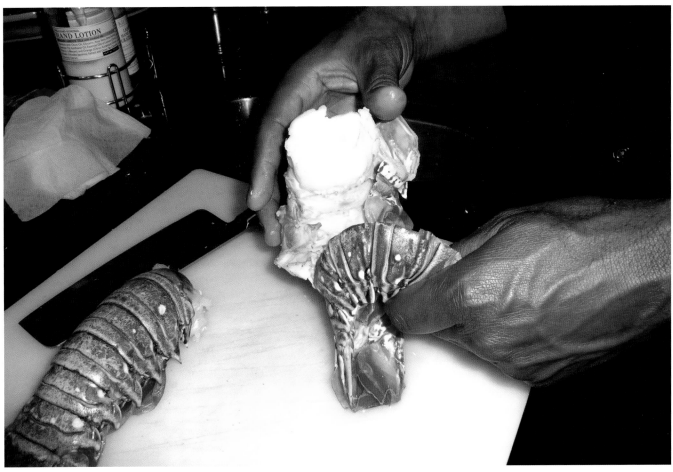

Trompe L'oeil Pork Tenderloin

Birth & Balance

Serves 4

The idea of this dish is to make you think it is a sweet dish although it is not. A play on the senses; trompe l'oeil of the palate!

Searing pork tenderloin is not our unique contribution. Our contribution to the pork tenderloin is in the unique way that we presented this fairly unhealthy meat in a very healthful manner. The concern with eating pork is the transfer of tapeworm and other unclean parasites as well as gallbladder and digestive issues found with regular pork consumption. There is also a concern of contracting influenza virus shared with humans via pigs' lungs frequently found in pork sausage.

Each ingredient in this dish counteracts these concerns in a stylishly flavorful way. It is not enough to say it ~ we sang it by encasing our tenderloins in colorful soy paper and pasta ~ watch out now!!!

Juice & Essence

Pork supplements kidneys, nourishes blood, and moistens dryness. The herb combination, especially thyme and rosemary, treats food and drink accumulation, headache, and indigestion. The herbs also enter and harmonize the stomach channels, move qi, resolve toxins, heal bodily aches and pain, and clear heat.

COMPLEMENT – This succulent festival deserves a velvety, elegant, well-balanced, dry red wine with light tannins, medium fruit and medium finish to complement this French-inspired dish. Solution: Pinot Noir from Burgundy or Tuscan Vino Nobile di Montepulciano.

Ingredients

- 1½ lbs. pork tenderloin, trimmed
- 4 large cloves of garlic, sliced
- 1 teaspoon minced fresh rosemary
- ½ teaspoon minced fresh thyme
- ¼ teaspoon fennel pollen
- Zest of 1 large orange
- ½ teaspoon sea salt
- 1 teaspoon freshly ground black pepper
- ¼ teaspoon freshly ground Grains of Paradise
- ½ lb. broccoli rabe, blanched for 30 seconds in boiling water, drained, and patted dry
- 4 scallions, green part only
- 20 fresh chives
- ¼ cup whole fresh basil leaves
- ¼ cup whole fresh mint leaves
- 1 egg white + 1 tablespoon water for egg wash
- 3 sheets of fresh pasta, 9"×11"
- 2 sheets each of spinach soy paper, turmeric soy paper, and paprika soy paper
- ¼ cup extra virgin olive oil
- ¼ cup water
- Paprika
- 2 scallions, green part only, finely chopped
- 3 chives, minced
- 1 tablespoon minced fresh oregano

Directions

1 Preheat oven to 400°F.

2 Make several small slits in the pork using a paring knife.

3 Stuff garlic slices into the holes.

4 Mix together the rosemary, thyme, fennel pollen, orange zest, sea salt, black pepper, and Grains of Paradise in a mortar and pestle.

5 Combine well and then rub all over the pork and let rest at room temperature for 30 minutes.

6 Sear the pork on all sides until brown.

7 Let the pork rest at room temperature for 15 minutes to cool.

8 Cut the pork in half crosswise and then lengthwise into strips 1" wide.

9 Take a pasta sheet and place two pieces of soy paper on top (use the same flavor).

10 Place a third of the broccoli rabe, scallions, chives, basil, and mint on top of the soy paper.

11 Place one-third of pork on top.

12 Brush edges of pasta with egg wash to help seal.

13 Working with the long side facing you, roll up the pasta tightly around the ingredients.

14 Press the edge together to seal.

15 Place in a casserole dish lightly coated with oil.

16 Repeat the process with the remaining ingredients.

17 Once all of the rolls are placed in the casserole dish, drizzle the ¼ cup of extra virgin olive oil and ¼ cup water over the tops and sprinkle with paprika.

18 Cover and bake for 15 minutes.

19 Remove from the oven.

20 Uncover and squeeze the juice from the zested orange over the dish and sprinkle the top with the finely chopped scallions, chives, and oregano.

21 Slice each roll into serving size pieces and serve immediately.

Bellini Basted Grilled Shrimp & Asparagus

Birth & Balance

Serves 4

The circular and linear shapes of the shrimp and asparagus seemed to work to balance each other. The goal this time was to make a visually interesting dish with unique tastes while exhibiting the essence of spring. When we look back at spring, this dish has a special place in our hearts.

Juice & Essence

Shrimp nourishes the liver, invigorates the kidneys and treats impotence and scanty lactation. Asparagus clears heat and lungs and eliminates dampness. Peaches moisten the intestines, move qi, aid the circulatory system and disperse accumulations. Onion treats the common cold and diarrhea. By strengthening the lungs and spleen, the coriander aids bloating, constipation and excessive phlegm.

CONTRAST – We need steel fermented, citrusy Chardonnay with a little oak and fruit. This wine with its loving nature cradles the individually strong components that are apparent here.

Prepare the Shrimp and Asparagus

Ingredients

- 16 jumbo shrimp with shells
- Peanut oil for frying the shells
- 1 lb. asparagus, trimmed and cleaned
- ¼ cup extra-virgin olive oil
- ¼ teaspoon crushed red pepper flakes
- ½ teaspoon sea salt
- ¼ teaspoon freshly ground black pepper
- Bellini Basting Sauce

Directions

1 In a large pot or deep fryer, heat some peanut oil to 350°F.

2 Heat grill to medium.

3 Remove the shells from the shrimp, being careful to keep them intact since they will be fried for the garnish.

4 Clean, devein, and butterfly the shrimp.

5 Season the shrimp with ¼ teaspoon of the sea salt and ⅛ teaspoon of the ground black pepper.

6 Drizzle the shrimp with a tablespoon of the olive oil and set aside.

7 Clean and trim the asparagus.

8 Mix together with the remaining olive oil, salt, pepper, and crushed red pepper flakes.

9 Set aside.

10 Once the fryer is up to temperature, add the shrimp shells (be sure they are dry so they do not spatter the hot oil).

11 Fry until crisp, about 2 minutes.

12 Drain on paper towels and set aside.

13 Grill the shrimp and asparagus and baste with the *Bellini Basting Sauce* for 8 to 10 minutes until done.

14 We set up this dish using our recipes for *Porcini & Sage Risotto* (page 212) and *Tomato Stuffed Peppers* (page 190) as follows: Set up the plate with the risotto in the center. Surround with 4 shrimp per person and garnish with the fried shrimp shells. Add some asparagus and a pepper. A beautiful addition would be to add some red and black caviar for contrast on the plate.

Prepare the Bellini Basting Sauce

Ingredients

- ¼ cup extra-virgin olive oil
- 1 teaspoon clarified butter
- 2 garlic cloves, pressed
- ½ cup peach nectar
- 1 teaspoon onion powder
- ½ teaspoon ground coriander
- ¾ teaspoon dried Mexican oregano
- ¼ teaspoon crushed red pepper flakes
- 1 teaspoon sea salt
- ½ teaspoon white pepper
- 1 cup Prosecco

Directions

1 Mix all of the ingredients except the Prosecco in a small saucepan.

2 Bring to a boil over high heat.

3 Boil the mixture for 5 minutes.

4 Add the Prosecco and boil to reduce by half, stirring occasionally for about 30 minutes.

5 Set aside to cool slightly.

Spring Accompaniments

Chapter 3

Spring Accompaniments

These accompaniments are gorgeous mates to the flavor notes and visual canvases of Juice & Essence entrées. These accompaniments are a fresh take on vegetable combinations that, as is customary with Juice & Essence, have an unpredictably delicious twist!

Green Bean & Beech Mushroom Sauté

Birth & Balance

Serves 6

The mushrooms are the star of this side dish and green beans were chosen for color. We liked the combination that these two veggies mingling would create. The safflower oil theme was of the essence. In the end, our anticipation proved correct. You will love this simple duo.

Juice & Essence

Green beans strengthen the spleen/pancreas and kidneys. They are helpful in treating diabetes and the frequent urination and thirst accompanied by this condition. Green beans are helpful for male vitality and beneficial for digestive complaints such as diarrhea. Mushrooms of this variety help decrease fat levels in the blood and rid the respiratory system of excess mucus. Additionally, the antibiotic properties found in mushrooms increases white blood cell count and thereby boosts immunity against disease producing micro-organisms. Mushrooms help treat contagious hepatitis, have anti-tumor capability and can help stop post-surgery cancer metastasis. Safflower oil assists with balancing hormones, cholesterol, blood sugar and inflammation complaints.

Ingredients

- 1 tablespoon safflower oil
- 1½ lbs. fresh green beans, trimmed
- 1 medium garlic clove, thinly sliced
- ¼ teaspoon crushed red pepper flakes
- 3.5 ounces fresh beech mushrooms, trimmed
- ½ teaspoon sea salt

Directions

1 Heat a large sauté pan over medium-high heat.

2 Add the oil and the green beans.

3 Sauté until the beans are just beginning to soften, about 8 to 10 minutes.

4 Add the garlic and crushed red pepper flakes.

5 Sauté for 4 minutes while constantly stirring so the garlic does not burn.

6 Add the mushrooms and salt.

7 Stir the mushrooms into the green beans and continue to cook for 1 to 2 minutes, just until the mushrooms are heated through. Serve immediately.

Tomato Stuffed Peppers

Birth & Balance   Serves 4

These decorative peppers will set any plate apart. We used the pepper as a cup to cradle the beautiful, succulent heirloom tomatoes as if to say that food represents love and spring the abundance of it.

Juice & Essence

Tomato stimulates the circulatory and digestive systems, and aids in lowering blood pressure and cholesterol. The garlic helps in cases of hardening of the arteries, asthma, flu, colds, and ear infections. It is also full of antioxidants and reduces the risk of heart disease.

Ingredients

- 2 large bell peppers, 1 red and 1 yellow
- 2 pints heirloom cherry tomatoes
- 1 large clove of garlic, thinly sliced
- 1 tablespoon fresh oregano, chopped
- ½ cup Kalamata olives, halved
- ½ teaspoon sea salt
- ¼ teaspoon freshly ground black pepper
- 3 tablespoons extra-virgin olive oil, divided
- 3 tablespoons balsamic vinegar

Directions

1 Preheat oven to 425°F.

2 Cut the peppers in half, clean out seeds and membrane.

3 Coat the inside and outside of the peppers with 1 tablespoon olive oil.

4 Place, cut side up, in an oil-coated casserole dish just large enough to hold the peppers.

5 Place the sliced garlic in the pepper shells, distributing evenly.

6 Cut the tomatoes in half and place in a medium-size mixing bowl along with the oregano, olives, salt, and pepper.

7 Drizzle with the remaining olive oil and the balsamic vinegar.

8 Fill the pepper shells with the tomato/olive mixture.

9 Bake the peppers uncovered for 20 to 25 minutes, or until they are cooked through.

J&E Ratatouille

Birth & Balance   Serves 4

We were looking for something to work with our *Trompe L'oeil Pork Tenderloin* (page 182) wrapped in soy paper and pasta. Ratatouille has a robust flavor with a simple feeling perfectly suited to accompany any dish searching for a fresh complement.

Juice & Essence

Zucchini resolves toxins and disperses accumulation and inflammation. Eggplant moves and rectifies qi and blood. Herbs and tomatoes harmonize the stomach and stimulate the circulatory and digestive systems.

Ingredients

- ¼ cup chopped fresh basil
- 1 tablespoon chopped fresh marjoram
- 1½ teaspoons chopped fresh thyme
- 2 teaspoons chopped fresh chives
- 1 large onion, diced
- 2 large cloves of garlic, thinly sliced
- 1 lb. eggplant, unpeeled and cut into ½"-cubes
- 1 lb. zucchini, unpeeled and cut into ½"-cubes
- 2 medium red bell peppers, cut into 1"-pieces
- 1 poblano pepper, cut into ½"-pieces
- 2 medium tomatoes, seeded and diced
- 1, 28-ounce can San Marzano whole plum tomatoes, strained, tomatoes coarsely chopped
- ½ cup extra-virgin olive oil
- 2 teaspoons sea salt
- Fresh ground pepper to taste

Directions

1 Preheat oven to 350°F.

2 Mix together all of the herbs, onion, garlic, eggplant, zucchini, peppers, tomatoes, canned tomatoes, oil, salt, and pepper in a large bowl.

3 Transfer to a lightly oiled 9"×13" glass baking dish.

4 Cover and bake for 1 hour.

5 Remove cover and stir.

6 Continue baking for another 10 to 15 minutes to reduce liquid.

7 Serve hot or at room temperature.

Springtime Eggplant Explosion

Birth & Balance

Makes 3 cups

Roasted goodness! The roasting process enhanced the explosion of flavors in this dish. The addition of fresh basil at the end with the fire-roasted tomatoes creates a pleasing peak for your palate. The lovely assortment of fresh herbs is finely assembled in a musical fashion. You can use this recipe as a tasty side dish or to stuff fresh artichokes like we did. It is also great as an appetizer with Parmesan toasts or as a pasta sauce.

Juice & Essence

Eggplant benefits the large intestine, stomach, and spleen. Food therapy attributes include clearing heat and cooling blood, improving circulation, healing canker sores, and easing swelling. The eggplant offers a rich source of bioflavonoids that help to renew arteries, prevent strokes and other hemorrhages. The star of this dish will also influence the liver and the uterus by moving liver qi and blood stagnation thereby easing lower abdominal discomfort. Eggplant, red bell pepper, and tomatoes are all members of the nightshade family known mostly for resolving stagnation of food and blood, promoting circulation, and reducing swelling. These, along with the onion, have potent anti-cancer and cancer symptom attributes.

Ingredients

- 1¼ lbs. eggplant, peeled and chopped into 1"-pieces
- 3 large plum tomatoes, chopped into 1"-pieces
- 1 large red bell pepper, chopped into 1"-pieces
- 1 small yellow onion, chopped into ½"-pieces
- 4 large garlic cloves, thinly sliced
- 1 teaspoon minced fresh marjoram
- ½ teaspoon minced fresh sage
- 1 teaspoon minced fresh thyme
- ½ cup extra-virgin olive oil
- 2 teaspoons sea salt
- ½ teaspoon freshly ground black pepper
- ¼ cup chopped fresh basil
- 1, 14-ounce can organic fire-roasted chopped tomatoes, drained

Directions

1 Preheat the oven to 400°F.

2 Line a rimmed baking sheet with foil.

3 In a large bowl, combine the eggplant, plum tomatoes, bell pepper, onion, garlic, marjoram, sage, thyme, olive oil, salt, and pepper.

4 Mix together well and spread out onto the prepared baking sheet.

5 Roast in the preheated oven for 1 hour.

6 Remove from the oven and let cool in the pan for 45 minutes.

7 Place the cooled vegetables in a large bowl.

8 Mix in the basil and the drained fire roasted tomatoes.

9 Can be served hot or at room temperature.

Springtime Stuffed Artichoke

Birth & Balance   Serves 4

There are so many reasons to try a version of stuffed artichokes. We took the best of our experiences over the years and combined them to make this amazingly tasty thistle!

Juice & Essence

This recipe, due to the artichoke, is strengthening to the liver and kidneys. It is also a blood cholesterol reducer due to the star of this dish. Immune boosting and antioxidant qualities are high because of the beautifully combined nutrients found in the artichoke, chicken stock, herbs, and spices. Other areas of assistance offered here are help with fertility and the common cold from the chicken stock, rosemary, artichoke, and basil. Ground white pepper helps with fatigue and digestion. Eggplant benefits the large intestine, stomach, and spleen. Food therapy attributes include clearing heat and cooling blood, improving circulation, healing canker sores, and easing swelling. The eggplant offers a rich source of bioflavonoids that help to renew arteries and prevent strokes and other hemorrhages. It will also influence the liver and the uterus by moving liver qi and blood stagnation thereby easing lower abdominal discomfort sometimes triggered by repressed emotions. Eggplant, red bell pepper, and tomatoes are all three members of the nightshade family, known mostly for resolving stagnation of food and blood, promoting circulation, and reducing swelling. These, along with the onion, have potent anti-cancer and cancer symptom associated attributes.

Ingredients

- *Springtime Eggplant Explosion* (page 194)
- 32 ounces chicken stock
- 1 cup water
- 1 cup Chardonnay
- 2 teaspoons minced fresh rosemary
- 2 tablespoons extra-virgin olive oil
- 1½ teaspoons dried tarragon
- 1 tablespoon ground white pepper
- 4 large globe artichokes, trimmed and choke removed
- 1 tablespoon chopped basil

Directions

1 Prepare *Springtime Eggplant Explosion.*

2 Set aside while preparing the artichokes.

3 In the bottom of a steamer pot, combine the chicken stock, water, Chardonnay, rosemary, olive oil, tarragon, and pepper.

4 Bring to a boil.

5 Place the trimmed artichokes on a steamer rack and put over the stock.

6 Cover and cook for 10 minutes.

7 Reduce heat to low and cook for 15 minutes more.

8 Remove the artichokes from the steamer rack and place on a cutting board.

9 Stuff the center of each artichoke with the *Springtime Eggplant Explosion.*

10 Stand the stuffed artichokes directly into the broth in the steamer pot.

11 Cover and cook over medium heat for 10 minutes, or until heated through.

12 Remove from heat and place each artichoke into a shallow soup bowl.

13 Ladle some of the stock into each bowl and sprinkle with the basil.

Mustard Roasted Radishes

Birth & Balance

Serves 4

We really enjoyed this surprise of a dish and were amazed at how incredibly attractive radishes can be when presented in the right manner. We chose to spotlight them by roasting them and including spicy Polish mustard. The texture and taste are delightful; nothing like you would imagine a radish to be.

Juice & Essence

Radishes have cooling properties with lung and stomach benefits. Radishes clear heat and assist with stagnation of food, qi and blood. Additional help via radishes range from treating distention and fullness to wasting thirst in diabetic cases and migraine headaches. The stimulating effects from the mustard benefit circulation and assist in reducing phlegm.

Ingredients

- 3 bunches of radishes with greens
- 1 teaspoon Pulaski Polish mustard
- 2 tablespoons extra-virgin olive oil
- ½ teaspoon minced garlic
- 1 tablespoon minced onion

Directions

1 Preheat the oven to 475°F.

2 Remove the greens from the radishes and reserve.

3 Cut the radishes in half.

4 Mix together the mustard, oil, garlic, and onion in a large bowl.

5 Add the cut radishes and mix together well.

6 Place the radish mixture on a rimmed baking sheet.

7 Roast the radishes in the preheated oven for 25 to 30 minutes until softened and caramelized.

8 Clean some of the radish greens in water.

9 Mince the greens and place on top of the roasted radishes. Serve immediately.

Beautiful Bulgur Chopped Salad

Birth & Balance

Serves 4

Merging interesting healthy ingredients should be the name of the game in any salad. This salad definitely got kudos in that department. We crammed in sprouts, bulgur, black radish, and even habanero pepper, then bathed the salad in coconut vinegar for a totally new and exciting living green experience.

Juice & Essence

Bulgur tonifies the kidneys, builds yin/fluids, and nourishes the heart-mind offering benefits in the areas of palpitations, insomnia, irritability, menopausal difficulty, and emotional instability. This dish is especially good for children and frail people, helpful with bed wetting, spontaneous sweating, night sweats, and diarrhea. Parsley improves digestion and detoxifies meat or fish poisoning. Parsley is a source of remarkable nutrition. It contains several times the vitamin C of citrus and is one of the higher sources of vitamin A, chlorophyll, calcium, sodium, magnesium, and iron. Parsley strengthens the adrenal glands and benefits the optic and brain nerves. It is great for treating ear infections, earache, and deafness and is also a great cancer preventative as well. Radish moistens the lungs and helps to diminish mucus and remove food stagnation. Radish is a preventative for viral infections such as the common cold and influenza. Cucumber is a mild diuretic, counteracts toxins, helps with depression, cleanses blood, and benefits the heart, spleen/pancreas, stomach, and large intestine. Cucumber purifies the skin and helps get rid of cellulite.

Ingredients

- 1 cup bulgur
- 1 cup boiling water
- ½ cup chopped parsley
- ¼ cup minced black radish
- ½ cup chopped, peeled, and seeded English cucumber
- 2½ teaspoons minced shallot
- ⅓ cup minced red bell pepper
- 1 teaspoon minced habanero pepper
- ⅓ cup minced celery leaves
- 1 cup quartered grape tomatoes
- 1 tablespoon minced fresh mint
- ¼ cup purple radish micro greens
- 1 teaspoon sea salt
- ½ teaspoon freshly ground black pepper
- 2 tablespoons extra-virgin olive oil
- 1 tablespoon coconut vinegar

Directions

1 In a large bowl, mix together the bulgur and the boiling water.

2 Cover and refrigerate for 30 minutes.

3 Uncover and fluff the bulgur with a fork.

4 Add the parsley, black radish, cucumber, shallot, red bell pepper, habanero pepper, celery leaves, tomatoes, mint, micro greens, salt, pepper, olive oil, and coconut vinegar and stir to combine.

5 Cover and refrigerate at least 1 hour and up to a day to let the flavors blend.

Herb & Spinach Couscous Stuffed Heirloom Tomatoes with Roasted Garlic Tomato Sauce

Birth & Balance

Serves 4

Couscous is a great change-up when it comes to sides and we enjoy the texture! The trick in making this attractive side dish was to give it a full flavor all its own by caramelizing the onions, roasting the garlic, choosing a well-balanced white wine, and bolstering the flavor of our grain choice with chicken stock. In addition, fortifying this dish with spinach, pine nuts and herbs created a lifeforce glow that was immediately felt on the palate and in the tummy.

Juice & Essence

Tomatoes are helpful to the stomach by clearing stomach heat while assisting in settling the liver and remedying indigestion. Other uses include moistening dryness and stopping thirst, invigorating blood circulation, and treating mouth sores, dizziness, and red eyes. Couscous is nourishing to the heart, spleen, and kidneys. It will also clear heat, stop thirst and assist with balancing digestion in cases of diarrhea and dysentery. Additionally this dish is energizing and blood building with immune boosting qualities. Pine nuts nourish fluids, moisten lungs, and large intestines thereby helping dry cough and constipation.

Ingredients

- 2 small heads of garlic
- 1 large sweet onion, chopped
- 2 tablespoons olive oil
- ½ cup white wine
- ½ cup chicken stock
- ½ cup water
- 1 teaspoon olive oil
- 1 cup whole wheat couscous
- 2½ cups chopped baby spinach
- ¼ teaspoon minced fresh thyme
- ½ teaspoon minced fresh marjoram
- 1 teaspoon minced fresh basil
- 3 tablespoons pine nuts, lightly toasted
- 4 large heirloom tomatoes
- ½ cup white wine
- Salt and pepper to taste

Directions

1 Preheat the oven to 375°F.

2 Place the heads of garlic on a sheet of aluminum foil and wrap the foil around the garlic to completely enclose the heads.

3 Place on the middle rack of the oven and roast for 40 minutes.

4 Unwrap the foil and set aside to cool.

5 Heat a large sauté pan over medium heat.

6 Add the onions and 2 tablespoons olive oil.

7 Sauté for 35 to 40 minutes until nicely caramelized, stirring occasionally and then set aside.

8 Place the wine, chicken stock, and water in a large saucepan.

9 Bring to a boil and add the 1 teaspoon of oil and the couscous.

10 Cover and cook for 2 minutes.

11 Uncover the pot and stir in the caramelized onions, chopped spinach, and the herbs.

12 Cover again and let the pot sit off the heat for 5 minutes.

13 Uncover and let cool for 30 minutes while you prepare the tomatoes and the sauce.

14 Cut ¼"-slice from the tops of the tomatoes and reserve.

15 Remove the flesh and seeds from the insides of the tomatoes leaving enough flesh to create a shell to be stuffed with the couscous and reserve the flesh for the sauce.

16 Lightly salt the insides of the tomatoes and set aside.

17 Once the couscous is cooled, stir in the pine nuts, salt, and pepper to taste and evenly stuff each tomato.

18 You can place the tops of the tomatoes back on top, slightly to the side, as a garnish.

19 Take the reserved tomato flesh and place in the bowl of a food processor fitted with the chopping blade.

20 Squeeze the roasted garlic cloves out of the heads into the food processor.

21 Process the garlic and tomatoes until smooth.

22 Transfer the mixture to a sauté pan and bring to a boil.

23 Add the white wine and continue to sauté for another 5 minutes.

24 Remove from heat and season to taste.

25 Pour sauce over the couscous stuffed tomatoes.

This sauce is also fantastic over the
Parmesan~Mustard Baked Chicken! (page 172)

Roasted Butternut Squash Puree

Birth & Balance   Serves 6

There is no wrong way to serve butternut squash. So we said let's roast it to bring out tons of inherent goodness and then puree it to give a supportive presence welcomed in almost any meal.

Juice & Essence

Butternut squash is a part of the winter variety of squashes that are generally helpful to the spleen and stomach channels. This squash will serve the function of strengthening digestion, energizing the body, detoxifying the body, ridding the body of worms, and reducing inflammation and pain. This is a lovely dish for nourishing and warming the body during cooler months. Onion, with some similarities to butternut squash, also warms the body, invigorates circulation, treats common cold, diarrhea, and worms. Honey assists with relaxing tension, ridding the body of toxins, and helping with dry cough and intestinal dryness causing constipation.

Directions

1 Preheat the oven to 425°F.

2 Cover a large rimmed baking sheet with foil.

3 Combine all of the ingredients into a large bowl and mix well.

4 Spread the mixture out in one layer on the prepared baking sheet.

5 Roast on the middle rack of the preheated oven for 30 minutes, or until the vegetables are soft.

6 Carefully transfer the vegetables to a food processor bowl fitted with the chopping blade.

7 Process until the mixture is a smooth puree.

8 Serve immediately or transfer to a covered casserole dish and refrigerate.

9 Bring to room temperature before reheating in a 350°F. oven for 20 to 30 minutes.

Ingredients

- 4 lbs. butternut squash, peeled, seeded, and cut into 1"-cubes
- 1 cup chopped white onion, chopped into ½"-pieces
- 2 tablespoons olive oil
- 2 tablespoons orange blossom honey
- 1 teaspoon minced fresh rosemary
- ½ teaspoon sea salt
- ¼ teaspoon ground white pepper

Red Quinoa

Birth & Balance   Serves 4

This is a colorful way to complement a dish without the typical starch as a side. We were happy to work in quinoa because of its tasty nutty flavor. It has a lightness that plays in your mouth.

Juice & Essence

Quinoa is a complete protein with essential amino acids that is gluten free. It is great for muscle building and high in cancer fighting antioxidants.

Ingredients

- ½ cup chopped sweet onion
- 1 tablespoon extra-virgin olive oil
- 1 cup red quinoa, washed and drained
- 1½ cups chicken stock, beef stock, or vegetable stock

Directions

1 Heat olive oil in a medium saucepan.

2 Add the onion and sauté for 5 minutes.

3 Add the quinoa and sauté, stirring constantly for 2 minutes.

4 Add the stock and bring to a boil.

5 Cover and lower heat to a simmer for 20 minutes.

6 Fluff with a fork before serving.

Sugar Snap Peas with Mint & Port Wine Vinaigrette

Birth & Balance   Serves 4

Since we paired this dish with our *Hog Snapper with Cocoa~Chili Rub & Strawberry~Lavender Sauce* (page 168), we carried on the sweet theme found in the main course, but with a nourishing, crunchy green this time. We chose the sugar snap peas with mint for their sing and zing!

Juice & Essence

Sugar snap peas and peas in general increase the health of, and tonify, the spleen/pancreas and stomach. Vinegar cleanses the blood. Mint is a cooling herb that will aid digestive processes.

Ingredients

- 4 cups fresh sugar snap peas, strings removed
- 2 tablespoons minced shallots
- 1 teaspoon coarse ground Dijon mustard
- 2 tablespoons port wine vinegar
- 4 tablespoons extra-virgin olive oil
- Salt and pepper
- 2 tablespoons chopped fresh mint

Directions

1 Steam the sugar snap peas for about 5 minutes, or until just cooked but still firm.

2 Whisk together the shallots, mustard, vinegar, and olive oil.

3 Add salt and pepper to taste.

4 Stir together the snap peas, vinaigrette, and mint to combine.

5 Set aside at room temperature for 30 minutes before serving so the flavors can blend.

Florida Sweet Corn Salad

Birth & Balance

Serves 4

This is a great salad for honoring corn when in season. Fresh and raw — this is a true vegan delight!

Juice & Essence

Corn is the part of this dish that benefits the heart and improves appetite. It aids digestion, strengthens kidneys, and increases vitality. Soybean adds to the heart benefits and strengthens the kidneys as well as being energizing, moistening dryness, stopping thirst, and treating mouth sores, dizziness, and poor digestion. Jalapeño pepper benefits the lungs. Overall this dish benefits lungs, relieves gallstones, and calms the heart. Immune boosting and enhances circulation. Cleanses lungs and disperses phlegm.

Ingredients

- 4 ears of fresh corn-on-the-cob
- ½ cup edamame
- ¼ cup chopped red onion
- ½ cup chopped jicama
- ¼ cup chopped fresh cilantro
- 1 teaspoon lime zest
- ½ teaspoon ground cumin
- 2 tablespoons extra-virgin olive oil
- 1 fresh jalapeño pepper
- 2 tablespoons lime juice
- Salt and pepper to taste

Directions

1   Cut the corn off the cob and place in a medium-size bowl.

2   Add the edamame, red onion, jicama, cilantro, lime zest, ground cumin, and olive oil.

3   Mix well and set aside.

4   Cut the jalapeño pepper in half.

5   Remove seeds and membrane from one-half and place them in a small bowl along with the remaining half.

6   Finely chop the seeded half and add to the corn salad.

7   To the bowl containing the rest of the jalapeño, seeds, and membrane, add the lime juice.

8   Set aside to allow flavors to blend for 30 minutes.

9   Strain the lime/jalapeno mixture through a fine sieve over the corn salad.

10 Discard the jalapeño and seeds.

11 Add salt and pepper to taste and mix the salad well.

12 Set aside at room temperature.

Can be made 6 hours in advance. Bring to room temperature before serving.

Porcini & Sage Risotto

Birth & Balance

Serves 4

This is risotto for people who don't like risotto! Italian in origin, risotto is an artful, slow, beautiful way to present rice; however, we are not fans of gummy, overly creamy foods. The result of this perfect medley was a tasteful, firmly textured, aromatic offering of risotto. Every bite is charming! This will be your show-off side for years to come!

Juice & Essence

Porcini mushrooms quiet the spirit. They also benefit the lung, stomach, and intestines, supplement the kidneys, and nourish the blood. Treats depression, anxiety, body fatigue, and qi weakness. Sage is an anti-parasitic.

Ingredients

- 1 ounce dried porcini mushrooms
- 1 cup boiling water
- 6 cups chicken stock
- 1 tablespoon olive oil
- 1 teaspoon clarified butter
- ½ cup diced pancetta
- ½ cup chopped shallot
- 1 cup Arborio rice
- 10 sage leaves, coarsely chopped
- ½ cup grated fresh Parmesan cheese
- Salt and pepper to taste

Directions

1   In a small bowl, mix together the dried porcini mushrooms and the boiling water.

2   Set aside to reconstitute for 20 minutes.

3   Strain the porcini from the liquid.

4   Finely chop the mushrooms and set aside.

5   Meanwhile, add the chicken stock to a large saucepan and bring just to a simmer. (Maintain the simmer while you make the risotto.)

6   Heat the olive oil and clarified butter in a large saucepan over medium heat.

7   Add the pancetta and sauté for 5 minutes.

8   Then add the shallots and sauté for 3 minutes until the shallots are translucent.

9   Mix in the rice and stir for a minute or so to coat the rice with the oil.

10 Add about ½ cup of stock and stir until it has been completely absorbed.

11 Keep adding the stock, a half a cup at a time and stirring until it is absorbed before adding more.

12 You will continue this process until the rice is al dente, about 20 to 25 minutes total.

13 When you are 15 minutes into the cooking time, add the porcini mushrooms and sage.

14 When rice is done, remove from the heat and add the Parmesan cheese and salt and pepper to taste.

Sprouted Salad with Strawberry~Dijon Vinaigrette

Birth & Balance   Serves 4

Spring has sprouted and the sunflower, sweet clover sprouts, and pea tendrils fit our *"tasteimony" to the resurgence of life. The strawberry-Dijon vinaigrette was formed using a strawberry balsamic vinegar that made a sweet splash when combined with Dijon mustard, and walnut and olive oils.

   *Definition: "tasteimony" = a validation whereas your taste buds are the witness to culinary perfection!

Juice & Essence

Strawberry is warming natured with benefits to the spleen/pancreas. Detoxifying qualities in the live elements of the red clover sprouts that represent the point of greatest vitality in the life cycle of the plant. One clearly experiences vitality when eating sprouts consistently. The sprouting process pre-digests the nutrients of this seed, making the proteins and sugars easier to assimilate and metabolize. Vinegar assists with cleaning blood and lymph. This dish will act as a general tonic due to sunflower seeds, which also lubricate the intestines and will assist with constipation. A very high antioxidant salad with large amounts of micronutrients assists with fighting cancer-forming cells while the additional high-fiber detoxifier and moistening apple content benefits the lung, stomach, and large intestines.

Ingredients

- 2 cups sunflower sprouts
- 1 cup sweet clover sprouts
- ½ cup pea tendrils
- ½ cup mixed micro greens
- 2 teaspoons Dijon mustard
- 2 tablespoons strawberry balsamic vinegar
- 2 tablespoons water
- 2 tablespoons roasted walnut oil
- 2 teaspoons extra virgin olive oil
- ¼ teaspoon black pepper
- ¼ teaspoon sea salt
- 1 cup slivered Granny Smith apple
- ½ cup roasted sunflower seeds

Directions

1   In a large bowl, mix together the sprouts, pea tendrils, and micro greens and set aside.

2   Prepare the vinaigrette in a small bowl by whisking together the mustard, vinegar, water, walnut oil, olive oil, pepper, and salt until emulsified.

3   Mix a tablespoon of the vinaigrette into the slivered apples and mix well to coat.

4   Then place them on top of the greens and sprouts.

5   Drizzle the salad with some of the vinaigrette and top with the sunflower seeds. Serve immediately.

Spring Desserts

Chapter 4
Spring Desserts

The surprisingly astounding Juice & Essence dessert world is an amazing place! We feature satisfying and creative inventions with nutritionally balanced and in most cases gluten-free ingredients. Enjoy!

Banana~Chocolate Dream

Birth & Balance   Makes 12

Thinking of things to do with phyllo dough and chocolate…we figured we would throw banana in the mix. In doing this, we created an amazingly childlike, awe-inspiring, creamy, tasty, tempting dream.

Juice & Essence

Bananas offer heart-healthy fiber, lubricate the lungs and large intestines, treat constipation and ulcers, and are good for reducing edema. Use bananas for assisting with colitis and hemorrhoids; they help detoxify the body and are useful in the treatment of drug addiction, especially alcoholism marked by heat symptoms and sugar cravings. Rich in potassium, bananas are used universally for hypertension because they can reduce blood pressure. Coconut benefits the spleen, stomach, and large intestine. It also assists with difficult urination, edema, and additionally will help with severe dehydration and diarrhea. Ginger and cinnamon assist with nausea, digestion, circulation, and cold feet and hands. Both also help with inflammation and pain related to osteoarthritis. Walnuts benefit the kidneys and lungs. Walnuts are rich in omega-3 fatty acids — an essential oil that will assist in lessening rheumatoid arthritis symptoms. They are very helpful for moistening the intestines, treating wheezing and coughing, low back pain and lower leg weakness, impotence, and frequent urination.

Prepare Phyllo Shells

Ingredients

- 3 tablespoons ghee (clarified butter)
- 3 tablespoons wildflower honey
- ½ teaspoon cinnamon
- ⅛ teaspoon ground ginger
- 8 sheets of phyllo dough
- ¼ cup toasted, finely chopped walnuts

Directions

1 Preheat oven to 350°F.
2 In a small saucepan, put the ghee, honey, cinnamon, and ginger.
3 Place over low heat for 3 minutes to melt the ghee and blend the flavors.
4 Set aside to cool slightly.
5 Open the phyllo dough and place on a work surface.
6 Cover with plastic wrap and a damp cotton towel so it will not dry out.
7 Take one piece of the dough and place it on a piece of parchment paper (long side facing you).
8 Brush the dough lightly all over with a little of the spiced ghee mixture being sure to cover the edges well so they do not become brittle.
9 Take a second piece of phyllo and place it on top of the first one.
10 Brush the dough lightly with the ghee mixture.
11 Sprinkle with half of the walnuts.
12 Take another piece of dough and place it on top of the walnuts.
13 Brush again with the spiced ghee mixture.
14 Place the fourth piece of phyllo on top and brush lightly with the spiced ghee to cover.
15 Cut the dough into six circles that are 5" in diameter.
16 Put each circle into a 12-cup muffin pan and press lightly to form to the inside of the pan.
17 Cover the muffin tin with plastic wrap so the phyllo shells do not dry out.
18 Repeat the entire procedure with the remaining 4 pieces of phyllo dough. (You will have a total of 12 cups.)
19 Bake the shells in the center of the preheated oven for 8 minutes, or until they are a light golden brown.
20 Remove the shells from the pan and cool on a wire rack.
21 Place in an airtight container at room temperature.

Can be prepared 8 hours ahead.

Banana~Chocolate Dream ~ *continued*

Prepare Pudding

Ingredients

- ¼ cup dark rum
- ⅛ teaspoon ground ginger
- ¼ teaspoon cinnamon
- 2 tablespoons coconut sugar
- 3 tablespoons finely grated 60% bittersweet chocolate
- 2 very ripe bananas, chopped
- ½ teaspoon vanilla bean paste
- ¼ teaspoon coconut extract

Directions

1 In a medium saucepan, add the rum, ginger, cinnamon, and coconut sugar.

2 Bring to a boil over high heat and then turn down to low heat.

3 Add the chocolate, chopped banana, vanilla bean paste, and coconut extract.

4 Stir the mixture until the chocolate is melted.

5 Remove from heat and puree to a fine consistency using an immersion blender.

6 Put the pudding into a bowl and cover with plastic wrap.

7 Place in the refrigerator to chill.

Can be made 8 hours in advance.

Assembly

Ingredients

- Phyllo shells
- Pudding
- ⅛ cup organic shredded unsweetened coconut
- 1 ripe banana, sliced
- ⅛ cup (approximately) additional coconut sugar for topping
- 2 teaspoons clementine zest

Directions

1 When ready to serve, fill each phyllo shell with 1½ to 2 tablespoons of the pudding.

2 Sprinkle each with ½ teaspoon of the shredded unsweetened coconut.

3 Top with some of the sliced banana and sprinkle with a very thin layer of coconut sugar.

4 Caramelize the sugar using a small kitchen torch or by placing them under the broiler for a few seconds.

5 Garnish with a little of the clementine zest on top. Serve immediately.

Fresh Creamy Delight Juice or Sorbet

Birth & Balance

Serves 4

This juice combines an assortment of green ingredients that we happily recommend. This juice is a healing alternative to a typical dessert. Further exploration granted us the magical mechanics produced by the ice cream maker rendering a wonderful, creamy sorbet.

Juice & Essence

Kiwi benefits the spleen and stomach, helps get rid of heat and diarrhea as well as treats fever with dry, sore throat. Kiwi helps with jaundice and painful urination. Pears moisten lungs, treat chronic thirst, cough and constipation. Apples benefit the lungs, stomach and large intestines. They also moisten the lungs and help with dry cough. Fennel is beneficial to the liver, kidneys, spleen, and stomach. Fennel is mostly balancing to the liver while helping to dispel gas, abdominal bloating, indigestion and vomiting and menstrual pain due to qi stagnation. Figs benefit the spleen, stomach and large intestine. Treats lack of appetite, indigestion and also assists with sore throat and dry cough. Avocado is balancing to the liver and moistens the lungs and large intestines. Avocado is a natural source of lecithin (a brain food), rich in copper which aids in red blood cell formation and a nutritious protein source often recommended to nursing mothers. Use avocado as a remedy for ulcers; they are also known to beautify the skin. Key limes are a natural liver detoxer and anti-carcinogenic with antibiotic properties.

Juice Option

Ingredients

- 2 organic kiwi, peeled
- 2 organic Bosc pears
- 2 organic Fuji apples
- 1 small organic fennel bulb, trimmed
- 3 organic brown Turkish figs
- 2 organic key limes
- 1 organic Haas avocado

Directions

1 Cut the kiwi, pears, apples, fennel, figs, and limes into pieces that will fit into your juice extractor.
2 Put the kiwi, pears, apples, fennel, figs, and limes through the juicer according to the manufacturer's instructions.
3 Pour the juice into a blender.
4 Peel and pit the avocado and place into the blender with the juice.
5 Blend together well.
6 The juice can be served at room temperature or chilled.
7 Place into the refrigerator to chill if making the sorbet.

Sorbet Option

Ingredients

- *Fresh Creamy Delight Juice,* chilled
- ¼ cup Apple Schnapps Liquor

Directions

1 Mix together the chilled juice and liquor.
2 Put the mixture into an ice cream maker and process according to the manufacturer's instructions.
3 Put the finished sorbet into a container and freeze until firm, about 4 hours.

Leilani Love Elixir or Sorbet

Birth & Balance   Serves 6

With the **Leilani Love Elixir**, you can expect that we combined a perfect portion of sweet, tart, and sassy. We created this on Dr. Ken's oldest daughter Leilani's 10th birthday. Our intention with this juice was to reflect a bright, deliciously healing elixir to mirror her essence. You can serve this as a juice for dessert or use the sorbet option to create a truly magical frozen treat.

Juice & Essence

Strawberry benefits the lung, spleen, liver, kidney, and stomach. As strawberries are very tonifying to the liver and kidneys, they help with hangover from alcohol, frequent urination, dizziness, and fatigue from enduring disease. They treat dry cough and sore throat as well. Summer squash and cucumber are cooling, help with detoxing, and decrease inflammation. They are also great for treating difficulty urinating and issues with edema as well as thirst. Eating squash and cucumber helps the spleen, stomach, and large intestine. Pineapple assists with low blood pressure, lack of strength in hands and feet, inflammation, difficult urination, bloating, and indigestion. Blueberries keep your brain sharp and fight age-related brain problems. Blueberries contain plant pigments called anthocyanins that have anti-inflammatory and antioxidant properties. They also help to stop the degradation of skin collagen and are therefore helpful as an anti-aging remedy to the sun's UV-B rays. Ginger assists with nausea, digestion, circulation, cold feet, and hands. Use ginger to help with inflammation and pain related to osteoarthritis.

Elixir Option

Ingredients

- 1 pint organic strawberries, hulled
- 1 organic pineapple, peeled and cored
- 1 medium organic yellow squash, peeled
- 1 large organic cucumber, peeled
- 2 large organic carambola (star fruit)
- 1 cup organic blueberries
- 1"-piece organic fresh ginger, peeled

Directions

1 Cut all of the fruit into pieces that will fit into your juice extractor.
2 Put the strawberries, pineapple, squash, cucumber, carambola, blueberries, and ginger through the juicer according to the manufacturer's instructions.
3 Mix together well.
4 The elixir can be served at room temperature or chilled.
5 Place into the refrigerator to chill if making the sorbet.

Sorbet Option

Ingredients

- *Leilani Love Elixir,* chilled
- ¼ cup raspberry liquor
- 2 tablespoons coconut palm sugar

Directions

1 Mix together the chilled elixir, raspberry liquor, and coconut palm sugar.
2 Put the mixture into an ice cream maker and process according to the manufacturer's instructions.
3 Put the finished sorbet into a container and freeze until firm, about 4 hours.

Gus's Guava Cake

Birth & Balance

Serves 6 to 8

The impetus for this dessert was Dr. Gus Castellanos' birthday. A Cuban-American with a mission of mindfulness who so graciously took time out of his busy day early in the history of our cookbook to write our first review. In thinking Cuba, we felt guava would best represent her sweet and exotic nature. Our task then became one of making a healthful rendition of this classic and very popular Caribbean cake.

Juice & Essence

Guava has general hemostatic properties and is therefore helpful in stopping bleeding. Our base of flours offer health benefits to the pancreas, stomach, and heart via the garbanzo bean, which contains more iron than any other legume, and is somewhat shaped like a heart. Additional benefits to the heart stem from our use of coconut oil that improves cardiovascular health and increases the ratio of HDL to LDL cholesterol due in part to saturated, medium-chain fatty acids (MCTs) such as lauric. Using applesauce minimizes fat, adds fiber, assists with detox, and energizes.

Ingredients

- ¼ cup butter, softened
- ½ cup Garden of Life Living Foods Extra-Virgin Coconut Oil
- ⅔ cup sugar
- 2 eggs
- 1 cup unsweetened applesauce
- 1 teaspoon vanilla extract
- ½ cup whole wheat pastry flour
- ½ cup spelt flour
- ½ cup garbanzo/fava bean flour
- ½ cup all-purpose flour
- 1 teaspoon baking powder
- 6 ounces guava paste, thinly sliced
- ½ cup guava jelly, stirred to soften
- 1 cup sifted powdered sugar
- 1½ tablespoons fresh lemon juice
- ½ teaspoon lemon zest
- ½ teaspoon vanilla extract

Directions

1. Preheat the oven to 350°F.
2. Grease a 10" springform pan and set aside.
3. Cream together the butter, coconut, oil and sugar in a large mixing bowl until incorporated.
4. Add the eggs one at a time, beating well after each addition.
5. Add the applesauce and vanilla and beat well.
6. Sift all of the flours and the baking powder into a small bowl.
7. Then gradually add the flour mixture to the batter, beating until completely blended.
8. Spread half of the batter into the greased springform pan.
9. Place the slices of guava paste evenly on top of the batter being sure not to place the slices too close to the edge of the pan.
10. Evenly spread the guava jelly over the paste.
11. Top with the remaining batter to cover the guava paste and jelly.
12. Bake in the preheated oven for 45 minutes, or until a toothpick inserted in the center comes out clean except for the guava filling.
13. Let cake cool for 10 minutes in the pan on a rack.
14. Run a knife around the edge of the cake to loosen it from the pan.
15. Remove the outer ring from the springform pan and let the cake cool completely.
16. To make the glaze: whisk together the sifted powdered sugar, lemon juice, zest, and vanilla until smooth.
17. Spread the glaze over the top of the cake allowing some to drip down the sides.
18. Let the glaze set and serve.

Strawberry Spring Crisp

Birth & Balance   Serves 6

For a spring dish, this takes the cake! Provided that the oatmeal you buy is gluten-free, this is a Celiac-safe dessert. Spring and strawberries go hand-in-hand. The flavors of mint and basil bring out their sweetness while fennel pollen and arrowroot aid in digestion. We couldn't get enough of the macadamia nuts in the topping, so we combined them with coconut palm sugar, orange zest, and cinnamon to create the supreme strawberry crisp.

Juice & Essence

Strawberry benefits the lung, spleen, liver, kidney, and stomach. As strawberries are very tonifying to the liver and kidneys, they help with hangover from alcohol, frequent urination, dizziness, and fatigue from enduring disease. They treat dry cough and sore throat as well. Coconut benefits the spleen, stomach, and large intestine. It also assists with difficult urination, edema, and additionally will help with severe dehydration and diarrhea. Ginger and cinnamon assist with nausea, digestion, circulation, and cold feet and hands. Use either to help with inflammation and pain related to osteoarthritis. Quinoa flour is gluten-free, high in protein, and contains all of the amino acids necessary for our nutritional needs. It is also high in iron and calcium and a good source of manganese, magnesium, and heart-healthy fiber. Basil benefits the lungs, spleen, stomach, and large intestine, helps to eliminate dampness, get rid of toxins, and assist with headaches, menstrual irregularity, bloating, and gas. Mint aids the digestion of fats, soothes the stomach, and stimulates bile production and flow. Mint can also be used to assist with Irritable Bowel Syndrome. Macadamia nuts assist with reducing the severity of arthritis, menstrual cramps, and migraine headaches. They will also help lower your risk of heart disease, cancer, and osteoporosis. Oatmeal benefits the spleen, tonifies qi, lowers cholesterol, and helps with hot flashes. Oats are rich in a class of antioxidants known as avenanthramides, which may help reduce colon cancer risk. Arrowroot is a gluten-free substitute for a thickening agent.

Prepare the Filling

Ingredients

- 2 quarts organic strawberries, washed, hulled, and coarsely chopped
- 1 teaspoon minced fresh mint
- 1 teaspoon minced fresh basil
- 1 tablespoon fresh orange juice
- ½ teaspoon vanilla extract
- ½ cup coconut palm sugar (use more if berries are not sweet enough)
- 1 tablespoon arrowroot
- ⅛ teaspoon fennel pollen

Directions

1. Preheat oven to 375°F.
2. In a large bowl, mix together the strawberries, mint, basil, orange juice, vanilla, coconut sugar, arrowroot, and fennel pollen.
3. Set aside while preparing the topping.

Prepare the Topping

Ingredients

- ½ cup organic steel-cut oatmeal
- ½ cup quinoa flour
- ½ teaspoon cinnamon
- ¼ cup coconut palm sugar
- 1 teaspoon orange zest
- ¼ cup finely chopped macadamia nuts
- ½ teaspoon aged balsamic vinegar
- 4 tablespoons ghee (clarified butter)

Directions

1. In a large bowl, mix together the oatmeal, quinoa flour, cinnamon, coconut sugar, orange zest, and macadamia nuts.
2. Cut in the balsamic vinegar, and ghee until it resembles coarse crumbs.

Assembly

Directions

1. Take six 1-cup ramekins and place them on a rimmed baking sheet.
2. Divide the filling into each ramekin.
3. Sprinkle the topping over the filling.
4. Bake in the center of the preheated oven for 25 minutes, or until the tops are golden brown and the filling is bubbling.

Sunshine Parfait

Birth & Balance   Serves 6

We named this "sunshine" because of its sunny, light presence. Lots of goodness to be had in this one! We were thrilled to create a dessert surrounding one of our favorite fruits — mangos — and loved the process of inventing a healthy crunch to complement it. The additions of banana rum, coconut oil, and spice will transport your senses to a tropical oasis.

Juice & Essence

Lung, spleen, and stomach get a jolt from this one due to the very liberal use of mango in this dessert. Benefits include treatment for cough, poor digestion, panting, wheezing, and vomiting. Gelatin assists with nail growth and joint/tendon health. Oatmeal fortifies the spleen, energizes, and treats spontaneous perspiration due to yin deficiency.

Prepare the Mango Gelatin

Ingredients

- 5 honey mangos, peeled and chopped (approximately 4 cups)
- 1 cup banana rum
- 1 cup water
- 2, 1-ounce packages unflavored gelatin

Directions

1 Place the chopped mango into the bowl of a food processor fitted with the chopping blade.

2 Process until finely pureed (should equal 2 cups puree).

3 Place the puree into a large bowl.

4 Place the banana rum and the water into a small saucepan and heat just to boiling.

5 Sprinkle the gelatin into a small bowl.

6 Add the hot rum to the gelatin and stir to combine well.

7 Whisk the gelatin mixture into the mango puree.

8 Cover and refrigerate for at least 2 hours or overnight.

Prepare the Crisp

Ingredients

- ½ cup oatmeal
- ¼ cup spelt flour
- 2 tablespoons brown sugar
- ½ teaspoon roasted cinnamon
- ⅛ teaspoon sea salt
- ¼ cup Garden of Life Living Foods Extra-Virgin Coconut Oil

Directions

1 Preheat the oven to 350°F.

2 In a large bowl, mix together the oatmeal, spelt flour, brown sugar, cinnamon, and salt.

3 Rub the coconut oil into the oatmeal mixture with your hands to form clumps the size of peas.

4 Place the oatmeal crisp mixture on a cookie sheet in a single layer.

5 Bake the mixture on the middle rack of the preheated oven stirring occasionally for 20 minutes, or until golden brown and crisp.

6 Set aside to cool.

Prepare Yogurt

Ingredients

- 1, 2" vanilla bean, scrape out the seeds to equal ⅛ teaspoon
- 17.5 ounces of whole milk or 2% Greek-style yogurt
- 2 tablespoons Tupelo honey

Directions

1 Combine the vanilla bean and honey in a bowl.

2 Add the yogurt and mix well.

3 Cover and refrigerate until cold.

Assembly

Directions

1 Layer the mango gelatin and yogurt in parfait glasses.

2 Top with the crisp and serve immediately.

3 You can also layer the mango gelatin and yogurt 8 hours in advance.

4 Top with the crisp just before serving.

Spring Sauces & Spices

Chapter 5

Spring
Sauces & Spices

Juice & Essence Sauces & Spices are meant to be the perfect complement to our Juice & Essence recipes. This chapter will guide you through this part of the creative cooking process.

Cocoa~Chili Rub

Birth & Balance

Makes 1½ tablespoons

We wanted to use cocoa in a rub with the knowledge that cocoa has a beautiful way of bringing out flavors. New Mexican chili pepper is a flavorful and interesting full-bodied spice with heat that does not overwhelm. It makes sense to fit in cayenne pepper whenever possible for its many healing properties.

Juice & Essence

Cocoa is high in antioxidants and also a great source of iron. Cocoa is helpful in improving blood pressure, enhancing circulation, and the cardiovascular system. It reduces cholesterol levels in the body while offering energy. Cayenne pepper and chili peppers benefit the spleen and stomach, warm the body, treat indigestion, loss of appetite, and poor circulation. Cayenne pepper specifically is a powerful anti-inflammatory that also neutralizes acidity. Cayenne's healing properties include assistance with heartburn, ulcers, gout, gas, sore throat, hemorrhoids, mucus, and nausea. Sea salt benefits the stomach, kidneys, and large and small intestines. It can be used to induce vomiting and get rid of phlegm. Sea salt cools the blood and helps treat phlegm accumulated in the chest, poor urination, bleeding gums, sore throat, and toothache.

Ingredients

- 1 tablespoon cocoa powder
- ½ teaspoon ground New Mexican chili pepper
- ⅛ teaspoon cayenne pepper
- 1 teaspoon sea salt

Directions

Mix together the cocoa powder, ground chili, cayenne pepper, and salt in a mortar and pestle to combine.

Use as a rub on fish, seafood, meats, and poultry.

Carrot~Leek Sauce

Birth & Balance

Makes about 4 cups

These are two ingredients that speak to us and speak very well to each other. Carrots and leeks deliver a one-two punch of complementing nutrition, color, and taste. The simmering agents of sweet vermouth and sherry deliver a depth of flavor easily paired with a myriad of poultry, fish, pasta, or vegetable dishes. Leave it to us…we'll tell you what you can do with your sauce!!!

Juice & Essence

This sauce, due mainly to the leek content, is warming, with benefits to the spleen, lungs, and stomach. Treatments include indigestion, cough, and difficulty swallowing. The carrot component helps dissolve accumulations such as stones and tumors. Carrots are alkaline forming and clear acidic blood conditions including acne, tonsillitis, and rheumatism. Tomatoes offer benefits of healing to the stomach and cleanse the liver, purify the blood, and detoxify the body in general.

Ingredients

- 2 tablespoons extra-virgin olive oil
- 2 tablespoons clarified butter
- 3 cups diced carrots
- 1¼ cups cleaned, sliced leeks
- 4 cloves garlic, minced
- ½ cup sweet vermouth
- ½ cup dry sherry
- ½ cup hot water
- 1, 14.5-ounce can organic diced tomatoes
- Salt and pepper

Directions

1 Heat a large saucepan over medium heat.
2 Add the olive oil and butter to the pan.
3 Then add the carrots, leeks, and garlic and sauté for 2 minutes.
4 Cover and continue to cook for 20 minutes, stirring occasionally.
5 Remove cover and add the vermouth, sherry, water, and tomatoes.
6 Sauté the vegetables for 10 minutes over medium heat, stirring occasionally.
7 Put the carrot mixture into a food processor fitted with the chopping blade and puree until smooth.
8 Add salt and pepper to taste.
9 Put the mixture back into the saucepan and reheat the sauce until desired temperature.

Mango~Brandy Citrus Drizzle

Birth & Balance

Makes about 2 cups

Something so sunny and alive! This drizzle is an invigorating mix of tropical mango with the sensual nature of brandy.

Juice & Essence

Mango treats a cough, wheezing, nausea, vomiting, and indigestion. Cardamom, ginger, and cayenne aid in the circulation of energy and blood, warm the body, treat bloating, poor appetite, and menstrual pain. Benefits the liver, kidneys, and stomach.

Ingredients

- 1 cup fresh mango
- 2 tablespoons extra-virgin olive oil
- Juice of 1 small lime
- Juice of ½ orange
- ¼ cup brandy
- ¼ teaspoon pumpkin pie spice
- ¼ teaspoon caraway seeds
- ⅛ teaspoon ground ginger
- ⅛ teaspoon ground cardamom
- ⅛ teaspoon freshly ground Grains of Paradise
- ¼ cup heavy cream
- Pinch of ground cayenne pepper
- Salt

Directions

1 Puree the mango, olive oil, and lime and orange juices in a blender until smooth.

2 Place in a small saucepan and add the brandy, pumpkin pie spice, caraway seeds, ground ginger, cardamom, Grains of Paradise, and heavy cream.

3 Heat just to blend flavors. Do not boil!

4 Cool to room temperature and strain the mixture through a fine mesh sieve into a bowl so that the texture is very smooth.

5 Add a pinch of cayenne pepper and salt to taste.

Can be made 1 day in advance. Bring to room temperature before serving.

Bellini Basting Sauce

Birth & Balance

Makes about 1½ cups

Spring's effervescence was captured in this sauce. What better way to lift the spirits of a spring dish than to finish it off with Prosecco. We chose the herbs and spices that would allow the palate to play with the sweetness by creating veils with the camphorous nature of the oregano and the gentle but significant spice of the red pepper flakes.

Juice & Essence

Peaches moisten the intestines, aid the circulatory system, disperse accumulations, and move qi. Onion treats the common cold and diarrhea. Coriander strengthens the lungs and spleen thereby aiding with bloating, constipation, and excessive phlegm.

Ingredients

- ¼ cup extra-virgin olive oil
- 1 teaspoon clarified butter
- 2 garlic cloves, pressed
- ½ cup peach nectar
- 1 teaspoon onion powder
- ½ teaspoon ground coriander
- ¾ teaspoon dried Mexican oregano
- ¼ teaspoon crushed red pepper flakes
- 1 teaspoon sea salt
- ½ teaspoon white pepper
- 1 cup Prosecco

Directions

1   Mix the oil, butter, garlic, nectar, onion powder, coriander, oregano, red pepper flakes, salt, and white pepper in a small saucepan and bring to a boil over high heat.

2   Boil for 5 minutes and add the Prosecco and boil to reduce by half, stirring occasionally for about 30 minutes.

3   Set aside to cool slightly.

Use this sauce to baste grilled fish, poultry, pork or vegetables.

Summer

Summer is nature's season of growth and maturation. Our gardens and our bodies soak up the sun's very Yang solar energy. Yang energy causes action and outward movement and creates hot and dry climate.

We take in a lighter diet of fruits and vegetables filled with sunshine energizing us for our increased outdoor recreation and exercise. Observing summer as a time of energizing and growth keeps us in harmony with nature and away from illness, which is a process by which we become more open and receptive to change.

The *Fire* element characterizes summer in the Chinese Five Element theory and is the element governing the heart. Pericardium ("circulation sex"), protecting the heart and regulating blood flow, heat, and nourishment throughout the body, small intestine; and Triple Burner, which acts to maintain proper temperature and warmth.

The human energies related to the Fire element are creativity, intuition, and motion. So above, so below…when these areas are off in your life, look to the foods you consume or lack thereof for the answers.

Emotionally we connect these organs and respective elements to joy and sadness. This is relevant to our society due to the very prevalent use of antidepressants. During this time, bitter foods and herbs are recommended as they will strengthen the heart and small intestine; however, we must always employ the saying: everything in moderation, even moderation. Too much of a good thing is not good, so be careful not to consume too many bitter foods in an effort to benefit the heart and small intestine.

Summer Superfoods

AVOCADOS are loaded with healthy omega-9 fatty acids (the same fats found in olive oil, olives, and macadamia nuts). Avocados speed the conversion of fat into energy and boost the rate of metabolism. Avocados have also been shown to improve blood vessel health. They contain a nutrient called glutathione that blocks at least thirty different carcinogens and is required by the liver to properly detoxify many synthetic chemicals.

BERRIES such as strawberries, blueberries, and raspberries offer so many health benefits. Berries contain anti-pain compounds that are better than many drugs. They generally have the highest amount of antioxidants and are among the best preventatives against prostate cancer and guardians against heart disease and memory loss.

CHERRIES are another summer food that Traditional Chinese Medicine says help relieve liver chi (subtle energy) stagnation. Tart cherries help with gout and osteoarthritis and provide cardiovascular benefits.

GRAPES, purple or red, are an excellent source of the phytonutrient quercetin, which has been shown to prevent depression, improve mental functioning, and lessen breathing problems linked to asthma. Purple or red grapes also contain the phytonutrient resveratrol, which has many health benefits, including heart disease prevention and increasing longevity.

LEAFY GREENS are packed with vitamins, minerals, chlorophyll (the green color), phytonutrients, and enzymes; leafy greens deserve a prominent place in your diet. The darker the color, the more intense the nutrients will be. This is particularly true of chlorophyll — a good blood cleanser. Most leafy greens contain high amounts of calcium and magnesium to help build strong bones, muscles, and a relaxed nervous system.

PLUMS contain special phytonutrients — neochlorogenic acid and chlorogenic acid, both of which are well-researched, potent antioxidants. They are particularly effective at neutralizing a type of free radical called superoxide anion radical, which is a serious threat to healthy cells and tissues, including brain cells.

TOMATOES are packed with vitamin C and lycopene. Tomatoes are an excellent addition to your diet. Lycopene has shown tremendous anti-aging and anti-cancer properties in research. It even demonstrates the incredible capacity to protect genetic material against disease and damage. It is showing tremendous promise against colon and prostate cancers. Choose organic, non-GMO heirloom tomatoes for best results.

WATERMELON contains lycopene, a prostate-protecting, anti-aging, and disease-thwarting substance. Watermelon is also high in vitamin C, beta-carotene, and glutathione content — the latter of which helps to remove toxins from your blood and improve liver detoxification.

Summer Appetizers

Chapter 1
Summer Appetizers

Fine as a stand-alone meal or as a precursor to Juice & Essence entrées. Our appetizers add an exploratory jolt to the most scrutinizing culinary adventurer!

Poke

Birth & Balance

Serves 4

You can't think of poke without thinking about Hawaii! There is something about Hawaii that makes you think summer. It must be the days at the beach, the sunshine and the fresh fish. This is a Juice & Essence aloha!

Juice & Essence

Tuna is strengthening, energizing and tonifies body fluids/yin. It is also great for increasing circulation and brain function. Seaweed (nori) is useful in softening masses/tumors, removing residues of radiation from the body, cleansing the lymph and improving water metabolism. Seaweed aids in the treatment of thyroid dysfunction, helps lower cholesterol and is a useful dish in weight loss programs.

CONTRAST – A nice French Sauvignon Blanc with its crispness and medium fruit would complement the depth of the tuna mixed with the citrus of the marinade.

Ingredients

- 4 tablespoons low sodium soy sauce
- ½ teaspoon wasabi powder
- 2 teaspoons wasabi paste
- 1½ teaspoons clementine zest, divided
- 4 tablespoons mirin
- 1½ lb. fresh Yellow Eye tuna (tail section optional)
- 1 large lemon, juice and zest
- ¼ cup shallots, thinly sliced
- ¼ cup ponzu sauce
- 2 teaspoons hot chili oil
- 2 tablespoons seaweed sheet (nori), sliced into very thin strips
- ¼ teaspoon black sesame seeds
- ¼ teaspoon red pepper flakes
- ½ teaspoon rice seasoning, Noritamago Furikake
- 1 teaspoon Hawaiian coral salt

Directions

1   To make the sauce, mix soy sauce, wasabi powder, wasabi paste, and half of the clementine zest in a small bowl.

2   Set aside.

3   Place remaining clementine zest and the mirin in large bowl.

4   Set aside to marinate for 20 minutes.

5   Cut tuna into 1"-cubes and place into the same bowl with the zest and mirin.

6   Add the lemon juice and zest and stir to combine well.

7   Add shallot slices to tuna along with the ponzu, hot chili oil, seaweed, black sesame seeds, red pepper flakes, rice seasoning, and Hawaiian coral salt.

8   Mix well and serve immediately.

Summer Rolls

Birth & Balance

Makes 8 rolls

Our Juice & Essence take on a Thai staple. This dish is loaded with fresh veggies, chicken, shrimp, and tons of nutritional benefits. It's simply summer goodness rolled up in thin, juicy rice paper!

Juice & Essence

Using fish sauce creates a new dynamic in flavor that offers the enhanced probiotic/digestive benefits of fermentation along with the health benefits of anchovies which increase yin and energy, strengthen sinews and bones, act as a mild diuretic, and increase circulation. The hot peppers also increase circulation while boosting the immune system. The shrimp benefits the liver and kidneys. The chicken works to energize the spleen, stomach, and kidney channels. Both are high in protein and build blood. Shiitake mushrooms are high in fiber, aid in intestinal health, and are shown to help in the prevention of certain forms of intestinal cancers. Basil benefits the lungs, spleen, stomach, and large intestine channels. It also helps treat headaches, remove toxins, and regulate menses while reducing burping and belching. Mint and cilantro are cooling and assist with digestion of spicy foods. Kale is a great cancer fighter and benefits the lungs, liver, and stomach, reduces lung congestion, and is an exceptional source of chlorophyll. Carrots benefit the lung and spleen channels and assist with dysentery and cough. Micro greens offer loads of energy in a small package and are generally rich in chlorophyll and vitamins D, A, and K.

Complement or Contrast

COMPLEMENT – A cold dish with lovely herbs, crunchy veggies, shrimp, and chicken would go so great with a fun, bold, and dry fruit forward glass of ice cold Rose or Domestic Riesling…. Yes, I said ice cold. Some wine snobs say that white wine has to be served at a temperature around 60 °F…. I say go crazy and let it chill to 40–50°F. except for big, rich whites like Chardonnay that loses some of its complexity if the wine is too cold.

For the Sauce

Ingredients

- 1 small Serrano pepper, minced
- ½ Pimento di Cheiro pepper, seeded and minced
- 4 tablespoons fish sauce
- 1 tablespoon sesame oil
- 2 limes, juice only
- 1 teaspoon salt
- 1 teaspoon freshly ground black pepper
- 2 tablespoons water
- 1 tablespoon light brown sugar
- 1 tablespoon grated fresh ginger

Directions

1 In a small bowl, combine all of the above ingredients for the sauce.
2 Set aside for the flavors to blend.

For the Shrimp and Chicken

Ingredients

- ¾ lb. boneless, skinless organic chicken breasts
- ¾ lb. wild caught white shrimp
- 1 teaspoon sea salt
- 1 teaspoon freshly ground black pepper
- 1 teaspoon fish sauce
- 1 teaspoon sesame oil
- 2 cups chicken stock
- 2 cups water
- 2 teaspoon dried oregano
- 2 teaspoons freshly ground black pepper
- 3 garlic cloves, pressed

Directions

1 Thinly slice the chicken on the diagonal and place into a bowl.
2 Shell and devein the shrimp, reserving the shells.
3 Place the shrimp into a separate bowl.
4 Mix together the sea salt, pepper, fish sauce, and sesame oil.
5 Divide among the chicken and shrimp and mix to coat.
6 Set aside while preparing the stock.
7 In a medium size saucepan, bring to a simmer over medium-high heat the chicken stock, reserved shrimp shells, water, oregano, pepper, and garlic.
8 Simmer for 15 minutes and then remove the shells from the broth with a slotted spoon.
9 Add the shrimp to the simmering stock and cook for 3 to 4 minutes until cooked through.
10 Remove the shrimp from the stock with a slotted spoon and set on a plate to cool. (Refrigerate the shrimp if preparing ahead of time.)
11 Add the chicken to the simmering stock and cook for 5 to 7 minutes until it is cooked thoroughly.
12 Remove the chicken from the stock with a slotted spoon and set on a plate to cool.
13 Reserve 2 tablespoons of the stock to be used to cook the shiitake mushrooms. (Refrigerate the chicken if preparing ahead of time.)

Summer Rolls ~ *continued*

Prepare the Shiitake Mushrooms

Ingredients

- 2 teaspoons sesame oil
- ½ cup thinly sliced shiitake mushrooms
- 2 tablespoons reserved chicken/shrimp stock

Directions

1. Heat the sesame oil over high heat in a small sauté pan.
2. Add the mushrooms and cook for 1 minute stirring constantly.
3. Add the reserved stock and sauté for another 2 minutes, or until the mushrooms are cooked through.
4. Set aside to cool.

Assembly

Ingredients

- 8 sheets of rice paper rounds (spring roll wrappers) plus extra in case some tear
- 16 cilantro sprigs
- 16 basil leaves
- 16 mint leaves
- ¼ cup thinly sliced red bell pepper
- ½ cup grated carrots
- ½ cup English cucumber cut into 3"-matchsticks
- ¼ cup thinly sliced scallions
- Cooked shiitake mushrooms
- 1 cup micro kale greens
- Cooked chicken
- Cooked shrimp

Directions

1 Have the herbs, red bell pepper, carrots, cucumber, scallions, shiitake mushrooms, micro kale greens, chicken, and shrimp all set out on a work surface.

2 Set up a cutting board so you can roll the rice paper easily.

3 Place some warm water into a shallow bowl.

4 Dip one sheet of rice paper into the water for a couple of seconds just to soften.

5 Place the sheet onto the cutting board. To the bottom third of the sheet, place 2 cilantro sprigs, 2 basil leaves, 2 mint leaves.

6 Top the herbs with some of the red bell pepper, carrots, cucumber, scallions, shiitake mushrooms, and micro kale greens.

7 Add a few pieces of chicken and shrimp to the top of the vegetables.

8 Roll the bottom of the sheet up to the center to cover the contents, then fold in the two sides.

9 Continue to roll the sheet as tightly as possible to completely enclose the contents.

10 Place the roll on a parchment-lined baking sheet and cover with a damp towel so it will not dry out.

11 Create the remaining rolls by following the same procedure.

12 Serve the summer rolls with the dipping sauce.

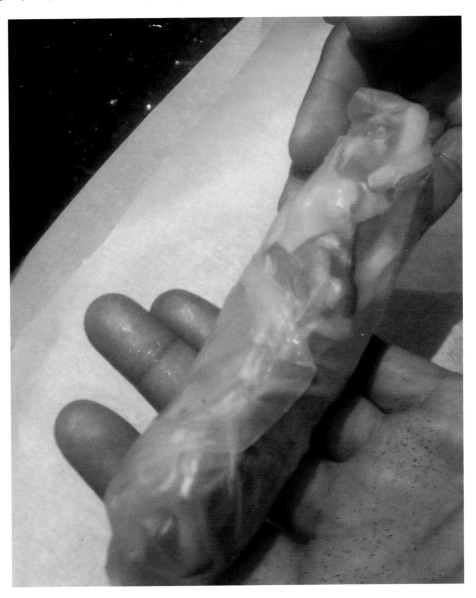

Smashed Avocado with Caviar on Petite Toasts

Birth & Balance

Serves 4 to 6

Who knew that four ingredients could be so perfect together? You will love the interplay of the creamy avocado, the crunchiness of the toast, the saltiness of the caviar, and the bite of the black pepper. Truly a dreamy combination!

Juice & Essence

Avocados are rich in vitamin E and lecithin — a brain food. Also rich in copper, which aids in red blood cell formation, a nutritional protein source also recommended for nursing mothers; builds yin, helps heal the liver, and lubricates the lung and large intestine. Caviar (fish eggs) is rich in omega-3 fatty acids which benefit the heart, brain, liver, joints, skin, and kidneys.

CONTRAST – Caviar = Champagne! Go with a cleaner/crisper Prosecco for this dish. A white wine such as a Pinot Grigio with solid acids or a dry Riesling will assist in cutting the fat of the avocado.

Ingredients

- 2 Haas avocados
- 1 package of petite toasts (Musette)
- 1, 2-ounce jar Paddlefish caviar
- Freshly ground black pepper

Directions

1. Peel and pit the avocados.
2. Place the flesh into a bowl and smash with a fork until completely smooth.
3. Stir in the black pepper.
4. Transfer the avocado to a decorative bowl.
5. Place the caviar into a decorative bowl also and put the toasts onto a serving platter.
6. To serve: put some avocado onto a piece of toast and top with some of the caviar.

Kick-a-My-Butt Jicama Tacos

J&E Time Signature

Birth & Balance:

Serves 12

Tacos are always fun! We were in the mood to create a light version that could stand alone or make a wonderful first course. A patient and mutual friend, lovingly named "Little Bundle of Fun", suggested we try jicama as the taco shell. We went with a vegetarian filling – high in protein and healing benefits. All the textures worked together beautifully!

Juice & Essence

Adzuki bean is healing to the heart and small intestine, tonifies the kidney-adrenal function, detoxifies the body, reduces heat, reduces swelling, assists with jaundice, diarrhea and prolonged menstruation. Grapeseed oil is high in vitamin C and is a significant source of omega-3 and 6 essential fatty acids. Celery is healing to the stomach and liver channels, clears heat, treats high blood pressure and dizziness. Corn is a healing agent to the heart, lung, spleen, liver, stomach, gallbladder and bladder. It also settles the heart while balancing stomach functions, treats difficult urination, gallstones, jaundice, hepatitis and hypertension. Red cherry peppers and Serrano peppers offer immune boosting, circulation increasing, body warming, antibacterial,

Complement or Contrast

CONTRAST – *Sturdy yet crisp and a little fruit to carry the spice of the tacos. I would choose a steel-fermented northern Italian Chardonnay or a good central California coast Chardonnay.*

antiviral, and digestion enhancing attributes as well as reducing joint pain. Avocados are rich in healthy fats and benefit the skin as well as the brain, liver, lungs and large intestine. Jicama is rich in B complex vitamins, folates, riboflavin, pantothenic acid and thiamin. It is a high fiber and antioxidant rich root vegetable filled with a significant offering of vitamin C. Watermelon rind reduces toxins and clears heat, treats summer heat symptoms, inhibition of urination, oral sores and the feeling of a blocked throat. Red onion is helpful for lung, spleen, liver and large intestine issues. Onion is warming and helps treat the common cold, diarrhea and worms.

Prepare the Filling

Ingredients

- 1 tablespoon grapeseed oil
- ½ cup minced red onion
- 1 teaspoon seeded and minced fresh hot red cherry pepper
- 1 teaspoon seeded and minced fresh Serrano pepper
- ⅓ cup chopped celery
- ⅓ cup minced tomatillo
- 2 teaspoons minced garlic
- 1 cup chopped tomato
- 2 cups fresh corn kernels, cut from about 4 cobs
- 1, 15-ounce can Adzuki beans, washed and drained
- 4 teaspoons minced fresh cilantro
- ½ teaspoon sea salt
- ½ teaspoon white pepper

Directions

1 Heat the oil in a large sauté pan over medium heat.
2 Add the onion, hot red cherry pepper, Serrano pepper, celery, and tomatillo.
3 Sauté for 3 minutes and add the garlic.
4 Continue to sauté for 1 minute.
5 Add the tomato, corn, beans, cilantro, salt, and pepper and sauté for 3 minutes more.
6 Remove from the heat and let cool to room temperature.

Prepare the Avocado

Ingredients

- 2 Haas avocados, peeled and pitted
- 1 lime, juiced
- ½ teaspoon sea salt
- ½ teaspoon freshly ground black pepper
- ½ teaspoon cumin

Directions

1 Place the avocados into a bowl.
2 Add the lime juice, salt, pepper, and cumin.
3 Mash the mixture until the avocado is smooth and everything is incorporated.
4 Set aside.

Kick-a-My-Butt Jicama Tacos ~ *continued*

Prepare the Jicama and Watermelon

Ingredients

- 2 large jicama, peeled
- 4 cups water
- 1 cup dry white wine
- Watermelon rind from about 2 slices that are 1" wide

Directions

1 Heat the water and the wine in a large saucepan until it boils.

2 Reduce heat to medium and maintain a simmer.

3 Using a mandolin, thinly slice the jicama to create rounds about ⅛" thick.

4 With the water at a simmer, drop a couple of the slices of jicama into the liquid. The slices will immediately sink to the bottom.

5 When the slices float up to the top, remove them to a wax paper-lined sheet pan.

6 Continue with the remaining jicama slices.

7 Set aside to cool to room temperature.

8 For the watermelon, use a vegetable peeler to thinly slice strips from the light green, inner part of the rinds.

9 Cut the strips into very thin 3"-long pieces and set aside.

Assembly

Ingredients

- Prepared jicama
- Prepared avocado
- Filling mixture
- About 50 cilantro leaves
- Watermelon rind strips

Directions

1   Place one piece of jicama onto a work surface.

2   Spread some of the avocado onto the middle of the jicama.

3   Top with the filling, some cilantro leaves, and a strip of watermelon rind.

4   Fold in half like a taco and place on a serving platter.

5   Tacos can be prepared 8 hours in advance.

6   Cover and refrigerate.

7   Remove from the refrigerator and let them sit, still covered, for about an hour before serving.

Greek Veggie~Feta Dip

J&E Time Signature

Birth & Balance

Serves 4

We created this quick and easy appetizer to be delicious as is but also found it to be very versatile. You can use many combinations of ingredients. We love the sweetness of the Peppadew peppers and the tomatoes mingling with the saltiness of the feta, capers and olives. Simply the sunshine and freshness of a beautiful day in Greece!

Juice & Essence

The kidney yin tonifying nature of cheese is somewhat overshadowed by the cold dampness of it, however we create a balance with the blood-moving, warming nature of the Peppadew peppers. Kalamata olives benefit the lungs helping with dry cough and the stomach in cases of dysentery. Tomatoes also benefit the stomach channel, clears heat, moistens dryness, treats mouth sores, red eyes and indigestion.

Complement or Contrast

CONTRAST – A medium-body, dry red wine is the ticket here. It will offset the saltiness of the feta and carry this dish. For fun, find a Greek or Turkish table wine! A safe bet here is a Riojo from Spain, Chianti, Rosso di Montalciano, or a Barbera from Italy.

Ingredients

- 6 ounces crumbled feta cheese
- 5 pickled Peppadew peppers, chopped
- 1 teaspoon capers
- ¼ cup diced Kalamata olives
- 1 cup grape tomatoes, chopped
- 1 tablespoon minced fresh oregano
- ¼ teaspoon sea salt
- ½ teaspoon freshly ground black pepper
- 1 tablespoon extra-virgin olive oil
- Pita chips or crackle bread

Directions

1   Brush 1 teaspoon of the olive oil into the bottom of an oven-safe baking dish.

2   Spread the crumbled feta cheese evenly in the dish and set aside.

3   In a small bowl, combine the peppers, capers, olives, tomatoes, oregano, salt, and pepper and stir to combine.

4   Spread on top of the feta cheese in an even layer.

5   Drizzle the topping with the remaining olive oil.

6   Broil about 5 inches from the heat for 5 to 6 minutes, or until the cheese is bubbly.

7   Serve with pita chips or crackle bread.

Crazy Crustacean Po' Boys

Birth & Balance

Serves 4 to 6

Reminiscent of a New Orleans BBQ Shrimp Po' Boy we simply added a decadent twist and included escargot and black garlic into our recipe, which in hindsight was not simple at all! There is a soulful interplay happening here and, although this is not our heart-healthiest dish, your heart will be happier for it. For in the end, a joyful life is a balanced life and "health is balance!"

Juice & Essence

Fennel balances this dish and protects the digestive process. Snails are rich in easily absorbable iron, B-12, and magnesium. They are high in potassium, low in sodium, and high in omega-3 fatty acids which, along with the shrimp, will offer health benefits to the liver and kidneys while treating complaints that include impotence, premature hair loss, low back pain, and fatigue. Black garlic is better than regular garlic as its fermentation process increases the benefits and decreases the drawbacks. Black garlic contains double the antioxidants of regular garlic, reduces cholesterol, and benefits the spleen, stomach, and lungs.

CONTRAST – Bring out the big guns! A lot of rich flavors call for a complex aggressive wine. Acid is important to handle the seafood, but the rest calls for an oaky, buttery Chardonnay. Think about the honey and straw color of a Bordeaux or deep Napa Valley, but don't forget the acid that is sometimes lacking in these wines.

Ingredients

- ½ cup unsalted butter
- 1 tablespoon extra-virgin olive oil
- 2 teaspoons minced black garlic
- ¼ cup sliced leeks
- ½ cup minced fresh fennel bulb
- 1 teaspoon minced fresh chervil
- 1 teaspoon minced fresh oregano
- 1 teaspoon paprika
- 2 teaspoons sea salt
- 1 teaspoon black pepper
- 1 lb. cleaned rock shrimp
- 1, 7.75-ounce can snails, roughly chopped
- ½ cup dry white wine
- 1 baguette, diagonally cut into slices

Directions

1   Melt the butter and oil in a sauté pan over medium heat.

2   Add the garlic and mix it into the butter for 1 minute.

3   Add the leeks, fennel, chervil, oregano, paprika, salt, and pepper.

4   Sauté for 5 minutes and remove from the pan into a bowl and set aside.

5   Add the shrimp and snails to the sauté pan and cook for 2 to 3 minutes, or until the shrimp are almost cooked.

6   Turn the heat to high, add the wine and sauté for 1 minute.

7   Remove the shrimp and snails from the sauce using a slotted spoon and set aside.

8   Add the vegetable/herb mixture to the sauté pan with the wine.

9   Continue to cook on high heat for 3 to 5 minutes, or until reduced by half.

10 While sauce is reducing, broil the baguette slices to toast them on both sides.

11 When sauce is reduced, return the shrimp and snails to the pan for a few seconds to warm them.

12 Spoon them over the baguette slices along with some sauce and serve immediately.

Asian Essence Grilled Purple Cauliflower & Shad Roe

Birth & Balance   Serves 4

Surprise, surprise, surprise!!! This is a lip smackin' treat! We crossed our fingers and went with the available oddities of ingredients in order to create something new and tasty. A wonderful mix of textures and flavors!

Juice & Essence

Cauliflower benefits the spleen and stomach channels, offers healing in the form of mild pain relief, and treats indigestion. Black sesame seeds are healing to the liver and kidney channels, help with dizziness, vertigo, mild paralysis, lack of milk when breast feeding, and premature whitening of hair. Millet offers healing to the kidney, spleen, and stomach. While balancing the stomach, it will strengthen kidneys and reduce heat and toxins. Uses include reducing or stopping vomiting, wasting thirst, and diarrhea. Shad roe is rich in omega-3 fatty acids and therefore offers healing to the liver, heart, and brain, enhances virility, restores luster to skin, and assists with joint health.

CONTRAST – The reason why we chose a California Sauvignon Blanc is because of the crispness, solid acids, and slightly grassy undertones that stand up nicely to the taste and texture of the Shad Roe.

Ingredients

- 1 head of purple cauliflower, chopped into flowerets as close to the same size as possible
- 1 tablespoon Asian Hot Chili Oil
- 1 tablespoon sesame oil
- 2 tablespoons Sriracha sauce
- 2 tablespoons ponzu sauce
- 2 tablespoons reduced sodium soy sauce
- 3 cloves garlic, pressed
- 2 teaspoons black sesame seeds
- ½ cup water
- ½ cup dry white wine
- ½ cup millet flour
- 1½ teaspoons sea salt
- 2 teaspoons freshly ground black pepper
- 1 set of Shad roe (4 lobes), carefully washed and dried
- 4 tablespoons unsalted butter

Directions

1 Preheat grill to medium heat.

2 In a medium size bowl, mix together the Hot Chili Oil, sesame oil, Sriracha sauce, ponzu sauce, soy sauce, garlic, black sesame seeds, water, and wine.

3 Add the cauliflower flowerets and let marinate for 10 minutes.

4 Stir together in a shallow dish the millet flour, sea salt, and black pepper.

5 Set aside.

6 Remove the cauliflower from the marinade and place the marinade into a sauté pan.

7 Reduce the marinade over medium heat for about 10 minutes.

8 Meanwhile, place the cauliflower into a grill sauté pan and grill for 10 to 15 minutes, or until the cauliflower is crisp/tender.

9 Transfer the cauliflower to a plate and cover to keep warm while preparing the Shad roe.

10 Heat the butter in a medium sauté pan over medium-high heat.

11 Carefully dredge the roe in the millet flour mixture so they are coated lightly.

12 Sauté the roe for 2 to 3 minutes on each side until they are still quite tender. *(Do not overcook!)*

13 Carefully separate the roe into 4 lobes, removing the membrane that held them together, and place one on each plate.

14 Divide the cauliflower among the 4 plates.

15 Top with the sauce and serve immediately.

Serrano Wrapped Figs with Truffle Honey & Parmesan Toasts

J&E Time Signature

Birth & Balance

Serves 4

How do you take something as interesting as a fresh fig and make it more interesting? There is already so much to be said about the unique flavor and texture it has to offer. We present this to be added to the list of supreme finger foods. Once your guests have tasted this dish, they will have either thoroughly enjoyed something pleasingly familiar or you would have created — in the form of a Serrano wrapped, truffle honey decorated gift — a newly developed palate.

Juice & Essence

Honey and figs are a sweet and salty way to positively influence the stomach, spleen/pancreas, and moisten the lungs and large intestine thereby healing certain cases of cough and constipation/sluggish digestion. The detoxifying and alkalizing nature of figs will help balance a body accustomed to a diet rich in meats and refined food.

Complement or Contrast

COMPLEMENT – Sweet and salty calls for the fruity elegance of Pinot Noir as a complement, Burgundy for elegance, and California for more fruit and spice.

Ingredients

- 12, ½"-slices from a whole grain baguette
- ½ cup freshly grated Parmesan cheese
- 12 fresh Turkish figs
- 12, slices ¼" thick × 1" wide of Prima Donna cheese
- 6 thin slices of Serrano ham
- 1 tablespoon toasted pumpkin seeds (pepitas)
- ½ teaspoon truffle honey
- Chopped parsley for garnish

Directions

1 Preheat the broiler to high.
2 Place the baguette slices on a baking sheet.
3 Broil until the bread just starts to brown.
4 Turn over the bread slices and mound the Parmesan cheese on top.
5 Place under the broiler again and cook until the cheese is melted and bubbly.
6 Remove from broiler and set aside.
7 Slit each fig in half, vertically, being sure not to cut all the way through.
8 Place a slice of cheese in each slit.
9 Lay out the slices of Serrano ham.
10 Cut them in half lengthwise to make two strips.
11 Wrap a strip of ham around the outside of each fig.
12 Stand them up on a platter.
13 Scatter the pumpkin seeds over the top of the figs and around the platter.
14 Drizzle the truffle honey over top of the figs.
15 Top with the chopped parsley.
16 Serve with the Parmesan toasts.

Royal Peking Duck Dumplings

Birth & Balance

Serves 8

This royal Peking duck will bring you luck if you're stuck in a rut and looking to stretch a buck! Serving duck breast in this delectable display gives you, as the host, the opportunity to enrich your evening's menu in a lovely and extravagantly frugal way. We crammed tons of nutritious herbs and texture into the dumplings and created a sauce that is sooo good!

Juice & Essence

Duck is mainly lung and kidney yin tonifying and helps with common issues such as dry cough, hot flashes, and constant thirst. Secondarily, mustard, garlic, mirin, ginger, and scallions offer circulatory, immune system boosting, and energizing properties.

Complement *or* Contrast

COMPLEMENT – *This dish needs a match for the spice, richness, and sweetness. We recommend Zinfandel, Shiraz/Syrah, and Malbec to complement this rich, pungent, and sweet dish.*

Prepare the Duck

Ingredients

- 2 whole duck breasts
- 1 tablespoon minced garlic
- 2 tablespoons mirin
- 2 tablespoons low sodium soy sauce
- 1 tablespoon Chinese hot mustard
- 1 tablespoon ponzu sauce
- 1 tablespoon Hoisin sauce
- 3 scallions, white and light green parts only, diced
- 1½ tablespoons grated fresh ginger
- ½ teaspoon ground white pepper

Directions

1 Remove the skin from the duck breasts.
2 Pound the skinned duck breasts between two sheets of plastic wrap until they are about ¼" to ½" thick.
3 Combine the remaining ingredients together and pour over duck.
4 Marinate for at least 1 hour or up to 4 hours.
5 Grill the duck breasts on very high heat for about 10 minutes, or until cooked to medium and grill marks are well defined.
6 Place on a platter to cool slightly.
7 Cut into a ¼"-dice and place in a medium size bowl along with the drippings from the platter.

Prepare the Dipping Sauce

Ingredients

- ¼ cup ponzu sauce
- 2 tablespoons soy sauce
- 1 tablespoon chili sauce with garlic
- 1 tablespoon honey
- ¼ cup vodka

Directions

1 Combine all ingredients in a small saucepan.
2 Heat on high to a boil and then reduce heat to simmer.
3 Continue to simmer for 15 minutes.
4 Remove from heat and set aside while preparing dumplings.

Royal Peking Duck Dumplings ~ *continued*

Assembly

Ingredients

- ¼ cup of ¼"-diced water chestnuts
- 2 tablespoons chopped fresh parsley
- 2 tablespoons finely chopped green onions, light green and white parts only
- 2 tablespoons hot sesame oil
- 2 tablespoons sesame oil
- 1, 12-ounce package wonton wrappers
- 2 egg whites
- Cornstarch
- Sesame oil

Directions

1. Place the water chestnuts, parsley, green onion, hot sesame oil, and sesame oil in the bowl with the duck.
2. Stir to combine well.
3. Sauté in a hot wok on high heat for 2 minutes.
4. Remove from heat and set aside.
5. Set up wonton wrappers on a towel and cover with plastic wrap so they do not dry out.
6. In a small bowl, whisk together the egg whites to make the egg wash.
7. Sprinkle some cornstarch in a thin layer on a baking sheet and set aside.
8. Place one wonton wrapper on a work surface (keep the remaining wrappers covered).
9. Add 1 teaspoon of the duck filling to the center of the wonton wrapper.

10. Brush the egg wash around the edges of the wonton.
11. Bring two opposite corners together and pinch to seal.
12. Bring the remaining corners together and pinch to seal.
13. Place on the cornstarch coated pan and cover with a towel to keep them from drying out.
14. Continue making the dumplings with the remaining wonton wrappers and duck filling.
15. Set up a steamer insert in a pot over simmering water.
16. Add some dumplings to steamer rack and cover.
17. Steam for 3 minutes.

18 While the dumplings are steaming, heat a frying pan over medium-high heat.

19 When pan is hot, add enough sesame oil to coat the pan.

20 Add the steamed dumplings to the oil and fry until the bottoms of the dumplings are well browned. (This can take about 3 minutes or more.)

21 Continue the steaming and the frying with the remaining dumplings.

22 Serve hot with the dipping sauce.

Smoked Wahoo Dip

Birth & Balance

Serves 8 to 10

Making a fish dip sounded extra fun! We knew that with our Juice & Essence dinner party on the horizon coming up with a signature Florida dish would be a sure winner. Finding smoked, fresh wahoo from our local fishmonger, Pinder's, was further inspiration. For texture we went out on a limb by adding water chestnuts, celery, and capers. Whoa! What an amazing triumvirate of taste!

Juice & Essence

The many arterial cleansing, cholesterol lowering, energizing, and brain stimulating qualities of fish are widely revered. Overall properties are warm and tonifying to the spleen/pancreas, kidneys, and liver. Our addition of water chestnuts balances this dip with a cooling nature. Water chestnuts benefit the lungs, spleen, stomach, large intestine, and bladder channels. Some key health benefits of water chestnuts are the lowering of blood pressure, the treating of hypertension, lung heat with sticky, difficult to expectorate phlegm, dry painful throat, fever with thirst, jaundice, and other heat/rash related complaints.

CONTRAST – I recommend Greco Di Tufo or Vermentino for their perfumy, refreshingly crisp flavors with good mineral content that will stand up nicely to the salty, smoky dip. If all else fails, a Chardonnay would do just fine.

Ingredients

- 1¼ lbs. smoked wahoo
- Zest of 1 lime
- Zest and juice of 1 lemon
- ¼ cup chopped shallots
- ½ cup thinly sliced celery
- ⅓ cup minced water chestnuts
- 2 tablespoons capers
- 1½ tablespoons chopped fresh chives
- ½ teaspoon cayenne pepper
- ½ teaspoon paprika
- ½ teaspoon freshly ground black pepper
- ¼ teaspoon sea salt
- 5 tablespoons mayonnaise
- To Serve: endive spears, crackers, celery sticks, toasted bread, etc.…

Directions

1   Flake the smoked wahoo into a large bowl.

2   Add all of the remaining ingredients and mix well.

3   Cover and chill at least 8 hours to allow flavors to blend.

Wahoo Ceviche

Birth & Balance

Serves 4

Wahoo keeps its composure well raw or cooked. We are blessed to have access to fresh wahoo in Florida. Ceviche by nature is the best summer afternoon dish. The recipe for ceviche is old and established; however, our measurements give a unique and thoroughly enjoyable take on this festive dish.

Juice & Essence

The omega essential oils in wahoo are arterial cleansing, great for stimulating circulation, and aiding with heart issues. It makes for a deliciously immune system boosting dish. The large amounts of fresh lime and lemon offer an antiseptic quality and is perhaps the most valuable fruit therapeutically for people who have eaten a high fat/protein diet. They also destroy unwanted bacteria thereby assisting with purifying the breath. The antiseptic, anti-microbial, and mucus resolving action make it useful during dysentery, colds, flus, hacking coughs, and parasite infestation. Beneficial to the liver, encourages formation of bile, improves absorption of minerals, promotes weight loss, cleanses blood, normalizes blood pressure, alleviates indigestion and gas.

COMPLEMENT – This high acid dish would do really well with the mild fruit and strong acids of Fumé Blanc or Albarino from Spain.

Ingredients

- ¼ cup chopped shallots
- 1 teaspoon minced garlic
- 1 tablespoon chopped fresh cilantro
- 1 jalapeño pepper, ½ seeded, minced
- 1 tablespoon minced Hungarian pepper
- ½ cup minced red bell pepper
- 1 tablespoon chopped green onion
- Juice of 1 orange
- Juice of 2 lemons
- Juice of 2 limes
- 1 lb. fresh wahoo, trimmed and cut into ¾"-cubes
- ¾ teaspoon freshly ground black pepper
- ½ teaspoon freshly ground Himalayan salt
- 1 avocado, chopped into ½"-pieces

Directions

1 Combine the shallots, garlic, cilantro, jalapeño, Hungarian pepper, red bell pepper, green onion, orange, lemon and lime juices, and the wahoo into a large bowl and mix well.

2 Set aside to "cook" in the citrus juice for about 10 minutes.

3 Add the pepper, salt, and avocado.

4 Stir to combine.

5 Serve immediately.

Soft-Shell Crab with Pepper Salad & Avocado Dressing

Birth & Balance

Serves 4

There was no rhyme or reason to this except why not take an in-season item like soft-shell crab which we do not usually eat and adventurize it!!!??? This turned out to be a tasty dish because of our efforts to combine fresh, lively greens with smooth, sweet, and tangy avocado dressing against the tender, crunchy backdrop of our scrumptious pan-fried soft-shell crab.

Juice & Essence

Crabs are bone building and restoring, beneficial to joints and tendons, very helpful for building blood, and overall nourishing to the liver. Avocado is lubricating to the lungs and intestines, a good source of brain food, and is beautifying to the skin. This is a yin nurturing dish.

Complement or Contrast

CONTRAST – Champagne!!! Fried seafood needs high acid, uncorked whites like Sauvignon Blanc, Sancerre, Pouilly Fumé.

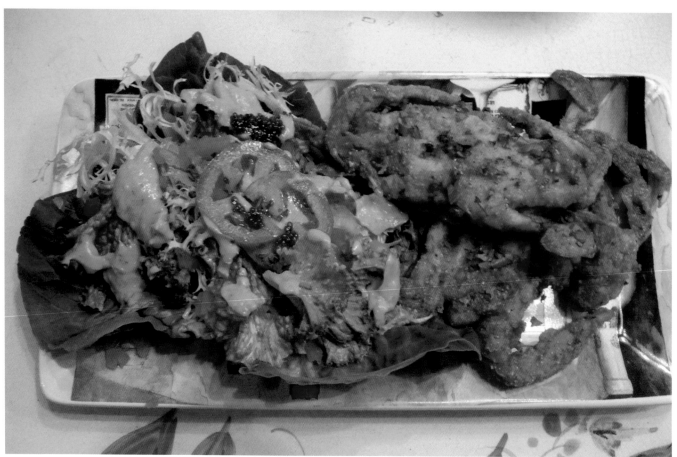

Salad and Dressing

Ingredients

- ½ cup finely chopped celery
- ⅔ cup finely chopped bell pepper, combination of yellow and red
- ½ teaspoon minced Scotch Bonnet pepper
- 4 tablespoons fresh lemon juice
- 2 avocados, cut into cubes
- 2 tablespoons fresh lime juice
- 2 tablespoons chopped fresh cilantro
- 1 tablespoon chopped fresh parsley
- 1 tablespoon minced shallot
- 1 garlic clove, put through garlic press
- 2 tablespoons sherry vinegar
- 4 tablespoons extra-virgin olive oil
- 4 tablespoons water
- Salt and pepper to taste
- 4 large leaves from Bibb lettuce (will be the bowl for the salad)
- 3 cups Frisée lettuce
- 3 cups red leaf lettuce
- 1 tomato, thinly sliced, for garnish

Directions

1. Combine the celery, bell pepper, Scotch Bonnet pepper, and lemon in a small bowl.
2. Add salt and pepper to taste.
3. Set aside.
4. Place the avocado, lime juice, cilantro, parsley, shallot, garlic, vinegar, oil, and water into a blender.
5. Puree the contents until very creamy and thoroughly mixed.
6. Add more water by the teaspoonful if too thick.
7. Add salt and pepper to taste.

Crab

Ingredients

- ½ cup all-purpose flour
- 1 tablespoon cornmeal
- 1 teaspoon ground cardamom
- ½ teaspoon ground white pepper
- 1 teaspoon freshly ground Grains of Paradise
- ¼ teaspoon Himalayan salt
- 1 teaspoon whole pink peppercorns, coarsely ground in mortar and pestle
- 8 soft-shell crabs, cleaned
- 2 eggs
- 2 tablespoons unsalted butter
- 2 tablespoons olive oil

Directions

1. Combine the flour, cornmeal, cardamom, white pepper, Grains of Paradise, salt, and pink peppercorns in a shallow dish.
2. Crack the eggs into another shallow dish and add 1 tablespoon of water, combine well.
3. Place a sauté pan over medium-high heat.
4. When hot, add the butter and oil to the pan.
5. Dip the crab in the egg wash and then into the seasoned flour to coat.
6. Add to the pan and cook for about 3 minutes per side until browned and crisp. (Add extra oil and butter as needed.)
7. Drain on paper towel-lined plate.
8. Arrange the Bibb lettuce leaves on 4 salad plates.
9. Tear the Frisée and red leaf lettuce into bite-size pieces and place inside the Bibb lettuce leaves, dividing evenly.
10. Top with the pepper mixture.
11. Drizzle with the avocado dressing.
12. Top with the sliced tomato for garnish.
13. Place 2 of the prepared crabs alongside the salad on each plate.
14. Drizzle with a little of the avocado dressing.

Summer Entrées

Chapter 2
Summer Entrées

We took the best the world has to offer and refined each contribution with respect to cultural ideals. We used our palates, taste experience, and history of chef interactions to lovingly create our entrées.

Lobster Salad Roll

Birth & Balance

Serves 4

In the spirit of summer simplicity and the northern states, we embarked on a flavorful vision with a Florida spin that could easily hold court at any scrutinizing picnic. Our palate of tastes is held tightly together with sweet local-caught lobster and zesty Meyer lemons, which are native to China and not Florida as commonly thought. Our healthful additions of red, yellow, and orange bell peppers, celery, and minced green onion add color and medicinal benefits.

Juice & Essence

Rich in omega-3 fatty acids, lobster meat is protein rich, very low in fat, and loaded with zinc and potassium. It is also a wonderful source of vitamins A, B, B12, and D that are great for bones, energy, and protein. Lemons assist the liver with detox and help alkalize the body, benefit the lungs, spleen, and stomach channels. Uses include assisting with cough, thirst, and sore throat. Celery is beneficial to the stomach and liver, helps clear heat, treats high blood pressure, dizziness and vertigo, and red face and eyes. Onion is warming and benefits the lungs, spleen, liver, and large intestine. It also assists in treating common cold, diarrhea, and worms. Using bell peppers aids in improving the appetite and resolving stagnant food in cancer cases where digestion is very poor. They also reduce swelling, promote circulation, and are rich in vitamin C. Bell pepper is part of the "night shade" family and caution should be taken if one is experiencing loose stools.

CONTRAST – Buttery lobster in mayonnaise needs an un-oaked, dry, citrusy Chardonnay to cut the richness of the lobster. (California/France/Italy) Sancerre since it is the all-around quintessential seafood wine.

Ingredients

- 2 lbs. Florida Lobster Tails, trimmed and cut in half lengthwise
- 2 tablespoons olive oil
- Salt and pepper to taste
- 1 teaspoon Meyer lemon zest
- ¼ cup minced celery, including some leaves
- 1 tablespoon minced green onion, white part only
- ¼ cup minced assorted red, yellow, and orange bell peppers
- ½ teaspoon Himalayan salt
- 1 teaspoon ground black pepper
- 1 teaspoon paprika
- 3 tablespoons mayonnaise
- 1 large whole grain baguette
- 1 large garlic clove, cut in half crosswise
- 1 large tomato, thinly sliced

Directions

1. Preheat grill to medium heat.
2. Coat the lobster tails with the olive oil and salt and pepper them to taste.
3. Place on the preheated grill and cook for about 15 minutes, or until cooked through.
4. Set aside to cool for 10 minutes then remove from the shell and chop into 1"-chunks.
5. Place the chunks into a large bowl and set aside.
6. In a small bowl, thoroughly mix together the zest, celery, green onion, peppers, salt, pepper, paprika, and mayonnaise.
7. Add the mixture to the lobster and carefully mix together being sure not to break up the lobster pieces.
8. Cut the baguette in half lengthwise and then into 4 serving sizes.
9. Toast the cut side on the grill or in the oven.
10. Lightly rub the cut side of the bread with the cut side of the garlic clove.
11. Place some of the lobster salad on the baguette and top with the tomato slices. Serve immediately.

Exotic Mushroom Strudel

Birth & Balance:

Serves 4 to 6

The art of making a sandwich can sometimes take you past simply placing varieties of food between two slices of bread. As we explored what a soup and sandwich combo meant to us, we decided that the actual bread portion could add to the excitement. We went with phyllo and created a strudel rich in flavor because of the fresh mushrooms, herb selection, and crumbled queso blanco cheese. Pairing this with our yellow gazpacho can easily make for a late lunch or early dinner.

Juice & Essence

The mushrooms in this strudel have anti-cancer benefits, also benefits the spleen and therefore digestion. These three mushrooms are high in fiber and share in detoxing, rash calming, and spirit quieting qualities. Shiitake mushrooms, as well as being a great anti-tumor, anti-cancer, and anti-viral resource, also enhance cellular oxygenation and overall immunity.

Complement or Contrast

COMPLEMENT – *Earthy deep flavors of mushroom respond nicely to the earthy notes of Pinot Noir and Malbec.*

Ingredients

- 3.5 ounces oyster mushrooms, cleaned and chopped into 1"-pieces
- 3.5 ounces shiitake mushrooms, cleaned, stemmed, and chopped into 1"-pieces
- 8 ounces crimini mushrooms, cleaned and chopped into 1"-pieces
- 2 tablespoons unsalted butter
- 2 tablespoons olive oil
- 1 leek, cleaned, white part only, thinly sliced
- ¾ cup diced fresh fennel
- 2 teaspoons chopped fresh fennel fronds
- 2 teaspoons chopped fresh thyme
- 2 tablespoons brandy
- 9 ounces fresh spinach, cooked, squeezed dry, and chopped
- ½ teaspoon sea salt
- ¼ teaspoon freshly ground black pepper
- ½ teaspoon minced fresh parsley
- ½ teaspoon minced fresh thyme
- ½ teaspoon minced fresh basil
- ½ cup extra-virgin olive oil
- ¼ teaspoon sea salt
- ¼ teaspoon freshly ground pepper
- ½ cup crumbled queso blanco cheese
- 12 sheets of phyllo dough

Directions

1 Preheat oven to 400°F.
2 Place a large sauté pan over medium-high heat.
3 When hot, add the butter and olive oil.
4 Add the leeks and diced fennel.
5 Sauté for 3 to 4 minutes, or until the fennel is beginning to soften.
6 Add all of the mushrooms.
7 Sauté for another 5 minutes, or until mushrooms have given off most of their liquid.
8 Add the fennel fronds, thyme, brandy, spinach, salt, and pepper.
9 Continue to cook until the liquid has evaporated, about another 2 minutes.
10 Set aside to cool slightly.
11 In a small bowl, mix together the parsley, thyme, basil, olive oil, salt, and pepper.
12 Set aside.

13 Open the phyllo dough and place on a work surface.
14 Cover with plastic wrap and a damp cotton towel so it will not dry out.
15 Take one piece of the dough and place it on a piece of parchment paper (long side facing you).
16 Brush lightly with a little of the herb-oil mixture.
17 Take another piece of dough and place it on top of the oiled one.
18 Brush again with a little of the herb-oil mixture.
19 Continue this procedure 4 more times. (You will have 6 sheets of the phyllo dough stacked together.)
20 Now take half of the mushroom mixture and place it down the center of the dough leaving a 2" border on each of the short ends of the dough.
21 Add ½ of the crumbled queso blanco cheese to the top of the mushroom mixture.
22 Wrap the dough, tightly, around the filling, using the parchment to help you.
23 Tuck the ends of the dough under the strudel and place on a parchment-lined baking sheet. (Leave room for the second strudel.)
24 Brush the top and sides with a little of the herb-oil mixture.
25 Follow the same procedure using the rest of the phyllo dough, herb-oil, mushrooms, and cheese.
26 Place next to the other strudel.
27 Bake for 25 minutes, or until the strudels are nicely browned.
28 Set aside to cool for about 10 minutes before slicing.

Yellow Gazpacho with Black Sesame Seed Mussels

Birth & Balance

Serves 4 to 6

Summertime is a great time to lighten up and try new combinations of readily available veggies. In this case, fresh ears of summer corn were around to keep with the theme of sunshine. We grabbed yellow tomatoes, sweet plantain, and yellow squash and threw them together with a bunch of fresh herbs. To add flavor, protein, and a fun texture, we added sweet mussels. This soup is fun to eat, goes down well, and feels very good inside!

Juice & Essence

The corn, mussels and black sesame seeds are very rich in kidney tonifying qualities. Strong kidneys equal strong back, knees, immune system and virility. Other attributes include nourishment to the heart and liver assisting in some cases of intestinal blockage, abdominal swelling, goiter and vertigo.

CONTRAST – We are looking for a wine that will respond equally well to the soup as it would to the fried mussels. My recommendation is a full, floral, peachy, straw-colored white wine such as Pecorino, Vermentino, New Zealand Sauvignon Blanc, or Viognier.

Ingredients

- 4 ears of yellow corn
- 3 lbs. yellow tomatoes
- 1 sweet plantain, peeled and boiled for 10 minutes, or until softened
- 1 English cucumber
- 1 yellow bell pepper
- 3 teaspoons finely chopped cilantro
- 1 teaspoon white vinegar
- 1 teaspoon extra-virgin olive oil
- ¼ teaspoon sea salt
- ½ teaspoon freshly ground Grains of Paradise
- 2 cups chopped yellow squash
- 5 cloves of garlic, pressed
- 1 cup chopped sweet onion
- 1 jalapeño pepper, ½ seeded or to taste
- 1 tablespoon sea salt
- 1 tablespoon sherry vinegar
- 2 dozen mussels, cleaned
- 1 egg white
- ½ cup whole wheat panko breadcrumbs
- 2 tablespoons black sesame seeds
- 1 cup olive oil

Directions

1 Remove the husks from the ears of corn and scrub with a stiff brush to remove silks.

2 In a pot large, enough to hold the corn, bring 3 cups of water to a boil.

3 Add the corn and then cover and remove from the heat. Let the corn sit in the covered pot for 15 minutes.

4 Remove the corn from the pot and, when cool enough, cut the kernels from the cob and set aside. *We are going to be chopping and separating the vegetables. Some will be going into the food processor for the base of the soup. The rest will be chopped a little finer and will be used in the finished soup.*

5 Take three of the tomatoes and seed and chop into ½"-pieces. Place in a large bowl which will be for the finished soup.

6 Place the rest of the tomatoes into the bowl of a food processor fitted with the chopping blade. Process until the tomatoes are pureed well. Remove to a separate large bowl.

7 Take ½ of the plantain and chop into a ¼" dice. Place them in the finished soup bowl.

8 Place the other half into the food processor bowl fitted with the chopping blade.

9 Take ⅓ of the cucumber and peel and chop into ½"-pieces.

10 Place in the finished soup bowl.

11 Chop the remaining cucumber and place in the food processor.

12 Seed the yellow pepper and chop ⅔ of it and place in the bowl of the food processor.

13 Take the remaining ⅓ and cut into a ¼" dice and place in the finished soup bowl.

14 Now take the finished soup bowl and add 1 teaspoon of the chopped cilantro, 1 teaspoon of white vinegar, 1 teaspoon extra-virgin olive oil, ¼ teaspoon sea salt, ½ teaspoon Grains of Paradise, and the corn kernels.

15 Mix together. Cover and place in the refrigerator.

16 Add the yellow squash, garlic, onion, jalapeño, 1 tablespoon sea salt, and 1 tablespoon sherry vinegar to the food processor bowl.

17 Process until the vegetables are pureed well. Add to the bowl with the tomato puree. Stir to combine well. Cover and place in the refrigerator to chill while preparing the mussels.

18 Steam the mussels in a steamer until the shells open. When cool enough to handle, remove the mussels from the shells.

19 In a small bowl, whisk the egg white well.

20 In another small bowl, combine the panko breadcrumbs and the black sesame seeds.

21 Place a wok over high heat and add the olive oil. Once the oil is very hot, dip each mussel into the egg white and then cover in the panko-sesame seed mixture and add to the oil. Flash fry for no longer than 1 minute. Remove from oil and drain on a paper towel-lined plate.

22 Remove the bowls of the soup mixture from the refrigerator.

23 Place the soup base in individual serving bowls.

24 Top with a scoop of the chopped vegetable mixture.

25 Add some of the hot mussels on top of the soup and serve.

Herbed Veal Chop with Raspberry~Chipotle Sauce

Birth & Balance

Serves 4

Flavorful and fun for summer with a bright and spicy twist. We wanted to create a veal chop dinner with more than just great texture…as veal chops do not have much flavor due to their young, lean nature. We took this boring piece of meat and made it exciting!

Juice & Essence

Veal is classified as having a sweet taste and respectively affecting the spleen. Other organs energetically affected by veal are the liver, kidneys, stomach, and large intestine channels. Overall the main ingredient of this dish builds qi and blood, benefits yin, strengthens the tendons, joints, and bones. Helps in many cases of low back pain, knee pain, and weakness. The use of fresh herbs such as thyme and rosemary will assist with immune system, indigestion, nausea, bloating, common cold, and cough. Raspberry has both a sweet and sour flavor with energetic tendencies toward the liver and kidneys. Builds blood and helps to detoxify it. Regulates menses and urination. The addition of chipotle will assist with poor circulation and lung issues as well as indigestion.

Complement or Contrast

CONTRAST – Big gun time! Bordeaux (Cab heavy; Haut Medoc), Barolo, Tempranillo (Ribera del Duero) or Tinta de Toro, if you can find it. It is not the young, tender, sweet veal that dictates this choice but the accompaniments and herbs.

Ingredients

- 4 veal chops, 1½" thick
- 2 teaspoons chopped fresh rosemary
- ½ teaspoon chopped fresh thyme
- ½ teaspoon chopped fresh marjoram
- 1 teaspoon chopped fresh parsley
- ½ teaspoon freshly ground Grains of Paradise
- 1 teaspoon sea salt
- 2 teaspoons roasted garlic
- ½ cup extra-virgin olive oil
- *Raspberry~Chipotle Sauce* (page 364)

Directions

1   Heat the oven to 400°F.

2   In a small bowl, combine the herbs, Grains of Paradise, salt, roasted garlic, and olive oil.

3   Brush all over the veal chops and let marinate for 30 minutes.

4   Heat a sauté grill pan over medium-high heat until very hot.

5   Sear the veal chops for 2 minutes on each side until nicely browned.

6   Place grill pan in oven to finish cooking the chops. (Approximately 10 minutes for medium.)

7   Serve with the *Raspberry~Chipotle Sauce.*

Scallops with Jalapeño Infused Walnut Oil Drizzle & Stuffed Leeks

J&E Time Signature

Birth & Balance

Serves 4

The idea of stuffing leeks stirred our interest. They are tasty, have a unique texture, and would serve as a lovely escort for our freshly seared scallops. The cheeses selected would have to support the creamy sweetness of the scallops above and the crunchiness of the leeks below. Once we assembled this creamy, crunchy, sweet dish, we further enhanced it with a sweet and spicy jalapeño~cherry honey drizzle. Enjoy!!!

Juice & Essence

Scallops are nourishing to yin and therefore moistening to the body with blood building and joint strengthening attributes. Leeks in this dish benefit the liver and especially add to medicinal qualities in the areas of difficulty swallowing, counteracting bleeding and diarrhea. The spices and honey help to detoxify the body while assisting in the healing of lung conditions such as cough and asthma.

Complement or Contrast

COMPLEMENT – *You know it by now… big Chardonnay for the rich scallops. To enhance the texture and richness of the scallops I chose the oaky and buttery California or French Chardonnay.*

For the Oil

Ingredients

- 1 large jalapeño pepper, cut in half, seeds and core removed from only half
- ⅔ cup walnut oil

Directions

1 Add to a small saucepan and simmer for 5 minutes.
2 Set aside to cool.
3 Once cool, pour through a fine mesh strainer to remove the jalapeño and seeds.
4 Set aside ¼ cup of infused oil to use in drizzle.

For the Drizzle

Ingredients

- ¼ cup *Jalapeño Infused Walnut Oil*
- 1 teaspoon cherry honey

Directions

Whisk the cherry honey into the infused oil and set aside.

For the Stuffed Leeks

Ingredients

- 4 leeks, white parts only
- 1 cup peanut oil
- 8 thin slices of Taleggio cheese
- 8 thin slices of Fontina cheese
- 8 fresh chives

Directions

1 Cut leeks in half lengthwise.
2 Remove root ends but do not remove the core since this will hold the leek together.
3 Clean very well in running water. Being sure to separate the leaves and get all of the dirt out.

4 Remove some of the center leaves to leave a space for the cheese to melt into.
5 Slice the center leaves into very thin strips.
6 Set aside.
7 Place the leek halves on a steamer rack set over boiling water and steam for 8 minutes, or until very soft and cooked through.
8 Meanwhile, heat the peanut oil in a large pot or wok until it reaches 350°F.
9 Add the thin strips of leeks and fry until crispy and browned.
10 Remove to a paper towel-lined plate to drain.
11 Once the leeks have been steamed, place them on a baking sheet, cut side up.
12 Cut the cheese to fit the leeks.
13 Place one slice of each cheese on top of the leeks.
14 Place a fresh chive on top of the cheese.
15 Broil on high until the cheese is melted and browned in spots.
16 Time the leeks so they are done at the same time as the scallops.

Scallops with Jalapeño Infused Walnut Oil Drizzle & Stuffed Leeks ~ *continued*

For the Scallops

Ingredients

- 2 tablespoons "Luke Mangan's Dukkah" seasoning: (mixture of ground hazelnuts, sesame seeds, coriander seeds, sumac, cumin seeds, mustard seeds, fennel seeds, chili and pepper)
- ¼ cup *Jalapeño Infused Walnut Oil*
- 1 teaspoon cherry honey
- 1 lb. wild caught sea scallops
- Olive oil

Directions

1 Grind the Dukkah seasoning in a mortar and pestle until very finely ground.

2 Mix in a medium bowl along with the oil and honey.

3 Add the scallops and toss to coat with marinade.

4 Set aside.

5 Heat a large sauté pan until very hot.

6 Add enough olive oil to coat the bottom of the pan.

7 Sear the scallops in hot pan for 10 minutes total.

8 Remove scallops and change heat to low.

9 Add the drizzle mixture that was made earlier to the pan and stir to pick up any browned bits in pan.

To Serve

Place two stuffed leek halves on the plate. Add two scallops. Top with the "drizzle" from the sauté pan. Sprinkle with the crispy leeks.

Phyllo Wrapped Sea Bass with Mediterranean Vegetable Sauce

Birth & Balance

Serves 4

How do you take a fish seemingly perfect in texture and improve on it? Well in this case we added a flaky crust. The trick was figuring out a way to bring texture to texture without ruining flavor. We chose phyllo dough...it worked!

Juice & Essence

Sea bass nourishes blood and, by extension, joints. It is highly nourishing, energizing, restorative, vitamin and mineral rich with anti-inflammatory attributes and helpful with brain function, including short-term memory loss. Sea bass moistens the lungs and is helpful with severe cough attacks. It is also strengthening to the spleen and pancreas. Olive and Omega oils in this dish will nourish the skin, nails, and joints and assist with bowel regularity. Shiitake mushrooms make this antioxidant high, cholesterol lowering, and immune system boosting. Circulation enhancing qualities from cloves, tomatoes, and onions further add to the dish's well rounded attributes.

Complement *or* Contrast

CONTRAST – We need a dry, crisp white wine with good fruit and minerality such as Terre di Tufo, Greco Tufo, Gavi di Gavi, French Sancerre, and Sauvignon Blanc to uplift the salty, flaky sea bass.

Phyllo Wrapped Sea Bass

Ingredients

- 1 teaspoon whole mustard seeds, finely ground in a mortar and pestle
- 1 teaspoon finely chopped fresh dill
- ⅔ cup extra-virgin olive oil
- 2 tablespoons clarified butter
- ½ teaspoon freshly ground Himalayan salt
- ½ teaspoon ground anise seed
- 2 lbs. sea bass cut into 4 equal portions
- 12 sheets of phyllo dough, laid out on and topped with a sheet of plastic wrap and a damp towel

Directions

1 Preheat oven to 450°F.

2 Combine mustard seeds, dill, olive oil, clarified butter, Himalayan salt, and anise seeds together in a small saucepan.

3 Bring to a simmer for 5 minutes and set aside.

4 Brush a little of the spiced oil mixture onto the fish.

5 Sear in a hot pan for 2 minutes on one side.

6 Flip the fish over and turn off the heat.

7 Leave for 2 more minutes in the hot pan, then remove from the pan and place on a plate. Set aside.

8 Meanwhile, take 1 phyllo leaf and place on a work surface with the long side facing you. (Be sure to cover remaining dough so it will not dry out.)

9 Quickly brush it lightly with some of the spice oil mixture.

10 Repeat procedure 2 more times. (You will have used 3 pieces of phyllo dough.)

11 Place 1 of the fish fillets in the center of the dough.

12 Fold the end nearest you to cover the fish.

13 Bring in the left and right sides of the dough to the center and then wrap the top end around to completely enclose the fish.

14 Place on a parchment-lined rimmed baking sheet (leaving enough room for the other three fillets), seam side down, and brush the top with a little more spice oil mixture to cover.

15 Lightly cover with plastic wrap so the dough of the wrapped fillet does not dry out while you prepare the remaining fillets.

16 Repeat this procedure with each of the remaining fish fillets.

17 Bake the wrapped fillets for 8 to 10 minutes or until nicely browned.

18 Serve with *Mediterranean Vegetable Sauce* on the side.

Mediterranean Vegetable Sauce

Ingredients

- 3 tablespoons extra-virgin olive oil
- 1 small onion, diced
- 3 garlic cloves, minced
- 1 yellow bell pepper, diced
- 10 ounces shiitake mushrooms, sliced
- 6 plum tomatoes, diced
- 1 cup kalamata olives, pitted and halved
- ¼ cup fresh oregano, chopped
- 3 tablespoons lemon juice
- 1 teaspoon lemon zest
- 1 tablespoon capers
- 8 ounces feta cheese, crumbled
- Salt and pepper to taste

Directions

1 Heat the olive oil in a large sauté pan over medium-high heat.

2 Add the onion, garlic, and pepper.

3 Sauté about 5 minutes, or until onion is translucent.

4 Add the mushrooms and sauté for 2 minutes.

5 Add the tomatoes, olives, oregano, lemon juice, zest, and capers.

6 Stir and reduce heat to low.

7 Add the feta cheese and salt and pepper to taste.

8 Remove from heat and serve alongside the fish.

Powerful Pungent Pork Chops

Birth & Balance

Serves 4

Good on the grill!!! When you are in the mood for pork chops, there is no substitute. We were definitely in the mood and simply could not pass up another opportunity to include the cherry honey. The rest was easy. We kept it simple with a healthy Asian marinade and let the grill do the work.

Juice & Essence

Pork is beneficial to the spleen, stomach, and kidneys, helps build blood, and strengthens weak kidneys, good for areas of yin deficiency where dry cough and dry intestines are concerned. Ample use of garlic, scallion, and ginger are antiparasitic, anitviral, and antibacterial therefore assisting where indigestion of pork or general digestive issues are in question.

Complement *or* Contrast

CONTRAST – What we need here are fruit forward, medium tannin, big red wines with hints of cherry, leather, and tobacco to compete with the powerful, pungent elements of these pork chops. I am very excited to introduce my Sardinian favorites: Carignano (example: Terre Brune) and Cannonau.

Ingredients

- ⅔ cup light soy sauce
- 4 teaspoons grated fresh ginger
- 4 teaspoons grated fresh garlic
- ½ cup scallions, white and light green parts only, finely chopped
- 4 teaspoons hot chili oil
- 3 tablespoons dark brown sugar
- Freshly ground black pepper
- 4 bone-in loin pork chops, 1½" thick
- 2 tablespoons cherry honey

Directions

1 Mix together in a glass dish large enough to hold the chops in a single layer the soy sauce, ginger, garlic, scallions, chili oil, and brown sugar.

2 Season chops with black pepper.

3 Add chops to marinade and turn to coat each chop well.

4 Refrigerate for 1 hour or as long as overnight.

5 Bring out of refrigerator 30 minutes before grilling.

6 Meanwhile, heat grill to medium high.

7 Pat chops dry with a paper towel to remove excess marinade.

8 Grill for approximately 6 to 8 minutes on one side.

9 Check for color and grill marks; then flip the chops.

10 Grill for about 2 to 3 minutes and coat with cherry honey and turn off heat.

11 Close grill and let chops sit for 5 to 10 minutes.

12 Remove from heat and serve.

Scotch Bonnet Sliced Lobster Tail in Butter~Herb Sauce with Caviar Dollops

Birth & Balance

Serves 4

As lobster lovers, finding ways to keep it interesting becomes a joyous task. This dish is as extravagant as main dishes get. We threw everything at these non-marinatable crustaceans but the kitchen sink hoping for a unique and unforgettable taste. Mission accomplished!

Juice & Essence

Lobster is very beneficial to the bones and brain. A very rich and nourishing dish with immune system and energy boosting properties. Can help restore harmony to the stomach. Restores appetite and assists with vertigo, some types of headaches, bloating, and high blood pressure. The yin nourishing cold nature of lobster is balanced in this dish by the warming blood moving qualities of cardamom, Scotch Bonnet, and white pepper.

CONTRAST – Lobster = Chardonnay... not today! The spices and herbs in this dish call for something more lively with fruit and grass yet dry and pretty. A central Napa Sauvignon Blanc or Albarino would be my choice.

Ingredients

- 1 teaspoon ground cardamom
- ½ teaspoon ground white pepper
- 1 teaspoon freshly ground Grains of Paradise
- ¼ teaspoon Himalayan salt
- 1 teaspoon whole pink peppercorns, ground in mortar and pestle
- ¼ cup extra-virgin olive oil
- 4, 8-ounce Florida lobster tails
- ¼ cup minced celery
- ½ cup minced red bell pepper
- ½ teaspoon minced Scotch Bonnet pepper
- ¼ cup minced shallots
- 2 tablespoons minced scallions
- 2 large garlic cloves, put through press
- ½ cup white wine
- 1 tablespoon chopped parsley
- 2 tablespoons unsalted butter
- 2 tablespoons olive oil
- Caviar as a garnish (optional)

Directions

1 To make the marinade, mix together the cardamom, white pepper, Grains of Paradise, salt, pink peppercorns and extra-virgin olive oil in a medium size bowl.

2 Remove the lobster from the shell and cut into 2" slices.

3 Add to the marinade and mix to coat the lobster well.

4 Heat a sauté pan with the 2 tablespoons of butter and the 2 tablespoons of olive oil.

5 Add the celery, red bell pepper, Scotch Bonnet pepper, shallots, scallions and garlic to the pan.

6 Cook for about 3 to 4 minutes until the vegetables are softened.

7 Add the lobster and sauté for 2 minutes.

8 Add the white wine and parsley.

9 Continue to cook for 6 to 8 minutes, or until the lobster is cooked through.

10 Transfer to serving platter and top each lobster medallion with a little bit of caviar.

Jerked Filet Roast Fajitas with Tropical Salsa & Meyer Lemon~Mint Cream

J&E Time Signature

Birth & Balance

Serves 4

This is a saucy, succulent summer lunch (or dinner) taking cues from the tropical influences of Jamaica and Mexico. We loved this dish and have not found its counterpart in our travels since. The balance of spice topped with cooling natured salsa and Meyer lemon cream give room for meditative culinary pause. Have fun in the sun as you make your own!

Juice & Essence

A thorough and tasty way to cover many bases, this beef dish benefits the spleen, liver, kidneys, stomach, and large intestine channels. This enriching combination tonifies yin, strengthens joints and bones, helps with some cases of low back and knee pain, and treats cough, wheezing, vomiting, and indigestion. The herb and seasoning content assists with digestion, boosts immune system, and invigorates blood flow. The Meyer lemons aid with indigestion, sore throat, excess phlegm, and bring beneficial healing to the spleen, stomach, and lungs.

Complement or Contrast

CONTRAST – I chose a wine to reign in the roast with the Meyer Lemon-Mint Cream and encompass all of the flavors: Tempranillo, Bordeaux or a young Merlot.

For the Jerked Filet Roast

Ingredients

- 1 teaspoon whole cloves
- 1 teaspoon whole allspice
- ½ teaspoon freshly ground nutmeg
- ¼ teaspoon ground cinnamon
- 2 teaspoons sea salt
- 1 teaspoon freshly ground black pepper
- 2 teaspoons grated fresh ginger
- 4 garlic cloves, pressed
- 3 Scotch Bonnet peppers (2 minced with seeds and ribs, 1 minced with seeds and ribs removed)
- 5 scallions (2 with greens, chopped fine; 3 with only the white part, coarsely chopped)
- 1 tablespoon finely chopped shallots
- 1 teaspoon finely chopped fresh thyme
- Juice of 1 lime
- 2 teaspoons tamarind concentrate
- ½ cup olive oil
- 2 lbs. beef filet roast
- Salt and pepper

Directions

1. Grind the whole cloves and whole allspice in a spice or coffee grinder.
2. Place in a small bowl.
3. Add the nutmeg, cinnamon, salt, pepper, ginger, garlic, peppers, scallions, shallots, thyme, lime juice, tamarind concentrate, and oil; mix well.
4. Coat the beef with the jerk mixture and cover well.
5. Refrigerate overnight.
6. Remove beef from the refrigerator 30 minutes prior to roasting.
7. Preheat oven to 400°F.
8. Adjust the oven racks so that one is at the very top and the other is all the way on the bottom.
9. Place the roast on a rack in a roasting pan.
10. Add more salt and pepper just to coat the top of the roast.
11. Place the pan on the bottom rack of the oven and roast for 40 minutes.
12. Turn the oven on broil and place the pan on the top rack.
13. Broil the roast for 10 minutes.
14. Remove from oven and let the meat rest for 15 minutes.

Jerked Filet Roast Fajitas with Tropical Salsa & Meyer Lemon~Mint Cream ~ *continued*

For the Meyer Lemon~Mint Cream

Ingredients

- 1 teaspoon Meyer lemon zest
- 2 tablespoons Meyer lemon juice
- ¼ teaspoon freshly ground black pepper
- ¼ teaspoon sea salt
- 1 small jalapeño pepper, minced
- 1 teaspoon chopped fresh mint
- 8 ounces sour cream

Directions

1 Mix all of the above in a small bowl.
2 Cover and refrigerate (can be made the day before).

For the Tropical Salsa

Ingredients

- 1 cup chopped mango
- 1 cup chopped pineapple
- 1 cup chopped red bell pepper
- 1 small Serrano chili, seeded and diced
- 4 green onions, white and light green parts only, sliced
- 2 tablespoons minced shallot
- ⅛ teaspoon paprika
- ½ cup chopped fresh cilantro
- Juice of 1 lime
- Cayenne pepper to taste
- Salt and pepper to taste

Directions

1 Mix all of the above in a bowl.
2 Stir to combine well.
3 Set aside at room temperature.

To Assemble the Fajitas

Ingredients

- 2 avocados, sliced
- 1 cup shredded Prima Donna cheese
- 10 flour tortillas

Directions

1 Place the tortillas in a stack on a sheet of aluminum foil.

2 Close the foil around the tortillas.

3 Place in a preheated 350°F. oven for 10 minutes to heat them.

4 Cut the roast into thin slices and place some on each of the tortillas.

5 Top with some of the cheese, avocado, salsa, and cream. Serve immediately.

Chicken & the Egg (Clay-Baked Cornish Hens with Liver~Oyster Mushroom Stuffed Polenta Eggs)

Birth & Balance

Serves 4

Which came first, the chicken or the egg? It's summer and everything is growing shiny and bright. Sometimes we don't feel so bright and shiny. We wanted to create something to engage us and make us respect the beginning and end of things. The sweetness of life reflected in birth and in the polenta. The wisdom and growth of life reflected in the Cornish hens. Ever young, supple, and tasty – that's us – Juice and Essence! Enjoy!

Juice & Essence

Using polenta was attractive for many visual, textural, and health enhancing reasons as it is nourishing to the heart, improves digestion and appetite, helps regulate digestion, promotes healthy teeth and gums, tonifies kidneys, and helps overcome sexual weakness. In addition, chicken makes this an overall energizing dish with benefits to the spleen/pancreas, stomach, and bone marrow. Chicken liver offers strengthening qualities for both the liver and kidneys, which help to treat impotence, blurred vision, tendencies for miscarriage, and urinary incontinence.

COMPLEMENT – I never thought I would say this…this dish calls for a young Amarone! The richness of the liver and mushrooms needs a dry, raisiny, deep passenger.

To Prepare Cornish Hens

Ingredients

- 4 Cornish hens, cleaned and dried
- 4 large garlic cloves, pressed
- 1 tablespoon chopped fresh parsley
- 1 teaspoon paprika
- 1 teaspoon dried tarragon
- 1 teaspoon dried marjoram
- 1½ teaspoons sea salt
- ½ cup extra-virgin olive oil
- 25-lb. block of fresh, low-fire terra cotta (purchased from a ceramic supplier)
- Parchment paper

Directions

1 Preheat oven to 400°F.
2 In a small bowl, combine the garlic, parsley, paprika, tarragon, marjoram, sea salt, and the olive oil.
3 Place the Cornish hens on a platter and pour the olive oil mixture over them.
4 Rub the oil onto each hen to coat them well.
5 Set aside to marinate while preparing the liver-oyster mushroom stuffed polenta eggs.

Liver-Oyster Mushroom Stuffed Polenta Eggs

Ingredients

- 1 teaspoon whole fennel seeds
- ½ teaspoon whole coriander seeds
- ¼ teaspoon pink peppercorns
- 1 lb. chicken livers
- 8 ounces oyster mushrooms
- 1 sprig each of fresh rosemary and sage, leaves removed from tough stems
- 1½ teaspoons chopped fresh chives
- 1 tablespoon chopped scallions, white and light green parts only
- 3 cloves of garlic, coarsely chopped
- 1 teaspoon lime zest
- 1½ teaspoon sea salt
- 1 teaspoon ground black pepper
- 1 tablespoon olive oil
- ½ lb. quick-cooking polenta
- Nonstick aluminum foil

Chicken & the Egg ~ *continued*

Directions

1 Prepare polenta according to the package directions for a firm texture.

2 Transfer to a large bowl to cool.

3 Toast the fennel seeds, coriander seeds, and pink peppercorns in a dry skillet over medium heat until fragrant.

4 Transfer to a mortar and pestle and grind well.

5 Add to food processor fitted with the chopping blade.

6 Add the livers, mushrooms, rosemary, sage, chives, scallions, garlic, lime zest, salt, and pepper.

7 Process until pureed.

8 Heat a sauté pan with the olive oil until shimmering.

9 Add the liver mixture and sauté until it is well browned and cooked through.

10 Set aside to cool.

11 Once the polenta is cool enough to handle, take an ice cream scooper full and form a patty in your hand.

12 Add 1 tablespoon of the liver to the middle.

13 Wrap the polenta around the liver to fully enclose and form an egg shape.

14 Make 3 more the same way.

15 Wrap the finished "eggs" individually in the nonstick aluminum foil.

16 This will allow the "egg" to hold its shape while cooking in the hens.

17 Place one foil wrapped "egg" into the cavity of each of the 4 hens and set them aside while preparing the clay.

Assembly

Directions

1   Cut four ¾"-thick slices from the short side of the block of clay.

2   Roll out a slice to a 9"×14" rectangle that is ⅛" thick.

3   Wrap a Cornish hen in parchment paper to cover.

4   Place in the middle of the clay and wrap the clay around the hen to cover removing excess clay as needed.

5   Rub the outside of the clay to smooth out.

Be creative and make markings on the clay for feathers and fashion a neck and head that looks like a chicken and attach to the clay. They can be prepared up to four hours ahead, covered and refrigerated.

6   Remove from the refrigerator an hour before baking (keep covered so as not to dry out the clay) or you can bake them immediately.

7   Place the clay wrapped hens on a parchment covered baking sheet and bake for one hour.

8   Remove from oven and let rest for 10 minutes.

9   Crack open the clay using a small hammer.

10   Remove the hen from the parchment paper being careful not to get any of the dried clay on the hen.

11   Remove the foil wrapped "egg" from the hen.

12   Take the "egg" out of the foil and carefully cut it in half.

13   Decoratively place it on a platter with the hens and serve.

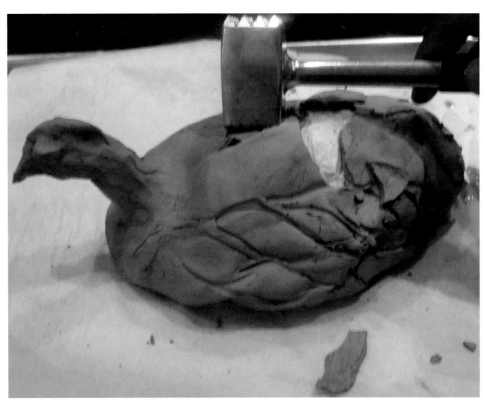

Chicken & Black Bean Enchiladas with Red Plum Tomato Sauce & Tomatillo Drizzle

Birth & Balance

Serves 6

Waste not, want not. This dish was created with some leftovers. We had leftover chicken, sauces, and cheese. To liven it up we furthered the Mexican influence and decided on an enchilada presentation. We dare you to find an enchilada this tasty and rich with healthy ingredients.

Juice & Essence

Chicken and black beans are blood building, iron and protein rich. They are beneficial to kidneys, spleen/pancreas, reproductive functions, moisten dryness, detoxify blood, and cooling to the body. Helpful in some cases of low backache, knee pain, male sexual malfunction, and infertility in both sexes. Black beans can be effective in treating laryngitis, kidney stones, urinary difficulty, hot flashes, and menopause.

COMPLEMENT – *A light and playful Pinot Noir will respond to the fresh herbs, acorn squash, and the red plum in the tomato sauce.*

Ingredients

- 1, 3- to 3½-lb. whole rotisserie chicken, cooked
- 2 tablespoons olive oil
- ½ cup chopped shallot
- 2 cloves of garlic, pressed
- 4 green onions; light green and white parts chopped, slice the dark green parts for garnish
- ½ cup finely chopped mushrooms
- ¾ cup finely chopped acorn squash
- ¾ cup finely chopped yellow bell pepper
- 1, 15-ounce can black beans, rinsed and drained
- 1½ tablespoons chopped fresh cilantro
- ½ teaspoon chopped fresh mint
- 1 teaspoon chopped fresh oregano
- Salt and pepper
- 16 corn tortillas
- *Red Plum Tomato Sauce* (page 370)
- *Tomatillo Drizzle* (page 372)
- 1 cup shredded Mexican cheese
- Sour cream

Directions

1 Preheat oven to 350°F.

2 Make the sauce and drizzle recipes.

3 Keep sauces warm on the stove while preparing the chicken and black bean filling.

4 Remove the meat from the cooked chicken and cut the meat into ¼"- to ½"-pieces.

5 Set aside.

6 Place a large sauté pan over medium heat until hot.

7 Add the olive oil, shallot, garlic, light green and white parts of scallions, mushrooms, acorn squash, and yellow bell peppers.

8 Sauté for 5 minutes until the vegetables are cooked through.

9 Add the black beans, cilantro, mint, oregano, and the chopped chicken.

10 Mix to combine and add salt and pepper to taste.

11 Continue cooking for 5 more minutes.

12 Remove from heat and set aside.

13 Place a medium-size frying pan over medium heat.

14 Once the pan is hot, begin dipping the corn tortillas one by one in the *Red Plum~Tomato Sauce* just to coat lightly.

15 Transfer immediately to the hot frying pan.

16 Heat the tortilla for just about 30 seconds on each side. You just want to soften them slightly so they will be easy to roll around the filling.

17 Remove the tortilla from the pan and place on a work surface.

18 Place about ⅓ cup of the filling down the center of the tortilla.

19 Roll the tortilla around the filling.

20 Place some *Red Plum~Tomato Sauce* in the bottom of a 13"×9" glass baking dish.

21 Place the filled tortilla in the baking dish.

22 Continue with the rest of the tortillas and filling.

23 Be sure to place the filled tortillas close together so they do not come apart.

24 Once all the filled tortillas are in the baking dish, cover them with more of the *Red Plum~Tomato Sauce.*

25 Top with some of the *Tomatillo Drizzle.*

26 Cover the top with the cheese.

27 Bake the dish for 20 to 30 minutes, or until the cheese is melted and the sauce is bubbling.

28 Remove from the oven and let rest for 10 minutes.

29 Garnish with the reserved green onion slices.

30 Serve with sour cream.

Very Zesty Veal Scallopini

Birth & Balance

Serves 4

We took a classic dish and added some zing. We figured we would lighten up this dish by omitting the flour and egg yolks. The end product was a very pretty, golden scallopini.

Juice & Essence

Veal is strengthening, blood building, and energizing. It also benefits the spleen/pancreas and stomach, and strengthens the connective tissue and bones. The secondary benefits of the supporting ingredients of lemon and capers are antibacterial and antiviral. Also will moisten the lungs and throat thereby assisting with a sore throat and dry cough.

CONTRAST – With a dish so light, a red or white wine would work. A Chardonnay will balance the pan-fried veal as well as the Dolcetto or Barbera, which are both red wines.

Ingredients

- 1½ lbs. veal top round thinly sliced (scallopini)
- Salt and pepper to taste
- Extra-virgin olive oil
- 3 large egg whites
- 6 tablespoons butter
- ¼ cup extra-virgin olive oil
- ⅓ cup diced shallots
- ½ cup dry white wine
- ⅓ cup fresh squeezed lemon juice
- 1 tablespoon capers
- Salt and pepper to taste
- Capers and lemon slices

Directions

1 Tenderize the veal slices by pounding lightly with a tenderizing hammer.

2 Place the veal slices in a shallow baking dish.

3 Sprinkle the veal with salt and pepper to taste and drizzle with a little olive oil.

4 Lightly beat together the egg whites in a shallow bowl.

5 Add salt and pepper to taste.

6 Set aside while preparing the sauce.

7 Heat a small saucepan on medium heat.

8 Add the butter and ¼ cup of olive oil to the hot pan.

9 Add the shallots and sauté for 5 minutes.

10 Add the white wine, capers and lemon juice.

11 Salt and pepper to taste.

12 Lower heat to simmer while sautéing the veal.

13 Place a large sauté pan over high heat.

14 Add olive oil to a depth of ½".

15 Dip each piece of veal into the egg whites to coat and add to the hot oil.

16 Cook on one side until you see that the edges are browned then flip over to the other side for about 2 minutes more.

17 Remove to a platter and pour the sauce over the veal.

18 Add additional capers and lemon slices for a garnish.

Sweet Ribs

Birth & Balance

Serves 4

Slow and low! Everything else after that when it comes to ribs is preference. Our preference was to create dynamic flavor by using everything from fig paste and anchovies to chipotle pepper and bourbon. We chose beef ribs over pork in the effort to minimize unnecessary fat content and maximize protein. We are aware that most rib dishes use baby backs, however, we wanted to try our hand at something different. This recipe can easily be converted for you baby back lovers.

Juice & Essence

This rendition of juicy, slow-cooked beef will benefit the spleen, liver, kidneys, stomach, and large intestine channels. Also contains blood building and energy (qi) restoring qualities, very good for strengthening the joints and all connective tissues. The beef along with warming circulatory and anti-inflammatory herbs and spices will also aid with digestive issues, low back pain, and boost your immune system. Fig and anchovy enhance and support these medicinal attributes by channeling the lung and large intestine. Figs have moistening qualities along with alkalizing and detoxing actions. Anchovies add a burst of warming, dampness eliminating benefits. Apples protect the lungs from cigarette smoke and assist with indigestion by inhibiting the growth of fermentation and disease-producing bacteria in the digestive tract.

COMPLEMENT – *Big Cabernet, California blend, or Amarone: The meaty, deep, dry flavors of these wines will enhance this respectively deep and meaty rib experience.*

Dry Rub

Ingredients

- 2 teaspoons sea salt
- ⅛ cup crushed red pepper flakes
- 2 tablespoons paprika
- 2 tablespoons ground black pepper
- 1 teaspoon pressed garlic
- 1 teaspoon minced onion
- 1 teaspoon celery salt
- ½ cup olive oil
- 2 racks of beef ribs, trimmed

BBQ Sauce

Ingredients

- 2, 6-ounce cans tomato paste
- 1 cup olive oil
- 1¼ cups brown sugar
- 4 teaspoons sea salt
- 1½ tablespoons chopped fresh rosemary
- 1 tablespoon chopped fresh oregano
- 1 tablespoon chopped fresh thyme
- ¼ cup balsamic vinegar
- ¼ cup apple cider vinegar
- 2 gala apples, peeled, cored, and chopped
- 3 sundried tomato halves
- 1 shallot
- 5 cloves of garlic
- 2 tablespoons honey
- 3 tablespoons fig paste
- 3 anchovies
- 10 whole cloves; 1 star anise; 1 dried hot chili pepper, ground together in a spice mill
- ¼ teaspoon ground chipotle pepper
- 1 cup good bourbon

Directions

1 Preheat grill to low (300°F.).
2 Mix together all of the dry rub ingredients in a small bowl.
3 Spread evenly all over the beef ribs.
4 Set aside and let marinate for 2 hours or overnight.
5 Place ribs on top rack of preheated grill.
6 Close the lid and grill for 1½ hours.
7 Meanwhile, prepare the BBQ sauce.
8 Combine all of the BBQ sauce ingredients in the bowl of a food processor fitted with the chopping blade.
9 Process on high until the sauce is well pureed.
10 Place in a medium saucepan over medium heat and cover.
11 Bring to a boil.
12 Turn heat down to simmer and continue to cook for 30 minutes, stirring occasionally.
13 Use to baste the ribs once the ribs have cooked for the 1½ hours.
14 Continue to baste with the sauce over the course of 2½ hours, or until the ribs are fork tender.

Grilled Vegetable Napoleons

Birth & Balance

Serves 4 to 6

The star of this dish was the homemade ricotta cheese. It is not common to take time out of your day to make cheese, but it is a great way to put your love into a dish. This meal, when done, will look a lot like love. It is rich, light, tasty, and filling all at the same time. The juiciness of our Napoleon arrangement is further enhanced by the flavorful dressing.

Juice & Essence

Green zucchini, also known as summer squash, is cooling in nature and works great to reduce swelling and heat conditions affecting digestion and female processes. Eggplants are rich in bioflavonoids, which renew arteries and prevent strokes and other hemorrhages. The positive influences to the liver and uterus help in resolving repressed emotions and their harmful effects on these organs. Our homemade ricotta is beneficial to the kidneys, specifically kidney yin which will thereby moisten lungs, aid with skin tone, and build blood. Tomatoes are also a beneficial ingredient for building yin, assists with chronic thirst issues while aiding the liver in detox and purifying blood. Additional complaints relieved by regular use of tomatoes include lowering high blood pressure, relief for red eyes and headaches.

CONTRAST – This inherently savory dish calls for a largely savory experience. I chose a wine with a playful sweetness with influence of fruit to play off the savoriness of the dish. Riesling is a harmonious addition to unlock all of the amazing flavors.

Vegetables

Ingredients

- ½ cup extra-virgin olive oil
- 3 large garlic cloves, pressed
- ½ teaspoon crushed red pepper flakes
- 1 teaspoon sea salt
- ½ teaspoon freshly ground Grains of Paradise
- 1½ lbs. eggplant, peeled and sliced crosswise into ¼"-slices
- 1 lb. zucchini, cut in half crosswise then sliced lengthwise into ¼"-slices
- 2 yellow bell peppers, cut into planks and seeded
- 1 large beefsteak tomato, cut crosswise into ½"-slices

Directions

1 Preheat oven to 350°F.
2 Spray grill with cooking spray and set to high heat.
3 Combine the oil, garlic, crushed red pepper flakes, salt, and Grains of Paradise in a small bowl.
4 Brush the vegetables with the oil mixture as you grill them.
5 Grill each of the eggplant, zucchini, and peppers until browned nicely and cooked through.
6 Grill the tomato slices just for a couple of seconds so you can get nice grill markings on them. Do not overcook or they will become too mushy.
7 Set grilled vegetables on a platter and set aside.

Filling

Ingredients

- 1½ cups homemade ricotta cheese (We used the recipe from *Cooking Light* magazine.)
- ½ cup shredded Fontina cheese
- ⅓ cup chopped sundried tomatoes
- 1 tablespoon chopped fresh basil
- 1 teaspoon minced fresh rosemary
- 1 teaspoon minced fresh thyme leaves
- ½ teaspoon sea salt
- ¼ teaspoon freshly ground black pepper

Directions

Prepare the filling by combining in a medium-size bowl the ricotta, Fontina, sundried tomatoes, basil, rosemary, thyme, salt, and pepper. Mix well and set aside.

Dressing

Ingredients

- 1 garlic clove, pressed
- Juice of 2 lemons
- 1 tablespoon balsamic vinegar
- 2 anchovies, minced
- ¼ cup extra-virgin olive oil
- Dash of crushed red pepper flakes
- Salt and pepper to taste
- ½ cup freshly grated Parmesan cheese

Directions

Prepare the dressing by whisking together the garlic, lemon juice, balsamic vinegar, anchovies, olive oil, crushed red pepper flakes, salt, and pepper in a small bowl.

Assembly

1 Line a baking sheet with parchment paper.
2 Begin layering the Napoleons by placing 6 slices of the eggplant next to each other but 2" apart on the baking sheet.
3 Top with about a tablespoon of the filling.
4 Place a zucchini slice on top of the filling.
5 Top zucchini with another tablespoon of the filling.
6 Place a slice of tomato on top of the filling.
7 Top the tomato with another tablespoon of the filling.
8 Place a slice of the pepper on top of the filling.
9 Finish off with another slice of eggplant on top.
10 Sprinkle the tops with the Parmesan cheese.
11 Bake the grilled vegetable Napoleons in the oven for 10 minutes. Broil on high until the Parmesan cheese on top is nicely browned, about 2 minutes.
12 Place each Napoleon on a platter or individual serving plate and drizzle with the dressing. Serve immediately.

Pappardelle Carbonara with Peas, Mushrooms & Truffle Butter

Birth & Balance   Serves 4 to 6

We thought, "let's do pasta carbonara!" It is like pasta soul food. We chose to switch it up with the enhancing earthiness of the white truffle butter, the texture of the pappardelle pasta, and the nutritious medley of sautéed veggies.

Juice & Essence

The energy and properties of this dish deal with "earth"; this includes the spleen and the stomach. Both peas and mushrooms have a strong tonifying action on the spleen, stomach, and intestines. This dish will regulate the flow of energy, rectify weakness, strengthen muscles, build blood, and detox the body while assisting with water metabolism. Mild help with calming rashes and measles can be found with the mushroom component.

Complement or Contrast

CONTRAST – The richness of the pasta is perfectly balanced with the Chianti Riserva Classico. Even a Brunello or a Sangiovese strong Super Tuscan for their dry, good tannin, medium finish qualities that offset the rich creaminess of the pasta.

Ingredients

- 2 tablespoons extra-virgin olive oil
- 1 cup diced pancetta
- ¼ cup thinly sliced shallots
- 1 cup assorted wild mushrooms, small ones left whole, large ones sliced
- 1 cup fresh peas, fully cooked and drained
- ½ cup dry white wine
- ½ cup grated Parmesan cheese
- ¼ cup grated Romano cheese
- 4 egg yolks
- 1 tablespoon finely chopped fresh parsley
- 1 lb. dried pappardelle pasta
- 2 tablespoons white truffle butter
- Salt and pepper to taste

Directions

1 Bring 4 quarts of water to a boil in a large pot.

2 Meanwhile, heat the olive oil in a sauté pan.

3 When hot, sauté the pancetta until it is browned.

4 Remove from pan and drain on a paper towel-lined plate.

5 Add the shallots to the sauté pan and cook until softened.

6 Add the mushrooms, peas, and white wine.

7 Continue to cook until the wine has reduced by half.

8 Set aside.

9 In a large serving bowl, place the Parmesan, Romano, egg yolks, and parsley.

10 Stir to combine well.

11 Add 1 tablespoon of salt and pasta to the boiling water and stir to submerge all of the pasta.

12 Cook the pasta according to the package directions until just al dente and drain well.

13 Add to the serving bowl with the cheese and eggs.

14 Add the shallot, pea and mushroom mixture along with the drained pancetta to the pasta.

15 Mix well to combine all of the sauce to the pasta.

16 Add the truffle butter, salt and pepper to taste and mix again. Serve immediately.

Linguine with Clams & Herbed Pesto Baked in Parchment with Tomato-Brushed Crostini

Birth & Balance

Serves 4

We decided to do Carol's favorite dish found at her local restaurant. This is a combination of linguine with clam sauce and a traditional pesto sauce. What we did to put our own stamp on this traditional dish was to cook it in parchment paper. The timing of the ingredients for this dish was a significant task to manage. Too much moisture and the pasta would overcook; too little and it would be dry.

Juice & Essence

Eating clams is a sweet way to aid the body in getting rid of damp conditions while nourishing yin substances of the body. For instance: excess mucus, edema, and feminine imbalances. A strengthening dish that will help restore vessel integrity while supporting in the treatment of hemorrhoids, lengthy and excessive female monthly visits, and goiter. Pine nuts moisten lungs and intestines which aid in dry cough and constipation. Pine nuts help alleviate some forms of dizziness mainly due to liver qi imbalances. Thyme and other herbs will offer warming qualities with immune system enhancing benefits to help alleviate symptoms of the common cold.

CONTRAST – Quintessential seafood wines like Albarino or Verdelho go great with clams. The briny salty aspects of the clams meld well with the dry-light fruit of these wonderful wines.

Ingredients

- 3 large garlic cloves
- 1 teaspoon chopped fresh thyme
- ¼ cup fresh parsley leaves
- ¼ cup chopped fresh basil leaves
- 1 tablespoon chopped fresh chives
- 1 tablespoon chopped fresh oregano
- 1 tablespoon chopped fresh mint
- 3 tablespoons pine nuts, lightly toasted
- ½ cup freshly grated Parmesan
- ¼ cup freshly grated Locatelli cheese
- ¾ cup extra-virgin olive oil

- ¼ lb. proscuitto, sliced into thin strips
- 1 lb. linguine
- 1 tablespoon salt
- 4 tablespoons butter
- ¼ cup extra-virgin olive oil
- 1 cup of the pasta cooking water
- 36 little neck clams, washed
- Parchment paper, cut into two sheets 20" long, each placed on a rimmed baking sheet
- Kitchen twine

Linguine with Clams ~ *continued*

Directions

1. Preheat oven to 400°F.
2. Place the garlic, thyme, parsley, basil, chives, oregano, mint, pine nuts, and Parmesan and Locatelli cheeses into a blender and puree until just mixed together.
3. With machine running, slowly pour olive oil in a thin stream through the feed tube.
4. Blend until all of the oil is incorporated with the herbs.
5. Set aside.
6. Place proscuitto into a sauté pan over medium heat.
7. Sauté until proscuitto is very crisp.
8. Remove from pan and drain on a paper towel-lined plate.
9. Set aside.
10. Bring 4 quarts of water to a boil in a large pasta pot with strainer insert.
11. Add the linguine and salt to the pot.
12. Stir and then remove after approximately 3 minutes. You just want the pasta to start to soften since it will finish cooking in the parchment package. *Be sure to save 1 cup of the pasta cooking liquid.*

13. Combine the pasta cooking water, butter, and olive oil.
14. Divide the pasta and clams between the prepared parchment papers on the pans.
15. Add half of the pasta cooking water mixture to each and gather the ends to the center and tie closed, tightly, with the kitchen twine.
16. Place in the preheated oven for 25 minutes.
17. Meanwhile, gently heat the pesto sauce in a small saucepan (do not boil).
18. After the 25 minutes, open the packages and take any clams that have not opened and place in with the pesto sauce and cover pan for a few minutes.
19. Discard any clams that do not open.
20. Spoon the pesto sauce and clams over the pasta, dividing evenly.
21. Top with the crispy proscuitto slices and extra cheese if desired.
22. Serve with tomato brushed crostini.

Tomato-Brushed Crostini

Ingredients

- 1 baguette
- 2 ripe tomatoes cut in half
- 2 cloves of garlic put through a garlic press
- ½ cup extra-virgin olive oil

Directions

1 Bring garlic and oil to a simmer in a small saucepan for 5 minutes.

2 Set aside.

3 Cut baguette in 1"-slices, lengthwise.

4 Brush the cut sides with the garlic/oil mixture.

5 Toast the bread in the 400°F. oven on both sides until nicely browned.

6 Remove from oven and immediately rub one side of the bread with the cut side of the tomato. (Some of the pulp from the tomato should stick to the bread.)

7 Season to taste with salt and pepper.

8 Return to the oven for about 2 minutes more. Serve immediately.

Cedar Plank Grilled Rabbit with Red Plum Tomato Sauce & Tomatillo Drizzle Pizza

Birth & Balance

Serves 4

We wanted to keep the rabbit simple ~ scallion, lemon, coriander, Himalayan salt ~ all good! So beautiful on top of the cedar plank! Rabbit is a peculiar form of protein because it is not readily available in our society, yet it is very tasty and very clean. Generally they are farm raised and there are no hormones or antibiotics used in their rearing. We went crazy in the area of peppers for spice to match the delicious smoky sweetness of the rabbit and the San Marzano tomatoes.

Juice & Essence

Rabbit has a high protein to fat ratio: approximately 20.8% protein to 4.5% fat, and 795 calories per pound. It also has a very low cholesterol content. The red plums and the plum tomatoes are beneficial to the stomach while calming the liver. The tomatoes function on the stomach rests in the area of reparation of indigestion. They also help to get rid of heat and parchness (dry mouth). Red plums are cooling in nature, clear heat, and assist with constipation and overall production of body fluids. This pizza has blood building stomach, spleen, kidney, and lung strengthening benefits. The use of hot peppers/chilies will stimulate digestion, reduce phlegm, and assist with lung health reducing asthmatic complaints and frequency of moist coughs.

COMPLEMENT – *Flowery and slightly sweet Pinot Noir, Amarone, and Syrah match very well with the richness of gamy meats like rabbit.*

Prepare the Red Plum~Tomato Sauce

Ingredients

- 2 large red plums, peeled and coarsely chopped
- 1, 28-ounce can San Marzano plum tomatoes
- Salt and pepper
- ¼ cup Patron tequila
- 1 tablespoon honey
- ¼ cup chopped, rehydrated sundried tomatoes
- 1 teaspoon ground New Mexican chili pepper
- 1 teaspoon dried Mexican oregano
- ½ teaspoon ground, dried jalapeño pepper
- ½ teaspoon ground ancho chili pepper
- ½ teaspoon ground chipotle chili pepper
- 1 tablespoon chopped fresh parsley

Directions

1 Place the plums and the tomatoes with their juices in a medium saucepan.
2 Bring to a boil over medium-high heat.
3 Add the remaining ingredients and simmer for 30 minutes.
4 Set aside.

Tomatillo Drizzle

Ingredients

- 1 lb. tomatillos, husked and cut in half
- 1 fresh jalapeño, seeds and veins removed, sliced
- ¼ teaspoon ground, dried jalapeño
- ½ teaspoon coriander seed, ground in a mortar and pestle
- 1 cup water
- 1 cup dry white wine
- ½ cup chopped cilantro
- 3 tablespoons olive oil
- ½ teaspoon sea salt

Directions

1 Place the tomatillos, fresh and dried jalapeño, coriander, and water in a medium saucepan.
2 Bring to a boil over high heat.
3 Reduce heat to medium and add the white wine.
4 Continue to boil for 15 minutes.
5 Remove from heat and drain, discarding the liquid.

6   Let the tomatillo mixture cool for 10 minutes.

7   Then place the tomatillo mixture in a blender with the remaining ingredients.

8   Blend on high until it is pureed.

9   Set aside.

Prepare the Rabbit

Ingredients

- ½ rabbit, debone the breast piece only, leave the bone in the remaining pieces
- ¼ cup scallion greens, thinly sliced
- ½ cup olive oil
- ½ teaspoon Himalayan salt
- ½ teaspoon ground coriander
- 2 tablespoons lemon juice
- 1 grilling cedar plank, soaked in water for at least 2 hours or overnight.

Directions

1   Place the rabbit, scallions, olive oil, salt, coriander, and lemon juice in a medium-size bowl and mix well.

2   Let the rabbit marinate for 10 minutes.

3   Meanwhile, prepare the grill.

4   Heat the grill to 400°F.

5   Place the plank on the grill and close the cover.

6   When the plank starts to smoke, it is ready.

7   Place the rabbit parts on top of the plank.

8   Leave the cover off and grill the rabbit for 30 minutes, or until done.

9   Remove from the grill. (Keep temperature at 400°F. to grill the pizza.) When cool enough to handle, remove the meat from the bones.

10 Chop the meat into 1"-pieces.

11 Set aside while preparing dough.

Pizza Dough & Assembly

Ingredients

- 1 teaspoon chopped fresh thyme
- 1 teaspoon chopped fresh sage
- 1 teaspoon chopped fresh chives
- ½ teaspoon chopped fresh rosemary
- ½ cup olive oil
- 1 lb. organic, unbleached wheat flour pizza dough
- Cornmeal
- 1½ cups grated mild Mexican cheese
- 2 tablespoons scallion greens, sliced

Directions

1 Combine the herbs and olive oil in a small bowl.

2 Roll out or stretch the pizza dough into a thin round on a floured work surface.

3 Transfer to a pizza paddle that is coated liberally with cornmeal. Brush the top of the dough with the herb/oil mixture.

4 Carefully transfer the dough to the grill, oiled side down.

5 Grill until the dough is bubbling on top.

6 Brush the top of the dough with some of the herb/oil mixture to coat.

7 Flip the dough over.

8 Spread the red plum~tomato sauce on the dough.

9 Top with the scallions, cheese, and rabbit pieces.

10 Cook for 2 minutes then shut off the gas and close the lid.

11 Let the pizza sit on the grill for 7 to 10 minutes, or until the cheese has melted.

12 Transfer to a serving platter and drizzle with the tomatillo sauce. Serve immediately.

Mediterranean Veggie Pizza

Birth & Balance

Serves 4

For our vegetarian readers, we wanted to provide a fun and interesting salute to pizza. We packed this one full of antioxidant-rich spices and veggies. It is bright and appealing to the eyes and palate. Looking back at this daring achievement, it is still amazing that we could take tamarind, balsamic vinegar, and honey and combine them successfully into a veggie marinade.

Juice & Essence

A variety of high antioxidant, cancer-fighting veggies and spices combining circulation enhancing and joint strengthening attributes. Using chickpeas in this pizza was a creative way to boost low, unsaturated fat/high protein content. Chickpeas contain more iron than any other legume and have beneficial healing qualities for the pancreas, stomach, and heart.

CONTRAST – Chianti Riserva Classico or a nice fruit forward Chardonnay goes well with this pizza due to its playful relationship with the spice from seeds, the balsamic vinegar, and honey.

Prepare the Vegetables
Ingredients

- ½ teaspoon cardamom seeds
- ½ teaspoon fennel seeds
- ¼ teaspoon cumin seeds
- 1 teaspoon honey
- 2 teaspoons tamarind concentrate
- 1 teaspoon balsamic vinegar
- ½ teaspoon reduced-sodium soy sauce
- ½ teaspoon chopped fresh parsley
- 3 tablespoons extra-virgin olive oil
- 1 medium zucchini
- 1 medium yellow squash
- 1 medium red bell pepper
- ½ cup grape tomatoes
- 6 scallions, light green and white part only (reserve dark green tops for the chickpea puree)

Directions

1. Toast the cardamom seeds, fennel seeds, and cumin seeds in a small sauté pan until fragrant, about 3 minutes.
2. Place in a mortar and pestle and coarsely grind the seeds.
3. In a large bowl, put the ground seeds, honey, tamarind, vinegar, soy sauce, and parsley.
4. Slowly whisk in the olive oil to emulsify.
5. Reserve 1 tablespoon of the dressing in a small bowl to be used for the crust and set aside.
6. Slice the zucchini and yellow squash lengthwise into ¼"-slices.
7. Core and seed the bell pepper and cut into ½"-slices.
8. Place the vegetables, along with the tomatoes and scallions, in the large bowl of the dressing and mix well to coat each piece.
9. Let marinate for 15 minutes.
10. Meanwhile, heat grill to medium.
11. Grill the vegetables until just softened, about 5 to 8 minutes.
12. Remove from grill.
13. Coarsely chop the scallions.
14. Set aside. (Can be made 6 hours ahead, covered at room temperature.)

Prepare the Chickpea Puree
Ingredients

- 1, 15-ounce can chickpeas, rinsed and drained
- ¼ cup chopped scallion greens
- 2 small garlic cloves, chopped
- ¼ cup extra-virgin olive oil
- ¼ teaspoon crushed red pepper flakes
- ¼ cup dry white wine
- ¼ cup parsley leaves
- Salt and pepper to taste

Directions

Combine all of the ingredients in a food processor. Blend until pureed well. (Can be made 1 day ahead. Bring to room temperature before proceeding with the pizza.)

Pizza Dough & Assembly
Ingredients

- Reserved 1 tablespoon of dressing from veggies
- 3 tablespoons olive oil
- 1 lb. organic, unbleached wheat flour pizza dough
- Cornmeal
- 8 ounces feta cheese
- 2 tablespoons coarsely chopped parsley
- Pizza stone

Directions

1. Place pizza stone on rack in upper third of oven.
2. Preheat oven to 500°F.
3. In a small bowl, combine the reserved dressing and olive oil.
4. Roll out or stretch the pizza dough into a thin round on a floured work surface.
5. Transfer the dough to a pizza peel that has been liberally coated with cornmeal.
6. Brush the top of the dough with the oil mixture.
7. When the oven is heated, carefully transfer the dough to the pizza stone.
8. Lower oven temperature to 475°F.
9. Bake for 5 to 8 minutes, or until the dough starts to crisp on the edges and center is bubbly and slightly cooked.
10. Spread the chickpea puree over the dough, leaving a slight border.
11. Top with the grilled veggies and crumble the feta cheese all over.
12. Continue to bake until the crust is nice and browned and the cheese is bubbling.
13. Sprinkle with the parsley and serve.

Mango~Tarragon Ravioli with Galliano~Beet Drizzle

Birth & Balance

Serves 4

Keeping with the propensity of Ken to venture into insane flavor combinations, this was created as a side dish for the *Very Zesty Veal Scallopini* (page 306). The intention was to keep within the sweet flavor spectrum contrasting to the tartness of the veal. This is also a light and refreshing main course on its own.

Juice & Essence

Mango is beneficial to the lungs, spleen, and stomach. In this dish mango, adds the health benefits of treating cough, wheezing, vomiting, and indigestion. The beet juice helps improve circulation, strengthening the heart, purifying the blood, moistening the intestines, and assisting with balancing liver health.

COMPLEMENT – I decided to elevate the sweet and tropical mango flavors with a dry yet fruity Alsacean Gewürztraminer. The effervescence of a Prosecco would also be nice.

Ingredients

- 1 cup diced honey mangoes, approximately 3
- 1 tablespoon chopped fresh tarragon
- 1 teaspoon extra-virgin olive oil
- 1 teaspoon cardamom seeds, toasted and finely ground in a mortar and pestle
- ¾ cup part-skim ricotta cheese
- 2 tablespoons dark rum
- ¼ teaspoon sea salt
- 1 egg white
- 12 ounces wonton wrappers
- 3 teaspoons Galliano liquor
- ⅓ cup fresh beet juice
- 2 teaspoons ghee

Directions

1 In the bowl of a food processor fitted with the chopping blade, combine the mango, tarragon, oil, ground cardamom, ricotta cheese, rum, and salt.

2 Process until you have a smooth puree, about 2 minutes.

3 Remove to a small bowl.

4 In a small bowl, whisk the egg white to make the egg wash.

5 Set up the wonton wrappers on a towel and cover with plastic wrap so they do not dry out.

6 Place one wonton wrapper on a work surface (keep the remaining wrappers covered).

7 Add about 1 teaspoon of the filling to the center.

8 Brush the egg wash around the edges of the wrapper.

9 Take another wonton wrapper and place on top of the filling.

10 Press all around the filling to seal.

11 Be sure the seal is tight so that they do not break apart while cooking.

12 Place on a baking sheet and cover with a damp towel.

13 Continue making the ravioli with the rest of the filling and wrappers.

14 Meanwhile make the Galliano~beet sauce.

15 Combine the Galliano, beet juice, and ghee in a small saucepan.

16 Bring to a simmer and cook for 10 to 15 minutes to combine the flavors.

17 Bring a large pot of water to a boil.

18 Once boiling, add the ravioli and cook until they are floating to the top, about 3 minutes.

19 Remove with a slotted spoon to the serving platter.

20 Spoon the Galliano~beet sauce over top of the ravioli.

Summer Accompaniments

Chapter 3
Summer Accompaniments

These accompaniments are gorgeous mates to the flavor notes and visual canvases of Juice & Essence entrées. These accompaniments are a fresh take on vegetable combinations that, customary with Juice & Essence, have an unpredictably delicious twist!

Baby Summer Squash & Cipollini Onion Sauté

Birth & Balance

Serves 4

Our local market had the most beautiful baby summer squash. To complement the squash, we chose a select type of onion called "cipollini." They are a small and not so intimidating onion. The cipollini mirrored the size and shape of the sunny yellow pattypan squash creating a circular, sumptuous summer surprise!

Juice & Essence

Baby summer squash benefits the spleen, stomach, and large intestines; helps clear heat; and reduce pain, edema, and inflammation. Cipollini onion, spices, and herbs increase qi, energy, and circulation. Also lowers blood pressure, calms the brain, and decreases sinus and throat congestion.

Ingredients

- 16 baby zucchini, cut in half lengthwise
- 16 baby pattypan squash, cut in half through stem
- 12 cipollini onions, boiled and peeled to remove the skins, cut in half
- 1½ teaspoons chopped fresh chives
- ½ teaspoon chopped fresh thyme
- 1 teaspoon chopped fresh marjoram
- 1 teaspoon chopped fresh parsley
- ½ teaspoon lemon zest
- 2 teaspoons lemon juice
- ½ teaspoon roasted garlic, mashed
- ½ teaspoon sea salt
- ½ teaspoon freshly ground black pepper
- 2 tablespoons extra-virgin olive oil

Directions

1   Mix all of the ingredients together and marinate for ½ hour at room temperature.

2   Heat a large sauté pan over medium-high heat.

3   Add the vegetables to the pan, cut sides down.

4   Brown well and continue to cook for about 10 minutes total, or until just softened.

5   May be served hot or at room temperature.

Beet Infused Turnip Fritters

Birth & Balance

Serves 4

In looking for a starch, we found a way to create fritters with turnips. The trick was to temper the excess turnip moisture by combining root vegetables. This ended up being a wonderful way to get people that would never eat turnips or beets to enjoy their flavors and immense medicinal value.

Juice & Essence

Turnips have pungent, sweet, and bitter flavors and have influence on the spleen, stomach, and lungs. As a member of the mustard family, turnips are a good source of sulphur, a warming, purifying element. Its pungent nature will help induce sweating thereby relieving heat. Turnips help to reduce body heat, assist in food elimination, stop cough, treat heat-oriented body issues, and detoxify the body. Turnips help with indigestion, hoarseness, diabetes, and jaundice. The addition of beets aids in blood building and heart strengthening and also assists in the healing of liver ailments.

First Step

Ingredients

- 2 lbs. turnips, cut into 1"-cubes
- 1 large potato, cut into 1"-cubes

Directions

1 Place in a large saucepan and add enough water to just cover the vegetables.
2 Bring to a boil and cook for 15 minutes, or until cooked through.
3 Drain and place back in hot saucepan for a few minutes to dry out excess water.
4 Place vegetables in a large mixing bowl.

Second Step

Ingredients

- 6 tablespoons unsalted butter, softened
- ½ teaspoon sea salt
- ¼ teaspoon fresh ground black pepper
- ½ cup fresh beet juice (use one medium-size beet in a juice machine)
- ¼ cup all-purpose flour
- 1 egg yolk

Directions

1 Put all of the above ingredients into the bowl with the turnips and potatoes.
2 Mash with a potato masher to incorporate well.
3 Heat 3 tablespoons of olive oil in a large sauté pan until shimmering.
4 Add the turnip mixture to the hot oil using about 2 tablespoons for each fritter.
5 Shape into circles or ovals as you place the mixture into the pan.
6 Brown well on each side.
7 Drain on paper towel-lined rack.
8 Serve while hot.

Oven Roasted Tomatoes

Birth & Balance

Serves 4

This is a staple tomato dish that can be used with anything. Our first time making it for this book, we decided to use them in a salad. They also can be used as an appetizer stuffed with tasty creations from your imagination.... The sky is the limit!

Juice & Essence

Tomatoes help moisten the palate and cool the body while settling and cleansing the liver. Helpful in lowering blood pressure and detoxifying the blood, thereby also aiding with red eyes and tension headaches. Blood purifying and digestion enhancing will result, even though tomato is an acidic fruit. After digestion, they will alkalize the blood and therefore be helpful in reducing the acid blood of rheumatism and gout.

Ingredients

- 8 large plum tomatoes, cut in half lengthwise, seeds removed (can use grape tomatoes but only cut in half – do not remove seeds)
- 1 large garlic clove, minced
- 1 small shallot, minced
- 2 tablespoons extra-virgin olive oil
- 2 tablespoons balsamic vinegar

Directions

1   Mix all of the above ingredients together and season to taste with salt and freshly ground pepper.

2   Arrange on a rimmed baking sheet, cut sides up.

3   Roast the tomatoes for 2 to 3 hours at 250°F. until they are concentrated and lightly caramelized. (They may also be roasted at 400°F. for 1 to 1½ hours until concentrated and lightly caramelized.)

Spring Essence Salad

Birth & Balance

Serves 4

Capturing the essence of spring we combined most of our favorite spring flavors and wrapped them like little gifts. This salad is as pleasing to the eye as it is to your palate.

Juice & Essence

Asparagus is beneficial to the kidneys and, in stimulating the kidneys, will help eliminate excess water. Because of the asparagus, this salad will help cleanse the arteries of cholesterol and will be useful in vascular problems such as hypertension and arteriosclerosis. Olives are helpful in moistening the lungs and dealing with chronic bronchitis. Tomatoes make this a cooling salad with yin nourishing properties. Tomatoes are a significant part of this dish, offering additional help with constipation, sluggish circulation, high blood pressure, red eyes, and headaches.

Ingredients

- 2 tablespoons balsamic vinegar
- ¼ teaspoon sea salt
- ¼ teaspoon freshly ground pepper
- ½ teaspoon light agave syrup
- 1 teaspoon water
- 4 tablespoons extra-virgin olive oil
- 8 slices proscuitto
- 16 halves of *Oven Roasted Tomatoes* (page 332)
- 16 fresh basil leaves
- ¼ cup Parmesan Reggiano, thinly sliced
- 1 lb. asparagus, roasted until crisp tender
- 16 (or more if some break) fresh chives, to tie up the tomatoes
- 4 cups arugula
- 4 heads of red endive
- ½ cup pitted Niçois olives
- ¼ cup pine nuts, lightly toasted

To Make the Dressing

Directions

1 In a small bowl, whisk together the balsamic vinegar, salt, pepper, agave syrup, and water.

2 Slowly whisk in the olive oil in a very thin stream to emulsify.

3 Set aside.

Preparing the Proscuitto

Directions

1 Cut the proscuitto into 1½"-pieces.

2 Add to a small sauté pan and place over medium heat.

3 Sauté the proscuitto until it is very crispy.

4 Remove from pan and drain on paper towel lined-plate.

5 Set aside.

Preparing Tomato Bundles

Directions

1 Place 1 tomato half on work surface, cut side up.

2 Top with 1 basil leaf, slice of Parmesan and 1 asparagus spear.

3 Place 1 chive under tomato and tie in a knot to hold the bundle together.

4 Repeat the procedure with the remaining tomatoes, basil, Parmesan, and asparagus.

5 Set aside at room temperature.

6 Divide the arugula, endive, and olives among four salad plates.

7 Top each with 2 tomato bundles.

8 Drizzle with the dressing to taste.

9 Sprinkle with the pine nuts and crispy proscuitto. Serve immediately.

Haricot Vert, Arugula & Radicchio Salad with White Peaches in a Clementine Dressing

Birth & Balance

Serves 4

Sometimes we are given gifts. It is up to us to see them, accept them, and use them. This was the case with the beautiful white peaches that were given by a patient. Pairing them with the complementary textures and tastes of the haricot vert, arugula, and radicchio came by way of "Veggie Queen," Carol, selecting fresh offerings at the market. The readily available clementines added a bright, tangy finish.

Juice & Essence

Haricot vert, the star of this medley, has a neutral nature and sweet flavor with benefits ranging from spleen/pancreas and kidney strengthening, to assisting with the frequent urination and thirst accompanying most cases of diabetes. Haricot vert will help with some cases of reproductive imbalances and imbalances in the area of food elimination. Overall this salad will create harmony in the areas of yin deficiency by helping to build body fluids thereby assisting with conditions stemming from dryness of the lungs such as dry cough and dry skin. The peaches in this dish help to lower blood pressure while helping to limit perspiration and tighten tissues.

Clementine Dressing

Ingredients

- ⅔ cup grapeseed oil or other neutral oil
- 1 orange, zest removed in strips from whole orange, reserve orange for another use (Bring oil and orange zest to a simmer in a small saucepan. Simmer for 5 minutes then set aside to cool. Once cool, strain out the orange peel and discard. Reserve 1 tablespoon of the orange-infused oil for roasting the haricot verts.)
- 3 clementines, grated zest from all and juice from all
- 2 scallions, finely chopped, white and light green parts only
- 1 teaspoon Dijon mustard
- Pinch of salt
- ⅔ cup (less 1 tablespoon) orange-infused oil

Directions

1   Combine the clementine zest and juice, scallions, mustard, and salt in a small bowl.

2   Whisk in the orange-infused oil in a thin stream until dressing is emulsified.

Salad

Ingredients

- 8 ounces of haricot verts
- 1 tablespoon orange infused oil
- ⅛ teaspoon freshly ground Himalayan salt
- ⅛ teaspoon freshly ground black pepper
- 8 ounces arugula
- 1 cup radicchio, sliced in strips
- 2 white peaches, thinly sliced

Directions

1   Preheat oven to 450°F.

2   Place haricot verts on a rimmed baking sheet.

3   Drizzle with orange-infused oil, salt, and pepper.

4   Mix to coat beans well.

5   Spread out in a single layer on baking sheet.

6   Roast for about 10 minutes until lightly browned.

7   Let cool.

8   In a large salad bowl, mix the arugula, radicchio, white peaches, and haricot verts together with enough dressing to coat.

9   Add salt and pepper if necessary. Serve immediately.

Asparagus~Shiitake Sauté

Birth & Balance

Serves 4

Fresh shiitake mushrooms looked good and we thought the crunch of lightly sautéed asparagus with its nuttiness would work well against the chewy, earthy, meatiness of the shiitake. We knew that our *Jalapeño Infused Walnut Oil* would safely connect these two vegetables. However, to add more flavor, we turned to Japanese staples: ponzu and mirin.

Juice & Essence

Asparagus touches on three flavors and three organs. The flavors are sweet, bitter, and cold. The organs are the lung, spleen, and kidneys. This dish is helpful in getting rid of excess heat from the body, frees up and eliminates damp conditions, and clears the lungs. The shiitake portion benefits the stomach and is said to be a natural source of interferon, a protein which appears to induce an immune response against cancer and viral diseases making its uses especially effective in treatment of stomach and cervical cancers. This is a great dish for lowering both fat and cholesterol in the blood.

Ingredients

- 6 ounces shiitake mushrooms, sliced
- 2 tablespoons ponzu
- 2 tablespoons mirin
- ¼ cup *Jalapeño Infused Walnut Oil* (page 366)
- 1 lb. asparagus, thinly sliced on the diagonal
- ½ Serrano pepper, seeded and minced
- 1½ teaspoons finely grated fresh ginger
- 2 garlic cloves, finely grated

Directions

1   Combine shiitake mushrooms, ponzu, and mirin together in a bowl.

2   Set aside.

3   In a heated wok, add the *Jalapeño Infused Walnut Oil.*

4   Add the asparagus, pepper, ginger, garlic, and mushroom mixture.

5   Sauté for 2 minutes, or until cooked through. Serve immediately.

Wasabi~Edamame Whipped Potatoes

Birth & Balance

Serves 4

The goal here was to take a boring and commonly used side and liven it up! We added the smooth texture and protein via edamame. Then we went with wasabi for an extra punch of "in your face" flavor!

Juice & Essence

Because of wasabi made from Japanese horseradish, this is a powerfully quick combo for strengthening the spleen and kidneys, cleansing the blood vessels and heart, improving circulation, relieving arthritis and rheumatism, and helping to restore pancreatic function (especially in diabetic conditions). Additionally, there are significant benefits from the cooling nature of edamame (soybean) in promoting clear vision, lowering fevers, alkalizing and detoxifying the body, and remedying dizziness.

Ingredients

- 2 lbs. Yukon Gold potatoes
- 5 ounces shelled (vacuum packed) edamame
- ½ teaspoon wasabi powder
- 1 teaspoon wasabi paste
- 1 tablespoon butter
- 2 tablespoons extra-virgin olive oil
- ¼ teaspoon ground white pepper
- ¼ teaspoon Himalayan salt

Directions

1 Peel and cut potatoes into 2"-pieces.

2 Put in medium-size saucepan and add water to cover potatoes by about an inch.

3 Bring to a boil over high heat.

4 Lower heat to medium and continue to cook for 15 minutes, or until softened.

5 While potatoes are cooking, place the edamame in a small saucepan with just enough water to cover.

6 Cook just to a simmer over medium heat.

7 Remove from heat and drain.

8 Place the edamame into a food processor with the chopping blade inserted.

9 Process until finely pureed.

10 Once potatoes are softened, drain and put back in the hot pot.

11 Add the pureed edamame along with the wasabi powder, paste, butter, oil, pepper, and salt.

12 Whip the mixture with a hand mixer until very creamy.

13 Add extra olive oil by the teaspoon if not creamy enough.

Daikon Radish & Carrot Slaw

Birth & Balance   Serves 4

Spice, spice, pungent, pungent, spice, spice! We felt called to make an Asian-influenced salad rich in energizing bright flavors and colors to perk up the mood, immune system, and vitality. This was our creation.

Juice & Essence

Carrots are beneficial to the lungs, spleen and liver. They are rich in cancer fighting properties and offer some assistance with night blindness, ear infections, ear aches and deafness. They also contain some cooling properties and help remove mucus while detoxifying the body. A great dish for helping to ward off viral infections such as the common cold and influenza. Daikon radish is helpful in clearing the sinuses, hoarseness, phlegm and sore throats. It will also help relieve indigestion and abdominal swelling. This is a decent remedy in assisting with the removal of gallstones, kidney and bladder stones.

Ingredients

- ½ cup cognac
- 2 tablespoons dried gogi berries
- 3 large carrots
- 1 medium daikon radish
- 4 teaspoons finely grated fresh ginger
- ¼ cup brown rice vinegar
- ¼ cup ume plum vinegar
- 1 tablespoon sesame oil
- 1 teaspoon coarse ground black pepper
- ½ teaspoon celery salt
- 1 tablespoon minced fresh cilantro
- 2 tablespoons slivered almonds, lightly toasted

Directions

1 Place cognac and gogi berries in a small saucepan.

2 Heat just to simmer.

3 Continue to cook for 10 minutes.

4 Drain berries from cognac and set aside to cool. (Save cognac for another use.)

5 Grate the carrots and the daikon radish in a food processor.

6 Place in a large bowl.

7 Add the ginger, vinegars, sesame oil, pepper, celery salt, cilantro, and gogi berries.

8 Stir until combined.

9 Set aside to blend the flavors.

10 Top with almonds when ready to serve.

Broccoli Rabe Succotash

Birth & Balance

Serves 4

Succotash – say that three times fast! It is such a fun word and we just basically wanted to create our take on this dish. This was Carol's Florida summer recipe that we amped up with the bitter broccoli rabe to further cool the body making this a great dinner side or a cold summer lunch.

Juice & Essence

Both onion and corn are helpful heals for the liver and related processes such as eye issues including eye inflammation and nearsightedness. The abundance of pantothenic acid and vitamin A in broccoli will help soften rough skin. The diuretic properties in this dish, due to the corn, assists with unwanted water and swelling. Corn is a very nourishing combination to the heart, kidneys, and spleen thereby improving circulation, sleep, appetite, virility, vitality, digestion, mental acuity, teeth, and gums.

Ingredients

- 1 medium white onion, chopped
- 1 tablespoon olive oil
- 1 teaspoon clarified butter
- 4 fresh corn on the cob, kernels cut from the cob
- ¼ cup celery leaves, coarsely chopped
- 1 small garlic clove, minced
- 1 Cubanelle pepper, diced
- 1 cup grape tomatoes, cut in half
- 2 cups broccoli rabe, chopped
- 2 teaspoons chopped fresh sage
- 1 teaspoon chopped fresh thyme
- 1 teaspoon lime zest
- 2 tablespoons fresh lime juice
- Salt and pepper to taste

Directions

1   Heat a large sauté pan over medium heat.

2   Add the oil and clarified butter to pan.

3   Add the chopped onions and stir to coat with the oil/butter.

4   Spread out the onions in a single layer.

5   Cook, stirring occasionally until brown and caramelized, about 30 minutes.

6   Add the corn, celery, garlic, and pepper to the onions.

7   Sauté for 3 minutes.

8   Add the broccoli rabe and sauté until wilted, about 5 minutes.

9   Add the tomatoes, herbs, lime zest, and juice.

10 Salt and pepper to taste.

11 Stir well to combine and continue to cook for 2 minutes more. Serve immediately.

Brussels Sprout Leaves with Scallion & Pumpkin Seeds

Birth & Balance

Serves 4

Brussels sprouts are so healthy for you. It is a wonder why we aren't all forced to eat more of them as adults. However, we hope that by deconstructing them and making it easier to eat, we will have ignited the Brussels sprouts craze!

Juice & Essence

Brussels sprouts are beneficial to the spleen, stomach, and large intestine channels, cleanse blood, strengthen the stomach, assist with constipation, and expel worms. Also helpful in treating motion sickness, nausea, impotency, and swollen prostate. Pumpkin seeds are a valuable source of zinc and omega-3 fatty acids.

Ingredients

- 1 lb. Brussels sprouts
- 1 clementine, all of the zest and juice
- 2 tablespoons olive oil
- ½ cup chopped scallions
- 1 garlic clove, minced
- ¼ cup pumpkin seeds
- Salt and pepper to taste

Directions

1 Wash and drain the Brussels sprouts.

2 Core the sprouts and remove all the leaves.

3 Place a large sauté pan over medium-high heat.

4 Once hot, add the olive oil, scallions, and garlic.

5 Sauté for 2 minutes and then add the Brussels sprouts.

6 Cook until the leaves start to wilt, about 3 to 5 minutes.

7 Add the clementine zest, juice, salt, and pepper.

8 Stir to combine.

9 Remove from heat.

10 Mix in the pumpkin seeds and place in a serving bowl. Serve immediately.

Summer Desserts

Chapter 4
Summer Desserts

The surprisingly astounding Juice & Essence dessert world is an amazing place! We feature satisfying and creative inventions with nutritionally balanced and in most cases gluten-free ingredients. Enjoy!

Watermelon Gelatin

Birth & Balance

Serves 6

For the longest time, we spoke about working with the medium of gelatin and watermelon rind. We knew that aesthetically the combination would be interesting and that texture-wise it would be a refreshing summer treat to the palate. We were very happy with this creation and look forward to experimenting by pairing this with some of our signature sauces.

Juice & Essence

Watermelon offers healing to the heart, stomach, and bladder. It clears heat and restores the body during summer as well as helping with difficult urination, cold sores, and the feeling of having a blocked throat. Gelatin is considered the most effective remedy for deficiency bleeding, particularly for menstrual and uterine bleeding, due to its yin tonifying and liver detoxing qualities. St. Germaine is made with fresh elderflower blossoms biked down from the Alps and is customarily one of the most refreshing drinks for the summer. Elderflower season is short — June to mid-July at the latest. Traditionally elderflower is used for the healing of colds, flu, fever, and pneumonia as well as inflammation of the brain, lungs, stomach, and bowels. Elderflower is a mild diuretic and will increase urine flow by building permeability of the kidney cells or by increasing blood flow. The flowers help the kidney action by relieving fluid retention. The relaxant quality of the flower is helpful to relieve bronchial spasms.

Ingredients

- 2, 1½"-wide slices of watermelon
- 2 packages unflavored gelatin (Knox)
- 1 cup boiling water
- ½ cup St. Germain liquor
- ½ cup cold water
- 12 small fresh mint leaves
- *Vanilla Bean Almond Sauce* (page 376)

Directions

1 Remove the pink flesh of the watermelon from the rind.

2 Cut the flesh into small ¼"-cubes.

3 Using a vegetable peeler, thinly slice pieces from the light green part of the rind, about 5 slices.

4 Cut the slices into 2"-pieces.

5 Place one piece of the watermelon rind into each section of a nonstick flexible mold (we used a nonstick flexible mold with 12, 2½"-wide openings) and set aside.

6 Whisk the gelatin in the hot water to dissolve.

7 Add the St. Germain liquor and cold water and continue to whisk to combine.

8 Immediately pour the gelatin into the molds over the watermelon rind about ¾ of the way full.

9 Place into the refrigerator for about 10 minutes, or until partially set.

10 *Do not let the gelatin set too much!*

11 Remove the mold from the refrigerator and top with some of the watermelon flesh and a mint leaf. The flesh and the mint will be partially submerged into the gelatin. This will create the layered look we are trying to achieve.

12 Place the mold back into the refrigerator to set up completely, about 30 minutes or up to 1 day.

13 Unmold the gelatin and serve 2 per person with the *Vanilla Bean Almond Sauce.*

Grilled Pineapple with Tropical Sauce

Birth & Balance

Serves 4

Grilling pineapple in the summer sounds deliciously decadent and tropical. Add a sauce filled to the brim with nature's rich sweetness and you get a simple yet powerful presence in our summer dessert selection.

Juice & Essence

Pineapple benefits the spleen and stomach, treats indigestion, vomiting, bloating, low blood pressure, weak hands and feet, fever, and difficult urination. Figs benefit the spleen, stomach, and large intestine. They treat lack of appetite and indigestion, constipation, sore throat, and dry cough. Coconut milk adds to the digestive qualities of this dish while the berries are high in antioxidants, energizing and blood building properties. Cinnamon and allspice aid with warmth and treat bloating, chills, and indigestion. Cinnamon is a natural antibacterial and antiviral. Banana clears heat and moistens the large intestine while assisting with muscle cramping, detox, thirst, and hemorrhoid bleeding.

Prepare Pineapple

Ingredients

- 1 organic pineapple, peeled and cored
- 4 small fresh Mission figs, peeled
- 1 tablespoon strawberry honey
- ½ teaspoon fresh lime juice
- ⅛ teaspoon freshly ground cinnamon

Directions

1. Preheat a grill to medium to medium-high heat.
2. Cut the pineapple into slices that are 1½" thick.
3. Mince the flesh of 4 Mission figs and place into a bowl.
4. Add the honey and lime juice and mix well to combine.
5. Sprinkle the freshly ground cinnamon over both sides of the pineapple slices.
6. Dredge the slices into the honey mixture to coat well. Grill for 3 to 4 minutes on one side to get nicely caramelized grill marks. Turn the slices over and grill for another 2 to 3 minutes while basting with the leftover honey mixture.

Tropical Sauce

Ingredients

- 2 small Honey mangoes, peeled and pitted
- 1 organic pineapple, peeled and cored
- 7 ounces organic coconut milk
- ¼ teaspoon allspice
- ¼ cup banana rum
- 1 large ripe organic banana

Directions

1. Process the mangoes through a juice machine according to manufacturer's instructions. Set the juice aside. Now process the pineapple through the juice machine as well. Add enough of the pineapple juice to the mango juice to make a total of 12 ounces. Reserve the remaining pineapple juice for another use.
2. In a small saucepan, combine the pineapple-mango juice, coconut milk, and allspice. Cook over medium-high heat for 8 minutes to slightly reduce. Add the banana rum and increase the heat to high. Continue to stir together to incorporate and cook for 2 minutes. Reduce the heat to medium and cook for another 5 minutes while constantly stirring.
3. Puree the banana in a food processor until smooth. Add the puree to the sauce and simmer for another 3 minutes while continuing to stir. (The sauce may be served warm or cold.)

Assembly

Ingredients

- *Tropical Sauce*
- Grilled pineapple slices
- ½ cup organic blueberries
- ½ cup sliced organic strawberries
- 4 small fresh Mission figs
- Fresh mint leaves for garnish

Directions

1. Pour some sauce on each of 4 serving plates.
2. Top each with the grilled pineapple slices, blueberries, and strawberries. Garnish with a fig and mint leaves.

Juice & Essence Strawberry Shortcake

Birth & Balance

Serves 4 to 6

This was our take on Strawberry Shortcake based on the desire to modify this classic dessert in such a way as to improve on the health benefits while preserving familiar flavors. In the process, we took chances on the use of almond meal and coconut flour that were new to us at the time and possibly new to you. Never fear! You'll love it!

Juice & Essence

Strawberries benefits the lung, spleen, liver, kidney, and stomach. It is a moistening agent to the lungs and extra nourishing to the liver and kidneys. They also help with complaints of sore, swollen throat, lack of appetite, indigestion, frequent urination, dizziness, and weakness after an enduring disease. Basil is beneficial to the lungs, spleen, stomach, and large intestine. A very helpful herb for balancing qi and blood, helps get rid of chills and dampness, aids with detox, treats headache, bloating, menstrual irregularities, diarrhea, and burping. Sheep's milk benefits the lungs, kidneys, and stomach. The warming and moistening properties assist with digestion while its energizing properties boost kidney essence. Sheep's milk also assists with weakness, wasting thirst, and mouth sores. Coconut milk and sheep's milk in yogurt form will have similar benefits. Coconut flour and almond meal benefit the lung, stomach, spleen, and large intestine while assisting with constipation, cough, and urination difficulty.

Prepare Strawberries

Ingredients

- 1 lb. organic strawberries, washed, stemmed, and coarsely chopped
- 1 tablespoon minced fresh organic basil
- ¼ teaspoon freshly ground white pepper
- 3 tablespoons xylitol sweetener
- 1 tablespoon vodka
- 1 teaspoon Meyer lemon zest

Directions

1 In a medium bowl, combine the strawberries, basil, white pepper, xylitol, vodka, and zest.

2 Mix well and set aside.

Prepare Yogurt

Ingredients

- 6 ounces organic Greek-style coconut milk plain yogurt
- 6 ounces organic sheep's milk plain yogurt
- ¼ teaspoon ground nutmeg
- ¼ teaspoon ground roasted cinnamon
- 2 teaspoons strawberry honey

Directions

1 In a medium bowl, whisk together the coconut yogurt, sheep's yogurt, nutmeg, cinnamon, and honey.

2 Mix well and set aside.

Prepare Pancakes

Ingredients

- ¼ cup organic coconut flour
- 1 cup organic almond meal
- 1 tablespoon xylitol sweetener
- 2 teaspoons baking powder
- ¼ teaspoon sea salt
- ½ vanilla bean, cut down the middle and seeds removed; reserve the bean for another use
- 1 egg
- 1 cup goat's milk
- 2 tablespoons Garden of Life Living Foods Extra-Virgin Coconut Oil plus additional to coat griddle

Directions

1 In a large bowl, whisk together the coconut flour, almond meal, xylitol, baking powder, salt, and vanilla bean seeds. Combine well.

2 In a separate bowl, combine the egg, goat's milk, and coconut oil.

3 Add the liquid to the dry ingredients and stir well to combine.

4 Heat an electric griddle to 400°F.

5 Brush the griddle with some of the coconut oil.

6 Place full tablespoons of batter onto the hot griddle and spread them out to be 3" in diameter.

7 Cook for 3 minutes per side, or until golden brown and cooked through.

Assembly

Directions

Place 2 pancakes on a serving dish and top with some of the yogurt and strawberries to taste.

Berrylicious Tantalizing Tart

Birth & Balance

Serves 8 to 10

We spoke about creating a tart for the longest time. This ended up being a gorgeous tart and well worth the wait. Every aspect of it was invented from an adventurous stance. Even the experimentation of the sauce produced a unique and lovely, awe-inspiring result. For us, this dessert revealed added mysteries to the science of baking and the gifts awaiting the culinary brave of heart.

Juice & Essence

Almond benefits the lung and large intestine, therefore it can assist with certain coughs and constipation due to intestinal dryness. Coconut oil benefits digestion and the heart. Cantaloupe and honeydew benefit the lungs, heart, large intestine, small intestine, and bladder by clearing heat, treating fever, dry cough, and constipation due to dryness. Chia seeds, next to flax, are the highest source of omega-3 fatty acids. They are an energy tonic that lubricate dryness and in so doing help also with constipation. St. Germain liquor is made from elderflower that is traditionally used as a detox to build the immune system by clearing toxins through the lymph glands. Additionally, allspice, thyme, and clementine zest benefit the immune system, circulation, and digestion. Raspberries and blueberries add to the antioxidant, blood building, and energizing qualities of this dish.

Prepare the Crust

Ingredients

- 2 cups almond flour
- ½ teaspoon iodized salt
- ¼ teaspoon ground allspice
- 1 teaspoon minced clementine zest
- ¾ teaspoon minced fresh thyme
- 2 tablespoons Garden of Life Living Foods Extra-Virgin Coconut Oil, warmed to liquefy
- 1 egg

Directions

1 Preheat the oven to 400°F. In a medium bowl, combine the almond flour, salt, allspice, zest, and thyme.

2 Add the coconut oil and egg to the flour mixture. Mix well until the dough comes together to form a ball.

3 Brush some coconut oil onto the bottom of a tart pan with a removable bottom.

4 Cut a piece of parchment paper to fit into the bottom of the tart pan and press it into place.

5 Place the dough into the tart pan. Evenly press the dough onto the bottom and up the sides of the tart pan. *It is important to make sure the dough is of an even thickness on the bottom as well as up the sides so that it will cook evenly.*

6 Put the tart pan onto a baking sheet and place in to the preheated oven.

7 Bake for 15 minutes, or until lightly golden brown and cooked through.

8 Cool completely in the pan placed on top of a wire cooling rack.

Prepare the Filling

Ingredients

- ½ large organic cantaloupe, peeled
- ½ large organic honeydew melon, peeled
- 2 tablespoons xylitol sweetener
- 2 teaspoons chia seeds
- ½ cup St. Germain liquor
- 2 tablespoons arrowroot
- 2 tablespoons water

Directions

1 Process the cantaloupe and honeydew melon in a juice machine according to the manufacturer's directions. You should get 3½ cups of juice.

2 Meanwhile, combine the chia seeds and St. Germain liquor in a small bowl and set aside.

3 Place the juice and xylitol sweetener into a saucepan and cook over medium heat for 15 minutes, or until reduced by ⅓.

4 Add the chia seeds and liquor to the juice and continue to cook for another 5 minutes.

5 Combine the arrowroot and water in a small bowl and mix well.

6 Add to the juice mixture and continue to cook for another 5 to 8 minutes until the mixture thickens.

7 Remove from heat and set aside to cool to room temperature.

Assembly

Ingredients

- Prepared crust
- 1½ cups fresh organic raspberries
- 2 cups fresh organic blueberries
- Prepared filling

Directions

1 Decoratively place the raspberries and blueberries in an alternating spiral pattern on the crust to cover.

2 Carefully pour the filling over the berries just to cover them. You will have some filling left over.

3 Place in the refrigerator for at least an hour to set.

4 Unmold the tart from the pan by first making sure that the sides of the dough are loosened from the tart pan.

5 Hold the tart from the bottom of the pan and the outside ring will fall away onto your arm.

6 Carefully transfer the tart to a serving platter.

7 Slice and enjoy!

Tart Cherry~Chocolate Mini Cupcakes with Coconut~Pecan Frosting

Birth & Balance

Makes approximately 72

The elements contained in these cupcakes were blended and measured without predictable forecast. The ingredient modifications came as a divine revelation. The result is a beautiful testimony to grace. Baking science met intuition and the desire to create an undeniable cupcake was formed. Mission accomplished!!!

Juice & Essence

Cherry benefits the spleen, stomach, lung, heart, and kidneys. Cherry is an energizer which also increases circulation and can help with dry sore throat and build blood. Coconut benefits the spleen, stomach, and large intestines, assists with difficult urination, severe diarrhea, digestion, dehydration, tapeworms, and edema. Cocoa aids in decreased blood pressure, improved blood vessel health, and improvement in cholesterol levels.

Ingredients

- 2¼ cup Bob's Red Mill All-Purpose Gluten-Free Baking Flour
- ½ cup unsweetened dark cocoa powder
- 1¾ teaspoon baking soda
- ¼ teaspoon iodized salt
- ¾ cup Garden of Life Living Foods Extra-Virgin Coconut Oil, solidified
- 1 cup organic raw coconut crystals
- 1 cup Demerara sugar
- ⅓ cup minced canned tart cherries (in water, drained)
- 1 teaspoon vanilla extract
- 3 eggs
- 1 cup organic unsweetened tart cherry juice
- ⅓ cup cold water

Special Equipment
- Mini cupcake baking pans
- Approximately 72 mini cupcake liners

Directions

1 Preheat the oven to 350°F.

2 Place the mini cupcake liners into the pans and set aside.

3 In a medium bowl, combine the flour, cocoa powder, baking soda, and salt. Set aside.

4 In the mixing bowl of a stand mixer, place the solidified coconut oil, raw coconut crystals sweetener, and Demerara sugar. Mix on medium speed for about 30 seconds to combine.

5 Add the tart cherries and vanilla extract. Beat for another 30 seconds to combine.

6 Add the eggs, one at a time, beating well after each.

7 Combine the tart cherry juice and cold water.

8 Add the dry mixture and juice mixture alternately to the beaten mixture. Beat on low speed after each addition just until combined.

9 Pour the batter into the cupcake liners until just over half full.

10 Bake for 12 minutes, or until the tops spring back when lightly touched.

11 Cool in the pans for 10 minutes.

12 Remove and let cool completely on a wire cooling rack.

Prepare the Frosting

Ingredients

- 1 egg
- ⅔ cup evaporated goat's milk
- ⅔ cup organic raw coconut crystals
- ¼ cup ghee (clarified butter)
- 1½ cup organic unsweetened coconut flakes
- ½ cup finely chopped roasted pecans

Directions

1 In a medium saucepan, combine the egg, evaporated goat's milk, coconut crystals, and ghee.

2 Stir to mix well. Cook while constantly stirring over medium heat for 10 to 12 minutes, or until thickened and bubbling.

3 Remove from the heat and stir in the coconut and pecans.

4 Set aside to cool to room temperature.

5 Spread the cooled frosting over the top of the cupcakes.

Zucchini~Kiwi Soufflé

Birth & Balance

Serves 4 to 6

Who puts zucchini in a dessert? We took a summer squash, juiced it, and with the comparable color of the kiwi, ventured into new territory that nailed it! The soufflé is delicate and demanding, so we did not recreate the wheel there. This is a daring and amazing offering for the most scrutinizing sweet tooth.

Juice & Essence

Kiwi is beneficial to the spleen and stomach, cool in nature, and helps clear heat. As it benefits the spleen, it can help stop diarrhea, treat fever and dry painful throat, along with jaundice due to deep heat. Kiwi also helps with painful urination. Zucchini is also cooling and great for summertime heat, offers mild diuretic properties, benefits the spleen/pancreas and stomach, and reduces inflammation and burns. Ghee strengthens kidney essence, balances the hormones, and promotes healing of injuries and gastrointestinal inflammations such as ulcers and colitis. Egg is a blood and yin tonic. Eggs help in certain cases of diarrhea and can help to secure the fetus when there is a tendency to miscarry.

Ingredients

- 6 organic eggs separated
- ½ small organic zucchini
- 1 organic kiwi
- 1 tablespoon clementine zest
- ¾ cup organic Demerara sugar
- Pinch of salt
- 1 teaspoon ghee (clarified butter)
- Approximately 1 tablespoon xylitol sweetener

Directions

1 Place oven rack in bottom third of the oven and preheat to 350°F.

2 Prepare a 2-quart soufflé pan by spreading the ghee all over the bottom and up the sides of the pan.

3 Sprinkle the xylitol sweetener on the bottom and sides of the dish. Invert to remove the excess.

4 Using a juice machine, process the zucchini and kiwi according to manufacturer's instructions.

5 You will need ⅛ of a cup of each juice to total ¼ cup. Set aside.

6 Whisk the egg yolks and ½ cup of Demerara sugar in a mixer at medium-high speed until they are lighter in color and thickened. This should take about 5 minutes. (The mixture will fall like a ribbon from the end of the whisk when you lift it out of the batter.)

7 Add the zucchini and kiwi juice as well as the zest.

8 Beat for another minute to incorporate.

9 In a new mixing bowl, whisk the egg whites and salt on medium-high speed until soft peaks form.

10 Gradually add the remaining ¼ cup of Demerara sugar.

11 Continue beating until the whites are holding stiff but not dry peaks. The whole process should take about 4 to 5 minutes.

12 Fold ⅓ of the whites into the yolk batter to lighten it.

13 Gently fold in the remaining whites, stirring lightly to just incorporate.

14 Pour the soufflé mixture into the prepared pan.

15 Bake for about 35 minutes, or until the center is just set.

16 Remove from the oven and serve immediately.

*Can be served with our **Vanilla Bean~Almond Sauce** (page 376) or our **Tropical Sauce** (page 374).*

Summer Sauces & Spices

Chapter 5
Summer Sauces & Spices

Juice & Essence Sauces & Spices are meant to be the perfect complement to our Juice & Essence recipes. This chapter will guide you through this part of the creative cooking process.

Raspberry~Chipotle Sauce

Birth & Balance

Makes about 1½ cups

We created this spicy, sweet ensemble to lather on our herbed veal chop dish found in our summer recipes.

Juice & Essence

Raspberry has both a sweet and sour flavor with energetic tendencies toward the liver and kidneys, builds blood, and helps to detoxify it. Also regulates menses and urination. The addition of chipotle will assist with poor circulation and lung issues as well as indigestion.

Ingredients

- 1 cup orange liquor, such as Cointreau
- 1 cup raspberry liquor, such as Chambord
- ½ cup sugar
- 2 pints fresh raspberries
- 1 whole chipotle chili in adobo sauce
- 1 blood orange, zest and juice
- ¼ cup raspberry balsamic vinegar

Directions

1   In a medium saucepan, bring the liquors, sugar, and raspberries to a boil.

2   Reduce heat to medium and simmer for 30 minutes.

3   Remove from heat.

4   Strain out the seeds using a fine mesh sieve.

5   Return to the same sauce pan.

6   Cut the whole chipotle chili in half and add to the raspberry sauce.

7   Also add the juice and zest from the blood orange and the raspberry balsamic vinegar.

8   Simmer for 30 minutes.

9   Remove the pepper halves and discard.

The sauce can be served with meat, pork, chicken or fish.

Jalapeño-Infused Walnut Oil

Birth & Balance

Makes about ⅔ cups

This was created to go with our *Scallops & Stuffed Leeks* (page 286) recipe. We've given it its own purpose and life due to its impressive, simple, and adaptable flavor. This can easily be part of a vinaigrette, marinade, or sauce.

Juice & Essence

This is a spicy combination with benefits for the lungs and kidneys. Walnuts energize the kidneys and help to restore kidney essence, which is the root of one's immune system and vitality. The lung warming nature of walnuts help to stabilize breathing and stabilize panting. Additional benefits include moistening qualities that help with intestinal flow, kidney strengthening properties that help reduce low back pain, knee weakness, and frequent urination. Spicy peppers in general help to alleviate phlegm throughout the body and especially the lungs, invigorate blood flow, and act as an antibacterial, antiviral immune boosting element.

Ingredients

- 1 large jalapeño pepper, cut in half, seeds and core removed from only one half
- ⅔ cup walnut oil

Directions

1 Add to a small saucepan and simmer for 5 minutes.

2 Set aside to cool.

3 Once cool, pour through a fine mesh strainer to remove the jalapeño and seeds.

Mango~Kiwi~Parsnip Spread

Birth & Balance

Makes about 4 cups

Sometimes we just like to see how creative we can get with what is available. We snuck in parsnip for its pungent nature and extensive health benefits. Mango, being one of the best fruits ever nutritionally, added the sweetness to the spectrum of taste. The kiwi came in with a light and bright tang.

Juice & Essence

This well-rounded tonic of a spread due to its star — mango — boasts benefits for the lungs, spleen, and stomach while specifically clearing obstructions from the liver and gallbladder. It also helps with restoration of appetite and the body in situations of colds, coughs, and shortness of breath. Parsnip tastefully treats headaches, dizziness, rheumatism, and arthritis. Mango and kiwi are rich in healing antioxidant vitamin A and beneficial to the digestion, spleen, builds blood, and assists with jaundice.

Ingredients

- ¾ cup grated parsnips
- 2 cups peeled and chopped mango
- 4 kiwi fruits, peeled and chopped
- 3 cups water
- 2 cups sugar
- ¾ cup banana rum
- ½ vanilla bean, cut in half lengthwise

Directions

1 Combine the parsnips, mango, kiwi, water, sugar, banana rum, and vanilla bean in a large saucepan over high heat.

2 Stir until the sugar has melted, about 5 minutes.

3 Once it has come to a boil, continue to cook over high heat for about 1 hour. (Adjust the heat if it begins to scorch.) The mixture should be thick and syrupy.

4 Remove the vanilla bean and lower heat to a simmer for 10 minutes.

5 Remove from heat and set aside to cool.

6 Serve with homemade crackers, breads, and cheeses, or even as part of a dessert.

Red Plum Tomato Sauce

Birth & Balance

Makes about 4 cups

The inspiration for this sauce was our *Cedar Plank Grilled Rabbit with Red Plum Tomato Sauce & Tomatillo Drizzle Pizza* (page 318). With rabbit, we knew we would need to temper its sweetness. From the sharpness of the sundried tomatoes, the tart-sweet flavors of the red plums, the burn of the jalapeño, and the smoky flavors of the ancho and chipotle chilis.... We were right!

Juice & Essence

The red plums and the plum tomatoes are beneficial to the stomach while calming the liver. The tomatoes function on the stomach rests in the area of reparation of indigestion. They both also help to get rid of heat and parchness (dry mouth). The red plums assist with constipation, dry throat, and overall production of body fluids. They are cooling in nature and help clear liver heat, which can aid in the treatment of fever and certain headaches. Both the tomatoes and the chili peppers invigorate blood circulation and boost the immune system. Chili peppers help unlock nutrients by stoking the stomach fire. Fresh oregano acts as an antibiotic. Its oils are an exceptional antiseptic and have potent antiviral, antifungal properties.

Ingredients

- 2 large red plums, peeled and coarsely chopped
- 1, 28-ounce can San Marzano plum tomatoes
- Salt and pepper
- ¼ cup Patron tequila
- 1 tablespoon honey
- ¼ cup chopped, rehydrated sundried tomatoes
- 1 teaspoon ground New Mexican chili pepper
- 1 teaspoon dried Mexican oregano
- ½ teaspoon ground, dried jalapeño pepper
- ½ teaspoon ground ancho chili pepper
- ½ teaspoon ground chipotle chili pepper
- 1 tablespoon chopped fresh parsley

Directions

1   Place the plums, the tomatoes,and the salt and pepper to taste in a medium saucepan.

2   Bring to a boil over medium-high heat.

3   Add the tequila, honey, sundried tomatoes, New Mexican chili pepper, Mexican oregano, jalapeño, ancho and chipotle chili peppers, and parsley.

4   Simmer for 30 minutes.

Tomatillo Drizzle

Birth & Balance

Makes about 2½ cups

Tart tomatillo felt right for our *Cedar Plank Grilled Rabbit with Red Plum Tomato Sauce & Tomatillo Drizzle Pizza* (page 318) and then the following night over enchiladas; however, the uses for this drizzle are infinite and it should be bottled due to its diverse and yummy nature!

Juice & Essence

Tomatillos, as part of the tomato family, offer high antioxidant, stomach tonifying, and liver settling qualities. The jalapeño and coriander invigorate blood flow and act as an antibacterial, antiviral agent. Cilantro balances the heat of this drizzle through its cooling qualities.

Ingredients

- 1 lb. tomatillos, husked and cut in half
- 1 fresh jalapeño, seeds and veins removed, sliced
- ¼ teaspoon ground, dried jalapeño
- ½ teaspoon coriander seed, ground in a mortar and pestle
- 1 cup water
- 1 cup dry white wine
- ½ cup chopped cilantro
- 3 tablespoons olive oil
- ½ teaspoon sea salt

Directions

1 Place the tomatillos, fresh and dried jalapeño, coriander, and water in a medium saucepan.

2 Bring to a boil over high heat.

3 Reduce heat to medium and add the white wine.

4 Continue to boil for 15 minutes.

5 Remove from heat and drain, discarding the liquid.

6 Let the tomatillo mixture cool for 10 minutes.

7 Place the tomatillo mixture in a blender with the cilantro, oil, and salt.

8 Blend on high until it is pureed.

Tropical Sauce

Birth & Balance   Makes about 1 cup

Created with grilled pineapple in mind, we discovered this yummy sauce could be paired easily with chicken, fish, and of course other desserts. Select ripe produce, a splash of banana rum, and you'll find yourself instantly transported to a tropical paradise!

Juice & Essence

Mangoes benefit the lung, spleen, and stomach. The strengthening action on the spleen and stomach translates to treating vomiting and indigestion while its action on the lungs treats cough. Pineapple is beneficial to the spleen and stomach thereby treating vomiting, abdominal bloating, low blood pressure, weak hands and feet, fever, and difficult urination. Coconut milk adds to the digestive benefits by energizing the spleen, stomach, and large intestine. Coconut milk assists with blood sugar, keeps skin and blood vessels flexible and elastic, aids in building strong bones, helps prevent anemia, relaxes muscles and nerves, decreases risk of joint inflammation, assists in lowering high blood pressure, helps maintain a healthy immune system, and promotes health of prostate gland. Bananas benefit the lungs and large intestines while clearing heat and helping to remove toxins, thirst, and hemorrhoid bleeding.

Ingredients

- 2 small honey mangoes, peeled and pitted
- 1 organic pineapple, peeled and cored
- 7 ounces organic coconut milk
- ¼ teaspoon allspice
- ¼ cup banana rum
- 1 large ripe organic banana

Directions

1   Process the mangoes through a juice machine according to manufacturer's instructions.

2   Set the juice aside.

3   Process the pineapple through the juice machine as well.

4   Add enough of the pineapple juice to the mango juice to make a total of 12 ounces. (Reserve the remaining pineapple juice for another use.)

5   In a small saucepan, combine the pineapple-mango juice, coconut milk, and allspice.

6   Cook over medium-high heat for 8 minutes to slightly reduce.

7   Add the banana rum and increase the heat to high.

8   Continue to stir together to incorporate and cook for 2 minutes.

9   Reduce the heat to medium and cook for another 5 minutes while constantly stirring.

10   Puree the banana in a food processor until smooth.

11   Add the puree to the sauce and simmer for another 3 minutes while continuing to stir.

12   The sauce may be served warm or cold.

Vanilla Bean~Almond Sauce

Birth & Balance

Makes 1 cup

We originally created this to go with the watermelon gelatin as a light, playful sauce. Later we found that this attractively bland but subtly sweet sauce would work wonderfully with many desserts.

Juice & Essence

Almond benefits the lung by specifically moistening the lungs and treats dry cough. Almonds moisten the large intestine thereby treating constipation due to intestinal dryness. Tapioca is gluten-free and a good source of a low cholesterol healthy starch. Tapioca is a good source of iron, B vitamins, including folic acid. The antioxidants in vanilla extract have anti-carcinogenic properties which by definition can prevent or delay the development of cancer.

Ingredients

- ½ vanilla bean
- 1 cup organic unsweetened almond milk
- ¾ teaspoon organic granulated tapioca
- 1½ teaspoon xylitol sweetener
- ¼ teaspoon almond extract

Directions

1   Cut the vanilla bean in half lengthwise and scrape out the seeds.

2   Place the seeds and the bean into a small saucepan along with the almond milk, tapioca, and xylitol.

3   Bring to a simmer over medium heat.

4   Turn the heat down a little to maintain a gentle simmer for 10 minutes.

5   Add the almond extract and remove from the heat.

6   Remove the vanilla bean

7   Place in a bowl to cool to room temperature. The sauce will thicken slightly as it cools.

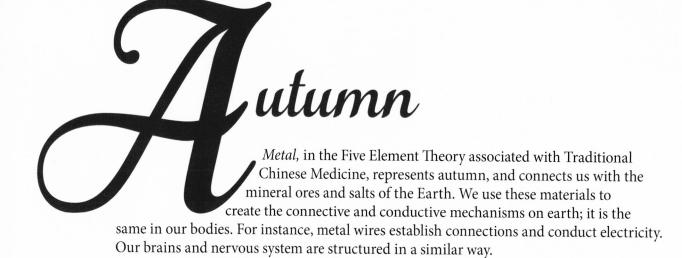

Autumn

Metal, in the Five Element Theory associated with Traditional Chinese Medicine, represents autumn, and connects us with the mineral ores and salts of the Earth. We use these materials to create the connective and conductive mechanisms on earth; it is the same in our bodies. For instance, metal wires establish connections and conduct electricity. Our brains and nervous system are structured in a similar way.

The sense organ for the Metal element is the nose, which is the opening to the lungs. The flavor corresponding to metal is pungent or spice — similar to flavors found in certain aromatic cheeses such as Roquefort, Brie, and Camembert, as well as peppers, mustard, and other spices. This flavor "opens up" the senses, clears the sinuses, and stimulates the lungs, but too much can be harmful to the lungs. Therefore craving spicy foods or a distaste for them may suggest an imbalance in the Metal element.

Complementing the lungs in the Metal element is the large intestine. Breathing involves both the intake of new air (energy) during aspiration, and the elimination of the old (that which is no longer needed) in expiration. The large intestine, like the lungs, has a down bearing energy taking things down and out, or in and out of the body. This heavy metal energy can be disrupted when we have caused imbalance to these organs via food, emotion, environment, or lifestyle. Autumn, or harvest time, is a time of work and assessing a reaping of what we have sown. Autumn is a great time to start paying attention to our health as manifested in our most obvious indicators: skin and hair, then make appropriate changes. The autumn diet includes more meats and dairy products than the summer diet, and includes grains, some nuts, beans, and seeds.

The general principles of free flowing intestines still apply, as a diet rich in too much bread and cheese, both clogging to the intestines, will also slow you down causing damage to your immune system and perpetuate unhealthy cravings. Meats are concentrated energy. They are not particularly easy to transform and transport. Meats create more density and body heat than fruits and vegetables. Fruits and vegetables are body cleansers in general, however, bananas have a congesting effect while avocados and mushrooms are nourishing and tonifying. The lungs and large intestine are two areas of the body which must stay clean for their best function. Their condition is reflected in the skin, body, and hair. An example of an important lung aid facilitating cleansing and healing is garlic. It is good to begin autumn with a week's cleansing diet of fruit and vegetable juice, or a grape fast (red preferred). As the weather grows colder, it is beneficial to turn to more vegetables as well as grains. Eating citrus fruits, grapes, apples, pears, tomatoes, walnuts, sunflower seeds, brown rice, corn, and wheat, along with squashes and pumpkins, which become plentiful by mid-autumn, nourish the Metal element, which is associated with autumn and the respective organs of lung and large intestine.

Autumn Superfoods

APPLES have a compound in the skin called quercetin, a powerful antioxidant that may fight a host of diseases, so don't discard the skin. Buy organic to avoid pesticide residue, but wash them well. Calcium, vitamin C, and folate make apples even sweeter.

PUMPKIN, when measured to a half a cup, has a full serving of vitamin A in the form of beta-carotene plus a healthy dose of potassium — more than 10% of the recommended daily amount.

BRUSSELS SPROUTS contain more vitamin C than an orange, plus vitamin K, calcium, and folate.

KALE is high in beta-carotene, an antioxidant which is believed to boost the immune system and even help ward off certain types of cancers. One cup of chopped raw kale offers more vitamin K than any other green.

CHESTNUTS are a snack you can feel good about thanks to their half-day supply of vitamin B6, which plays a role in boosting the immune system, keeping skin youthful, and possibly even fighting lung cancer. Chestnuts are also high in fiber, which helps fill you up so you eat less.

POMEGRANATES and their juice have been credited with everything from lowering cholesterol to managing Type 2 diabetes and helping to fight prostate cancer. The tasty red seeds called arils are a good source of fiber, vitamins B and C, potassium, and polphenols (antioxidants). They are loaded with antioxidants and compounds called tannins that may help keep the heart healthy.

TURNIP GREENS are the most nutritious part of this autumn root vegetable. One cup provides 441 mg or about half of the daily recommended amount of vitamin A in the form of beta-carotene which helps promote good vision, as well as fight illness and build strong bones. Turnip greens also pack vitamin C, folate, vitamin K, and calcium.

Autumn Appetizers

Chapter 1
Autumn Appetizers

Fine as a stand-alone meal or as a precursor to Juice & Essence entrées. Our appetizers add an exploratory jolt to the most scrutinizing culinary adventurer!

Shrimp Salad Stuffed Peppadews

Birth & Balance

Serves 4

This fun and fairly easy to make finger food draws your tastebuds to the present moment of any occasion. It's memorable in flavor and appearance. This made it into our first media-covered dinner!

Juice & Essence

The shrimp is warming and beneficial to the liver and kidneys. Enhances virility, energy, and moving joint pain, along with some aspects of immunity associated with wind conditions such as constant dry cough or cough with clear mucus. The peppers help with bloating, circulation, and improve appetite.

COMPLEMENT – Torrontes (Argentina or Spain). The acid, pepper, and sweetness of Peppadews and shrimp require the elegant, dry, yet peachy aspects of Torrontes that will "hold hands with this dish and skip down the road!"

Ingredients

- 1, 14-ounce jar Peppadew peppers, mild
- ¾ lb. cooked extra-large shrimp, diced
- 2 tablespoons minced mini bell peppers (about 1 red and 1 yellow)
- 1 teaspoon minced shallot
- 2 tablespoons minced celery hearts (include some leaves)
- 1½ tablespoons minced radishes
- 1 tablespoon freshly grated horseradish
- ¼ teaspoon lemon zest
- 1 tablespoon fresh lemon juice
- ½ teaspoon freshly ground Grains of Paradise
- ¼ teaspoon sea salt
- ½ teaspoon chopped fresh thyme
- 2 tablespoons extra-virgin olive oil

Directions

1 Remove the Peppadew peppers from the jar.

2 Place the peppers, cut side down, on paper towels to drain well.

3 Combine the shrimp, bell peppers, shallot, celery, radishes, horseradish, lemon zest, lemon juice, Grains of Paradise, salt, thyme, and oil into a bowl and mix well.

Note: The shrimp salad can be made up to 4 hours ahead. When ready to serve, fill each pepper with the shrimp salad.

Spice Baked Acorn Squash

Birth & Balance

Serves 4

There is something so poetic and fantastic about using the same family of vegetable in this creative way. The acorn squash as a bowl for the spaghetti squash presented visually and tastefully well. Choosing the Thai-influenced coconut milk curry stemmed from the desire to compile spices and a texture that could offer a rich soup without being too soupy. We are happy with this as is and, although some would read optional where the roasted, salted pumpkin seeds and raisins are concerned, we urge you to give it a whirl.... Delicious!

Juice & Essence

Spices play a key role in the fall as they warm the body, boost immunity, tonify digestion, and enhance circulation. Squash has a warming nature and is generally sweet in taste. Eating squash helps reduce inflammation, nervous energy, reduces pain, and along with its seeds helps rid the body of parasites. Winter squash varieties have more vitamin A. The mushrooms are cancer fighters, help decrease fat levels in blood, offer antibiotic properties, increase white blood cell count, and help balance toxic accumulations associated with a heavy meat eating diet. Mushrooms are generally beneficial to the stomach and lungs.

Complement or Contrast

COMPLEMENT – *Warm spices and the sweetness of the raisins call for a Northern Italian. A Valpolicella or an Amarone would be great with this dish. I know it's a little big for an appetizer, but I am going with it.*

Prepare the Curry Sauce

Ingredients

- ¼ cup extra-dry vermouth
- ¾ cup water
- 1 tablespoon dried chanterelle mushrooms
- 1 tablespoon Garden of Life Living Foods Extra-Virgin Coconut Oil
- ½ cup minced yellow onion
- 1 large garlic clove, pressed
- 2 tablespoons *J&E Curry* (page 134)
- 3.5 ounces oyster mushrooms, stemmed and coarsely chopped
- ½ cup organic coconut milk
- 1 teaspoon sea salt
- ½ cup ground white pepper

Directions

1. In a small saucepan, bring the vermouth and water to a boil.
2. Add the dried chanterelle mushrooms and cook for 3 minutes and remove from the heat.
3. Strain mushrooms and reserve ¾ cup of liquid.
4. Chop mushrooms into ¼"-pieces and set aside.
5. Heat a saucepan over medium heat.
6. Add the coconut oil, onion, and garlic.
7. Turn the heat to low and sauté for 2 minutes.
8. Add the *J&E Curry* and sauté for another minute.
9. Stir in the oyster mushrooms and turn the heat up to medium-low.
10. Sauté the mixture for 3 minutes and add the chanterelle mushrooms.
11. Continue to sauté for another minute.
12. Add the reserved ¾ cup mushroom liquid and cook for 5 minutes.
13. Slowly stir in the coconut milk to incorporate.
14. Season with the salt and white pepper and reduce the heat to a simmer.
15. Remove from the heat and set aside

Prepare the Spaghetti Squash

Ingredients

- 1, 1½-lb. spaghetti squash
- 2 large fresh thyme sprigs
- 2 tablespoons water

Directions

1. Preheat oven to 375 °F.
2. Line a rimmed baking sheet with foil.
3. Cut squash in half and clean out the seeds.
4. Place squash halves on baking sheet, cut side down.
5. Put a thyme sprig and a tablespoon of water under each half.
6. Bake the squash in the oven for 40 to 45 minutes, or until the squash is cooked through.
7. Set aside until cool enough to handle.
8. Scrape out the strands of squash into a bowl.
9. Measure out 1½ cups to be used in the recipe; set aside.
10. Reserve the remaining squash for another use.

Prepare the Acorn Squash

Ingredients

- 2 acorn squash (about 1 lb. each)
- 2 tablespoons extra-virgin olive oil
- ¼ teaspoon Salt-free Five Spice Powder

Directions

1. Preheat oven to 375°F.
2. Line a rimmed baking sheet with foil.
3. Cut squash in half and clean out the seeds
4. Combine oil and Five Spice Powder in a small bowl.
5. Brush onto the cut side of the squash.
6. Place the squash onto the foil-lined baking sheet cut side up and bake for 40 minutes, or until they are cooked through.

Assembly

Ingredients

- Curry sauce
- 1½ cups cooked spaghetti squash
- Cooked acorn squash halves
- ¼ cup raisins
- ¼ cup roasted pumpkin seeds

Directions

1. Gently rewarm the curry sauce over low heat.
2. Add the cooked spaghetti squash and stir to combine.
3. Place the acorn halves, cut sides up, on serving plates.
4. Divide the spaghetti squash-curry sauce evenly into the center of each acorn squash.
5. Sprinkle the tops with the raisins and roasted pumpkin seeds. Serve immediately.

Buffalo Pierogies

Birth & Balance

Serves 6

Why not pierogies? Such a fun food! Carol speaks of pierogies with an endearing smile. She calls them a great vehicle for sour cream. As a salute to Carol's childhood comfort food, we went with buffalo meat and gluten-free flour for a healthy, balanced, tasty twist.

Juice & Essence

Buffalo is raised without antibiotics or steroids. It has all of the great powers of beef without the toxins. Buffalo is a blood builder, joint and tendon strengthener, and low back and knee pain reliever. Eating buffalo benefits the spleen, liver, kidneys, stomach, and large intestine channels. Flour/gluten-free will have most of the benefits of wheat without the digestive hardships. Wheat is energetically beneficial to the heart, spleen, and kidneys. While nourishing the heat and boosting kidney energy, wheat will thereby help reduce stress levels, complaints of diarrhea and dysentery. Wheat in its cool nature helps get rid of excess heat and thirst. Potato is also cold in nature and while benefiting the spleen and stomach will help to reduce excess heat and offer detox assistance. Potatoes help treat acute hepatitis, breast abscesses, laryngitis, tonsillitis, mumps, and stomach and duodenal ulcers. The ground cloves, mustard, and black and white peppers will balance the cooling nature of the flour and potatoes while strengthening the digestion via spleen and kidney yang. The fresh thyme, rosemary, and marjoram will reduce bloating and bad breath due to food accumulation. Thyme especially will treat common cold, bodily aches, sore throat, headache, cough, vomiting, and indigestion.

Complement or Contrast

COMPLEMENT – *To embrace the herbs and spices in this dish, go with a Pinot Noir, Syrah, or Zinfandel*

Prepare the Dough

Ingredients

- 4 cups Bob's Red Mill Gluten-Free All-Purpose Baking Flour
- 1 teaspoon onion powder
- 1 teaspoon sea salt
- ½ teaspoon freshly ground white pepper
- 1 egg, at room temperature
- 1 cup lukewarm water

Directions

1 Sift together the flour, onion powder, salt, and pepper into a large mixing bowl.

2 Create a well in the center and add the egg and water.

3 Stir together the egg and water with a fork while incorporating the flour a little at a time until a loose dough is formed.

4 Transfer the dough to a lightly floured work surface and knead until it comes together and is not sticky, adding extra flour as needed.

5 Pat the dough into a flat circle, cover, and let rest for 30 minutes to 1 hour.

Prepare the Filling

Ingredients

- 1 medium russet potato, peeled and chopped
- 1 teaspoon sea salt
- 12 ounces organic, grass-fed ground buffalo
- 1½ teaspoons minced fresh marjoram
- ¼ teaspoon minced fresh thyme
- ¼ teaspoon minced fresh rosemary
- ½ teaspoon sea salt
- ¼ teaspoon ground black pepper
- ⅛ teaspoon ground mustard
- ⅛ teaspoon paprika
- ⅛ teaspoon celery salt
- Pinch of ground cloves
- 1 tablespoon minced oil-packed sundried tomatoes
- 1 leek, cleaned and minced
- 1 tablespoon olive oil
- 1 garlic clove, pressed

Directions

1 Place the potatoes into a small saucepan and fill with water to cover the potatoes by 1" and add the salt.

2 Bring to a boil and cook for 15 minutes, or until cooked through.

3 Drain well and mash the potatoes with a fork to create small pieces and set aside.

4 Gently combine the buffalo, marjoram, thyme, rosemary, salt, pepper, ground mustard, paprika, celery salt, cloves, and sundried tomatoes in a large bowl.

5 Sauté the leeks and garlic in the olive oil on medium-high heat for about 4 minutes to soften.

6 Add the buffalo mixture and stir to break the meat into small pieces until it is cooked through.

7 Mix in the potatoes and set aside to cool to room temperature.

Assembly

Ingredients

- Flour
- Dough
- 3" round cookie cutter
- Filling
- Grapeseed oil
- Sour cream

Directions

1 Lightly flour a work surface.

2 Divide the dough into 6 equal pieces and keep covered.

3 Roll out one piece at a time to about ⅛"-thickness and cut as many pieces as you can from the dough using the cookie cutter.

4 Place about 1 tablespoon of filling onto the center of the dough round, fold over the edge to cover the filling, and pinch the seams together to completely seal.

5 Put the pierogies onto a baking sheet lined with a towel sprinkled lightly with flour and cover with another towel so they do not dry out.

6 Continue this process for the remaining pierogies.

7 Bring a large pot of water to a boil and add a few of the pierogies at a time to the boiling water.

8 When they float to the top, remove them and drain well on a towel.

9 Meanwhile heat enough grapeseed oil to measure 1" in depth in a cast iron skillet or frying pan and fry the pierogies on both sides until they are golden brown.

10 Drain well on a towel. Serve with the sour cream while they are still hot.

Sweet & Sour Stuffed Sliders

Birth & Balance

Serves 6

These are no ordinary sliders. We set out to create one of the most awesome sliders ever and we succeeded! Our homemade kraut and catsup are super-duper must tries. When you try the catsup, a sort of trompe l'oeil of the mouth takes place. Everything about it says tomato is involved, however, there is no tomato!

Juice & Essence

The elements of the Cranberry Catsup are packed with vitamin C and antioxidants. Cranberries benefit the kidneys, urinary bladder, and urinary tract as an anti-adhesive to certain bacteria. Figs fortify the spleen and benefit the stomach and large intestines. Use figs for constipation, sore throat, dry cough, and sluggish appetite. Orange benefits the lungs and stomach; helps lessen excessive drinking of alcohol and stops thirst and certain types of vomiting. Cabbage cleanses the blood, treats constipation, strengthens the stomach, and lessens the thirst for alcohol. Cabbage and orange also treat tightness in the chest due to stagnant energy. Pork builds blood and energizes the kidneys. It can be used for dry cough, constipation, and overall dryness. Pork can benefit the spleen and stomach.

COMPLEMENT – This amazing dish opens the doors to so many wine choices. The slightly sour cabbage and slightly bitter cranberry catsup are amazing flavor enhancers that bring this dish to a different level. Dry, medium-body reds with low tannins would go perfectly. My favorite would be a Vecqueyras (Rhone) but a nice Cabernet would do, so would a Super Tuscan, an aged Chianti, and a Barbaresco or Barolo.

Prepare the Cranberry Catsup

Ingredients

- 1 navel orange
- 1 tablespoon orange zest (from the navel orange)
- 2 Bosc pears, peeled, cored, and diced
- 15 dried Black Mission figs, stemmed and chopped
- 1, 12-ounce bag fresh cranberries
- ½ cup light brown sugar
- ½ cup Lemoncello liquor

Directions

1 Zest the orange and peel and coarsely chop the flesh.

2 Combine the orange, zest, pears, figs, cranberries, brown sugar, and Lemoncello into a large saucepan.

3 Cover and cook over medium-low heat for 20 minutes. Reduce heat to simmer and continue to cook for another 40 minutes, or until the fruit is very soft.

4 Use an immersion blender to puree the fruit until it is completely smooth and let cool to room temperature.

Prepare the Cabbage

Ingredients

- ¼ teaspoon whole black peppercorns
- ¼ teaspoon whole pink peppercorns
- ¼ teaspoon whole white peppercorns
- ¼ teaspoon fennel seeds
- ¼ teaspoon caraway seeds
- ¼ teaspoon coriander seeds
- ½ teaspoon sea salt
- 1 teaspoon mustard seed
- 2 tablespoons grapeseed oil
- ½ of a small head of green cabbage, thinly sliced
- 2 tablespoons apple cider vinegar

Directions

1 Put all of the peppercorns, fennel seeds, caraway seeds, coriander seeds, sea salt, and mustard seeds into a spice grinder and process until finely ground.

2 Heat the oil in a large sauté pan over medium heat and add the ground spices.

3 Sauté for 1 minute until fragrant, then add the cabbage and vinegar and sauté for 5 minutes.

4 Reduce the heat to low and continue to cook for 5 minutes more, then cool to room temperature.

Prepare the Bread

Ingredients

- 3 tablespoons extra-virgin olive oil
- ½ teaspoon dried Italian herbs
- ¼ teaspoon sea salt
- ¼ teaspoon freshly ground black pepper
- Cocktail Rye Bread slices, 2 slices per slider

Directions

1 Combine in a small bowl the oil, Italian herbs, salt, and pepper.

2 Brush one side of the bread with the oil mixture and broil until lightly browned.

Prepare the Pork

Ingredients

- 1 teaspoon sea salt
- ½ teaspoon garlic powder
- ½ teaspoon onion powder
- 1 teaspoon Herbs de Provence (grind in a spice grinder if too large)
- ¼ teaspoon cayenne pepper
- 2 tablespoons extra-virgin olive oil
- 2 pork tenderloins, cut into 1½"-slices then butterflied (created 17 sliders for us)
- 1 tablespoon grapeseed oil

Directions

1 In a small bowl, combine the salt, garlic powder, onion powder, Herbs de Provence, cayenne pepper, and olive oil.

2 Brush both sides of the pork with the mixture.

3 Place about a tablespoon of the cabbage onto one side of the butterflied tenderloin and bring the other side together to close it.

4 Heat the tablespoon of grapeseed oil in a large sauté pan over medium-high heat and sauté the pork for about 20 minutes, turning to cook on all sides.

Assembly

Place the stuffed pork onto the untoasted side of toast, top with some of the Cranberry Catsup and another slice of toast. Enjoy!!!

Juice & Essence Pastels

Birth & Balance

Makes about 44

This little bundle of goodness stemmed from Dr. Ken's family tradition. The roots of this dish were shared with ready assistance by Mom, Yvonne, from Trinidad. We did our best to salute her and replicate a unique taste that could become a favorite at your family functions. Pastels, rich in taste and memories in their authentic form, were wrapped in dough, then banana leaves, and over the course of drinking, music, and laughter, prepared by many hands. Our way is a bit simpler, however, still very fun!

Juice & Essence

Pork is a tonifier to the spleen, stomach, kidneys, and lungs. Olives and capers are helpful with dry lungs, sore throat, dry cough, chronic digestive weakness, and hangovers.

Complement or Contrast

CONTRAST – *Olive and caper saltiness needs light, simple fruity awesomeness.... Dolcetto di Dogliani, Barbera, or Pinot Noir (California or Burgundy).*

Ingredients

- 2 tablespoons capers, minced
- 1, 5.75-ounce jar Spanish olives stuffed with pimento, minced
- 1 lb. ground pork
- ¾ teaspoon freshly ground black pepper
- 2 large garlic cloves, pressed
- 2 tablespoons extra-virgin olive oil
- ½ teaspoon fresh thyme leaves
- 1, 6-ounce can tomato paste
- 1 teaspoon sea salt
- 2 tablespoons extra-virgin olive oil
- 1, 12-ounce package wonton wrappers, cut into 3"-rounds
- 1 large egg white
- Cornstarch
- Olive oil

Directions

1 In a large bowl, mix together the capers, olives, pork, black pepper, and garlic.

2 Place a large sauté pan over medium-high heat and add 2 tablespoons of the olive oil.

3 Heat until the oil is shimmering.

4 Add the meat mixture and sauté until cooked through, about 10 minutes.

5 Carefully drain the fat from the pan.

6 Return to heat and add the thyme, tomato paste, salt, and the remaining 2 tablespoons of olive oil.

7 Cover and cook for 15 minutes to let the flavors blend.

8 Remove from heat.

9 Cool to room temperature if you are going to fill the wontons, or cover and refrigerate for up to 2 days.

10 Set up wonton wrappers on a towel and cover with plastic wrap so they do not dry out.

11 In a small bowl, whisk together the egg white to make the egg wash.

12 Sprinkle some cornstarch in a thin layer on a baking sheet and set aside.

13 Place one wonton wrapper on a work surface (keep the remaining wrappers covered).

14 Add ½ teaspoon of the pork filling to the center of the wonton wrapper.

15 Brush the egg wash around the edges of the wonton.

16 Fold over to enclose the filling and press the edges to seal the dumpling.

17 Place on the cornstarch-coated pan and cover with a towel to keep them from drying out.

18 Continue making the dumplings with the remaining wonton wrappers and pork filling. *Note: When all of the dumplings have been filled, the tray may be covered tightly with plastic wrap and foil and stored in the refrigerator up to 1 day. Bring to room temperature before continuing.*

19 Set up a steamer insert in a pot over simmering water.

20 Add some dumplings to steamer rack and cover.

21 Steam the dumplings for 3 minutes.

22 While the dumplings are steaming, heat a frying pan over medium-high heat.

23 When pan is hot, add enough olive oil to coat the pan.

24 Add the steamed dumplings to the oil and fry on both sides until they are well browned.

25 Continue the steaming and the frying with the remaining dumplings. Serve immediately.

Horseradish & Herb Encrusted Turkey Loin with Killer Kayenne Kale Krisps

Birth & Balance

Serves 4

We wanted to try our hand at making a turkey appetizer. While turkey is a loved fowl, creating an appetizer with turkey would require significant framing. Looking back, we'd have to say that this unusual combination is a perfect one with no one cultural origin. Imagination, divine intervention, and experimentation were the prominent forces here. *Kayenne Kale Krisps* seemed to offer the kick and "krunch" to complement the turkey!

Juice & Essence

Turkey, like chicken, builds blood, strengthens the body, and is used as a general tonic benefiting the spleen/ pancreas and stomach. Horseradish strengthens digestion, kills parasites, boosts libido, is a bronchodilator, and has antibiotic and anti-inflammatory properties. Kale eases lung congestion, benefits the stomach (can be used to treat ulcers), and builds red blood cells due to its high chlorophyll content. Cayenne also aids in the treatment of ulcers while treating indigestion, poor circulation, cold limbs, and loss of appetite. Caraway in the dip aids with spice and gas. Fresh rosemary, sage, and thyme are antibacterial, antiviral, anti-bloating, and antifungal.

COMPLEMENT (White) – CONTRAST (Red) – For the herbs, pungent horseradish and the mildly flavored turkey you could pull off a huge Chardonnay here... I mean huge! Bordeaux or central Napa. Otherwise go safe and serve a Rioja or an elegant, dry Argentinian Malbec or a blend from the central California coast. We are talking lower tannins, medium body, and medium fruit.

Prepare the Mustard Spiced Sour Cream Dip

Ingredients

- 1 tablespoon whole mustard seeds, ground in a spice grinder
- 1 tablespoon Sriracha hot chili sauce
- 1 cup reduced fat sour cream
- ¼ teaspoon whole caraway seed, ground in a spice grinder

Directions

Mix the ground mustard seed, chili sauce, sour cream, and ground caraway together in a small bowl and refrigerate to blend the flavors.

Prepare the Turkey Loin

Ingredients

- 1½ teaspoons chopped fresh rosemary
- 1½ teaspoons minced fresh sage
- ½ teaspoon minced fresh thyme
- ½ cup finely grated fresh horseradish root
- 2 teaspoons sea salt
- ½ teaspoon freshly ground black pepper
- ½ teaspoon ground white pepper
- 4 tablespoons grapeseed oil
- 1½ lbs. turkey tenderloins

Directions

1. Preheat the oven to 450°F. with the rack on the middle shelf.
2. Line a rimmed baking sheet with aluminum foil.
3. In a small bowl, combine the rosemary, sage, thyme, horseradish, salt, peppers, and grapeseed oil.
4. Rub the turkey loins all over with the herb mixture and place in the middle of the foil-lined baking sheets.
5. Bake for 20 minutes, or until just cooked through.

Prepare the Killer Kayenne Kale Krisps

Ingredients

- ¼ cup ground cayenne pepper
- ¾ teaspoon Himalayan salt
- 1 large bunch Tuscan Kale, stems removed and cut into 3" to 4" squares
- 1 teaspoon grapeseed oil

Directions

1. Line 2 large rimmed baking sheets with foil.
2. Preheat oven to 450°F.
3. Place the cayenne pepper and salt into a spice grinder. Process until finely ground.
4. Put the kale pieces into a large bowl and toss with the grapeseed oil until the kale is coated with the oil.
5. Spread the kale into one single layer onto the lined baking sheets and sprinkle all over with the cayenne and salt mixture.
6. Bake the kale in the preheated oven for 5 minutes, or until it is nice and crispy.
7. Set aside to cool.

Assembly

Directions

Slice the turkey loin into ¼"-slices and serve with the dip and kale chips.

Autumn Entrées

Chapter 2
Autumn Entrées

We took the best the world has to offer and refined each contribution with respect to cultural ideals. We used our palates, taste experience, and history of chef interactions to lovingly create our entrées.

Three-Peppercorn Encrusted Beef Tenderloin

J&E Time Signature

Birth & Balance

Serves 10

The focus of this dish was the tenderloin. Roasting a delicious cut of beef coated in three types of peppercorns sounded tasty and attractive. Any variance from this powerfully simple dish was diverted to our creative sauce using Prosecco, lime, capers, and rosemary.

Juice & Essence

Black peppercorns have a medicinal history of over 4,000 years. The use of peppercorns in this dish offer stimulation of the nervous, digestive, and circulatory systems which make it good for poor circulation, constipation, sluggish digestion, and drowsiness. It also has a laxative effect, tones the muscles of the colon, soothes the stomach, helps to prevent food poisoning, and stimulates the appetite. The combinations found in this dish (supported by the star: beef tenderloin), benefit the spleen/pancreas, stomach, build blood, increase energy, strengthen joints and bones, warm the body, boost the immune system, and increase muscle tone.

Complement or Contrast

COMPLEMENT – B.O.C.C. – (Big Ol' California Cabernet). The inherent spice and pepper of a Cabernet will go with the peppers in this dish. Choose something dry with tannins. Yum!

Ingredients

- ¼ cup pink peppercorns
- ¼ cup white peppercorns
- ¼ cup black peppercorns
- ¼ cup sea salt
- 2, 2½-lb. beef tenderloin roasts
- ½ cup extra-virgin olive oil
- ½ cup Prosecco
- Juice and zest of 1 lime
- 1 tablespoon Spanish capers, chopped
- ½ sprig of fresh rosemary, minced
- Olive oil

Directions

1 Place all of the peppercorns and sea salt in a spice grinder and process to a fine powder.

2 Rub the mixture all over the beef tenderloin roasts.

3 Place the roasts on a platter and cover completely with plastic wrap.

4 Refrigerate overnight or as long as 2 days.

5 Remove from the refrigerator 45 minutes prior to roasting.

6 Preheat two ovens to 400°F.

7 In a small saucepan, combine the extra-virgin olive oil, Prosecco, lime juice and zest, capers, and rosemary.

8 Bring to a boil and then turn down to a simmer.

9 Let the mixture simmer for 15 minutes to blend the flavors.

10 Keep warm while roasting the beef tenderloin.

11 Use two ovenproof sauté pans, large enough to fit a roast in each but still can fit in your oven.

12 Place the pans over medium-high heat.

13 Once the pan is very hot, add olive oil to just coat the bottom of the pans.

14 Sear the roasts on all sides then transfer them to the ovens.

15 Roast for 20 minutes for medium-rare.

16 Remove from the oven and let rest for 10 minutes.

17 Cut the roast into slices and serve with just a drizzle of the sauce.

Mediterranean Grilled Lamb Chops

J&E Time Signature

Birth & Balance

Serves 4

Every seasoning used in the marinade of these lamb chops has been used for years in the health conscious kitchens of Mediterranean families. We achieved balance in creating a superb grilled lamb chop. A lollipop of finger licking goodness!

Juice & Essence

Lamb is sweet natured and warming, with benefits to the kidneys and spleen, enhancing overall energy and strength while assisting with low back and knee pain. The spleen qi enhancing qualities will aid with abdominal pains and digestive imbalances ranging from hiccups to cold sensations in the abdomen. This dish will be helpful with increasing blood production when diagnosed with anemia. Commercial lamb is typically given fewer antibiotics and drugs than other red meat.

Complement or Contrast

COMPLEMENT – The unique herb signature and gamey flavors of the lamb speak volumes here. My palate remembers Greek and Turkish table wines that would be so great with this dish. They are simple, modest food wines that are easy and tasty. Try a well-stocked wine store and see if you can find some! If you cannot find any, a Rioja or Chianti would do.

Marinade

Ingredients

- 1 cup extra-virgin olive oil
- Zest and juice of 1 lemon
- 6 garlic cloves, pressed
- 2 teaspoons sea salt
- 1 teaspoon freshly ground
  black pepper
- ½ teaspoon finely ground fresh
  mustard seed
- 1 teaspoon paprika
- 1 teaspoon chopped fresh rosemary
- 16 lamb chops
- Honey

Directions

1 Combine the olive oil, lemon juice and zest, garlic, salt, pepper, mustard
   seed, paprika, and rosemary in a bowl.

2 Combine well.

3 Divide the lamb chops between two Ziploc freezer bags.

4 Divide the marinade between the two bags.

5 Close the bags and refrigerate overnight or for a minimum of 3 hours.

6 Heat a gas grill to high.

7 Grill chops for 5 to 10 minutes total, or until desired degree of doneness.

8 Place the chops that are done on the top shelf of the grill.

9 Drizzle the lamb with a little of the honey as desired. Serve immediately.

Life-Changing Oxtail & Root Vegetable Soup with Chanterelle~ Spaghetti Squash Medley

J&E Time Signature

Birth & Balance

Serves 6 to 8

The purpose of this soup was to boost the immune system in preparation for the fall season. The combination of vegetables, herbs, bone marrow, and oxtail meat work as strengthening agents with readily available nutrition for easily assimilated quick and long-term revitalizing energy. This soup will enrich and restore you. This is the life change we hope you will share and enjoy with your family time and time again.

Juice & Essence

Because of the bone marrow and oxtail, this dish is superbly energizing, pain relieving, and because of the squash, detoxing. This life changing soup is jam packed with ingredients that will help to restore joint health, alleviate constipation, cough, and chest blockages. Bone marrow-infused broth and oxtail will strengthen bones and tendons, help to aid lower back, knee pain, and migraine relief. This is a great cure for weakness, lack of virility, impotence, and infertility. The *Chanterelle-Spaghetti Squash Medley* increases the anti-cancer, anti-viral digestive benefits. The cooling nature of spaghetti squash and mushrooms will balance the heat and spice of the soup while decreasing fat levels and heat toxins accumulated from heavy meat eating.

Compliment or Contrast

CONTRAST – The richness of everything in this soup needs a richness to match it. A well-structured Shiraz, Cabernet, Malbec, or Zinfandel would do very nicely.

Soup

Ingredients

- 16 cups of water
- 2 tablespoons sea salt
- 1 tablespoon olive oil
- 1.5 lbs. marrow beef bones
- 2.25 lbs. oxtails
- ¼ teaspoon ground red pepper
- ½ teaspoon paprika
- ¼ teaspoon white pepper
- ½ teaspoon onion powder
- ½ teaspoon garlic powder
- ¼ teaspoon cumin
- ½ teaspoon celery salt
- ¼ teaspoon ground cloves
- ¼ teaspoon ground allspice
- 1 teaspoon sea salt
- 3 tablespoons olive oil
- ⅓ cup freshly grated horseradish root
- ¼ lb. salsify, peeled and chopped
- 1 parsnip, chopped
- 1 medium size turnip, chopped
- 1 medium size rutabaga, chopped
- 2 tablespoons Williams-Sonoma Beef Demi-Glace
- 8 multi-colored carrots, cut into 1" to 1½"-thick slices
- 1 large fennel bulb, chopped into 1"-pieces
- 1 large sweet onion, chopped into 1"-pieces
- 6 large garlic cloves, minced
- 2 cups ½"-diced Yukon Gold potatoes
- 2½ cups ½"-diced sweet potato
- 1 teaspoon chopped fresh oregano
- 1 teaspoon chopped fresh rosemary
- ½ teaspoon chopped fresh thyme
- Salt and pepper to taste

Directions

1 Add the water, 2 tablespoons sea salt, 1 tablespoon olive oil, and the beef bones to a large stockpot.

2 Bring to a boil over high heat.

3 Meanwhile, combine the ground red pepper, paprika, white pepper, onion powder, garlic powder, cumin, celery salt, cloves, allspice, and 1 teaspoon sea salt in a small bowl.

4 Rub all over the oxtails.

5 Heat a large frying pan over medium-high heat.

6 Add the 3 tablespoons of olive oil.

7 Brown the oxtails in the hot oil until they are nice and brown on all sides.

8 Add the oxtails to the stockpot.

9 Add the horseradish, salsify, parsnip, turnip, and rutabaga to the stockpot.

10 Cover with a lid and let cook over medium heat for 2 hours.

11 Remove the marrow beef bones and the oxtails from the soup and place in a large bowl.

12 Strain the vegetables from the broth (keep the broth in the stockpot) and place them in the bowl of a food processor fitted with the chopping blade.

13 Process the vegetables until they are finely pureed.

14 Add the pureed vegetables to the broth and stir to incorporate.

15 Remove the bone marrow from the beef bones and add to the broth also.

16 Return the oxtails and the beef bones to the broth.

17 Now add the remaining ingredients and stir to combine.

18 Reduce heat to low and continue to cook, stirring occasionally, for another 3 to 4 hours, or until the meat from the oxtails is very tender.

Life-Changing Soup ~ *continued*

Chanterelle-Spaghetti Squash Medley

Ingredients

- 1 lb. spaghetti squash
- 1 tablespoon olive oil
- 1½ cups fresh chanterelle mushrooms, sliced
- 1 large garlic clove, minced
- 1 teaspoon minced fresh sage
- ½ teaspoon minced fresh oregano
- 1 tomatillo, chopped into large chunks
- 1 yellow tomato, chopped into large chunks
- Salt and pepper to taste

Directions

1 Preheat the oven to 400°F.

2 Cut the spaghetti squash in half lengthwise and clean out the seeds.

3 Cover a baking sheet with sides with foil.

4 Sprinkle 2 tablespoons of water on the foil.

5 Place the squash halves, cut side down, on top of the foil.

6 Bake for 40 to 45 minutes until the squash is fully cooked.

7 Once the squash is cool enough to handle, use a fork to flake the strands of "spaghetti" into a bowl.

8 Set aside while cooking the mushrooms.

9 Heat a medium sauté pan over medium-high heat.

10 Add the olive oil, mushrooms, and garlic.

11 Sauté until the mushrooms are just cooked through.

12 Add the sage and oregano.

13 Remove from heat and add to the bowl with the spaghetti squash.

14 Mix in the remaining ingredients.

Assembly

Ingredients

16 ounces farfallini pasta (baby bow-tie), cooked

Directions

1 Place the desired amount of pasta into each serving bowl.

2 Ladle the soup on top of the pasta, being sure to include an oxtail.

3 Top the soup with a couple tablespoons of the Chanterelle~Spaghetti Squash Medley and serve.

Testimonials

Personally, I am immensely pleased to have had the Oxtail and Root Vegetable Soup, for it exploded an array of herbs and spices into my body that just knocked a cold completely out of my system. There was no more congestion, coughing, or fever. I have known Dr. Ken for over eight years now, through my position as Computer Specialist in the Office of Dr. Maya Angelou and various emails updating me on his art, family, and life's experiences.

As a holistic doctor, he has recommended various remedies and medications to treat my arthritis and other aliments with great success. I don't know of any other holistic cookbooks on the market, but I can't wait for Dr. Ken's; and upon viewing www.juiceandessence.com, I eagerly await the book's release.

In conclusion, I think once you reap the benefits from one of the recipes in the book, your palate will also want more; therefore, again, I personally and wholeheartedly recommend you consider his book request.

Warmly,
Patricia S. Casey

I had the unexpected pleasure of eating a most surprising lunch last week. Dr. Ken Grey and Carol Maglio have been working on a cookbook and made a wonderful soup of oxtail and marrow with a delicious relish of fall vegetables that went on the soup. I have eaten a large variety of foods over the years, but I had never tried oxtail, so I didn't know what to expect. The soup was truly delicious, which was surprisingly unexpected as there was a heartiness — as Ken explained a fall type meal — which suggested a blander taste to me. But this was truly enjoyable, appetizing, and delightful. In addition, Ken explained that this meal was designed to provide energy, a natural energy from the ingredients themselves, as they are incorporated in the soup and then into my own body. This should help avoid the usual post lunch drowsiness that I frequently get, especially after heavy meals.

I was somewhat skeptical of this, but sure enough, I was energized and alert for the rest of the afternoon and evening. Indeed my wife and I ended up Salsa dancing in Palm Beach. Then, to a night club for more dancing thereafter! It was then when I realized it was past midnight, that I truly did feel that energizing feeling that Ken had told me about! This is without a doubt what food should be about — nutritious, seasonal, with fresh ingredients, matched for taste and palatability, AND providing a natural source of energy. Thanks Ken and Carol, I look forward to the next recipe.

Dr. Gus Castellanos

Poached Salmon with Bay Scallops, Curried Pumpkin, Sautéed Kale & Purple Rice

Birth & Balance

Serves 4

We tried our hand at poached salmon and created unique complements to support the flavor. The most interesting component was choosing curry in our pumpkin puree, instantly elevating the overall sophistication of this dish. This rainbow of colors, flavors, and textures creates ecstasy on the plate.

Juice & Essence

Salmon is rich in omega-3 fatty acids thereby enriching brain and nervous system development and renewal. Anti-inflammatory properties from the root ingredients add to the overall tonifying of the liver, spleen, and kidneys. This dish is energizing and blood building. This is an interesting way of consuming kale, which eases lung congestion and benefits the stomach while treating duodenal ulcers. Adding pumpkin assists with regulating blood sugar balance, necessary for diabetics and those suffering from hypoglycemia. Pumpkin promotes discharge of mucus from lungs, bronchi, and throat. Regular use of pumpkin has been shown to assist with bronchial asthma.

Complement *or* Contrast

CONTRAST – A lot of things going on here. You need a wine that can stand up to this aromatic variety. A good Viognier would do it or a Torrontes. My favorite would be one of Jermann's big whites. They are a little expensive and hard to find, but WOW what a rush!

Prepare Salmon & Scallops

Ingredients

- 1 cup dry white wine
- ½ cup chicken stock
- 1 cup water
- ½ teaspoon sea salt
- 4, 6-ounce center-cut salmon fillets with skin
- ½ lb. bay scallops
- ¾ teaspoon *J&E Curry Spice Mixture*
- 2 teaspoons extra-virgin olive oil

Directions

1. Combine the white wine, chicken stock, water, and salt in a large skillet.

2. Place the salmon fillets, skin side down, in the skillet.

3. Cover the skillet tightly and simmer over medium-low heat for 8 to 10 minutes until the salmon is cooked to desired doneness.

4. While salmon is cooking, prepare the scallops.

5. Combine the scallops, curry spice mix, and 1 teaspoon of the olive oil in a small bowl.

6. Place a sauté pan over medium heat.

7. Once hot, add the remaining olive oil and the scallop mixture.

8. Sauté for 5 minutes, or until scallops are just cooked through.

9. Remove the salmon from the poaching liquid and place on a serving platter.

10. Top with the scallops and serve with the curried pumpkin, sautéed kale, and purple rice.

Prepare J&E Curry Spice Mixture

Ingredients

- 1 teaspoon black peppercorns
- ½ teaspoon mustard seeds
- 1 teaspoon fennel seeds
- ½ teaspoon celery salt
- 1 teaspoon cumin
- ½ teaspoon ground coriander
- 2 teaspoons fenugreek
- ½ teaspoon ground ginger
- ¼ teaspoon ground allspice
- ¼ teaspoon ground turmeric
- ¼ teaspoon paprika
- ¼ teaspoon cayenne pepper
- ⅛ teaspoon red pepper flakes

Directions

1. Place the black peppercorns, mustard seeds, and fennel seeds into a spice grinder.

2. Finely grind and place in a small bowl.

3. Add the celery salt, cumin, coriander, fenugreek, ginger, allspice, turmeric, paprika, cayenne, and red pepper flakes and mix well.

4. This will be more than you will need for the pumpkin and the scallops. Store the remaining curry in an airtight container.

Poached Salmon ~ *continued*

Prepare the Pumpkin

Ingredients

- 4 cups peeled and cubed sugar pumpkin
- 5 medium cloves of garlic, pressed
- ½ teaspoon sea salt
- ½ teaspoon fresh thyme leaves
- ½ cup water
- ¼ cup extra-virgin olive oil
- 1 teaspoon *J&E Curry* spice mixture

Directions

1 Combine the pumpkin, garlic, salt, thyme leaves, water, and olive oil in a medium saucepan.

2 Place pan over medium-high heat, cover, and bring to a boil.

3 Continue to cook, covered for 15 minutes.

4 Add the curry spice mixture.

5 Cover and continue to cook for 30 minutes, or until the pumpkin is cooked through.

6 Use an immersion blender to puree the mixture to a smooth consistency and serve.

Prepare the Kale

Ingredients

- 2 bunches kale (about 1 lb.), rinsed, stemmed, and coarsely chopped
- 1 tablespoon clarified butter
- 1 cup chopped sweet onion
- 2 garlic cloves, minced
- Salt and pepper to taste

Directions

1 Heat a large sauté pan over medium heat.

2 Add the clarified butter and onion and cook, stirring occasionally, until the onion is nicely caramelized, about 30 minutes.

3 Add the garlic and the kale to the pan.

4 Cook until the kale wilts, stirring often, for about 6 to 8 minutes until the kale is tender and still bright green.

5 Season the kale to taste with salt and pepper and serve.

Prepare the Purple Rice

Ingredients

- 1 tablespoon olive oil
- 1 cup purple rice
- 2 cups chicken stock
- ½ teaspoon sea salt
- ½ teaspoon freshly ground black pepper

Directions

1. Preheat oven to 375°F.
2. Place medium-size saucepan over medium-high heat.
3. When heated, add the olive oil and purple rice.
4. Sauté rice in olive oil for 1 minute, stirring to coat rice in the oil.
5. Add the broth, salt, and pepper.
6. Bring to a boil.
7. Cover and place on the middle rack of the oven for 40 minutes, or until rice is cooked through.
8. Remove, place in to a bowl, and serve.

Candied Blood Orange Veal Tenderloin with Port Wine~Morel Mushroom Sauce

Birth & Balance   Serves 4

This was an accident in the loveliest of ways. We found ourselves shopping together for veal shanks on our cooking night however they were frozen. At first we were contemplating a Juice & Essence take on Osso Buco and had to shift gears. We took a deep breath and opened ourselves to feeding off of what was readily available to us in the market. First was the rare offering of veal tenderloin. Next, some beautiful blood oranges followed by a bottle of port wine and dried morel mushrooms. The rest is history!

Juice & Essence

Veal is beneficial to the spleen, liver, kidneys, stomach and large intestine channels. It is also strengthening to the body and digestion with energizing qualities, helpful for weak joints and in the wasting stages of diabetes. This is a useful dish for low back and knee weakness. Mushroom content boosts the immune system benefits, while increasing anti-tumor activity, decreasing fat level in blood, ridding the respiratory system of excess mucus and assisting with treating contagious hepatitis. Candied blood orange peel will help aid repair of digestion, increase energy, decrease mucus and assist with weak gums and teeth.

COMPLEMENT – To further the dining experience, we will pair a wine that will work well with the fragrant, sweet, and slightly bitter aspects found in this complex creation. I recommend a wine that can neutralize each bite so you can look forward to the next one. Big, deep, cherry fruit with raisiny finish would do the trick. My go-to was a good Amarone.

Ingredients

- 2 medium size blood oranges
- ⅓ cup Cointreau liquor
- ½ cup water
- ⅛ teaspoon fennel seeds
- 1 teaspoon cherry honey
- ¼ cup extra-virgin olive oil
- ½ teaspoon whole black peppercorns, ground in a spice grinder
- 1 teaspoon sea salt
- 2 lbs. veal tenderloins (should have 2 tenderloins)
- ½ cup all-purpose flour
- 2 tablespoons olive oil
- .65 ounces dried morel mushrooms, rehydrated and finely chopped
- ¾ cup port wine
- 2 tablespoons minced fresh parsley
- 1 cup water
- ⅓ cup beef stock
- 2 tablespoons cold butter, cut into 6 pieces
- Salt and pepper to taste

Directions

1 Peel the zest from the blood oranges in long strips.

2 Juice the oranges to make ½ cup of juice.

3 Place the peels, juice, liquor, water, fennel seeds, and honey in a saucepan and bring to a rolling boil for 7 minutes.

4 Lower heat to simmer for 30 minutes.

5 Remove from heat.

6 Place the peels on a cooling rack and discard the liquid.

7 Take a hair dryer and dry the peels for 5 minutes.

8 Finely mince the peels and place in a small bowl; add the olive oil, ground pepper, and salt.

9 Mix to combine well and rub the mixture on the veal tenderloins.

10 Let the veal marinate for 1 hour or overnight.

11 Preheat the oven to 425°F.

12 Remove the veal from the marinade and pat lightly to remove excess liquid.

13 Dredge veal tenderloins in the ½ cup flour, shaking off excess.

14 Heat a sauté pan over medium-high heat until hot.

15 Add the 2 tablespoons of olive oil and sear the veal on all sides until browned nicely.

16 Remove the veal tenderloins to a roasting pan and place in the oven for 20 minutes.

17 Meanwhile, add the chopped mushrooms, port, parsley, water, and beef broth to the sauté pan and bring to a boil, scraping up any brown bits on the bottom of the pan.

18 Lower heat and reduce the mixture for 20 minutes.

19 Remove veal tenderloins from the oven.

20 Add any liquid from the roasting pan to the mushroom mixture in the sauté pan and continue to reduce for an additional 5 minutes.

21 Tent the veal with foil to keep warm while letting the meat rest.

22 Strain the mushroom~port wine mixture into a small saucepan, discarding the solids.

23 Add the butter, one piece at a time, whisking until thoroughly incorporated before adding the next piece.

24 Season the sauce with salt and pepper to taste.

25 Cut the veal tenderloins into serving size pieces and drizzle with the sauce.

Lamb Shanks Osso Buco with Saffron Wheatberries

Birth & Balance

Serves 4 to 6

Our original intention was to make veal Osso Buco; however, we ended up using veal the week before in our **Candied Blood Orange Veal Tenderloin** (page 408) dish. We chose lamb shanks with great caution as Carol is not fond of lamb. To create a superior lamb shank Osso Buco, our plan would include a pressure cooker and a chemistry of flavors never before seen! This included pears cooked with rum, additions of caraway seeds, clementine zest…the list goes on! The results in our own words: Carol: *I don't like lamb. You know I don't like lamb. But this lamb shank…mmmmmm!* Ken: *Mmmmmmmmmmmmmmmmmmmm!!! That's what this is all about!*

Juice & Essence

Lamb has supportive health benefits for the spleen, heart, and kidneys. It is also helpful in treating low back pain and weak knees. This is an energizing dish with middle and lower abdominal warming qualities. A generous helping will work to restore overall bodily warmth in the case of the chills. Consuming this dish will assist with stopping hiccups stemming from abdominal cold and weakness. Saffron will stimulate the liver energy and help remove liver qi stagnation. Wheatberry is more tolerable to individuals allergic to glutinous, processed wheat grain and strengthens the kidneys, restores calmness to the heart thereby reducing irritability and menopausal difficulty.

I am taking this dish and giving it both attributes because it is very complex. You can choose to COMPLEMENT the deep, rich, soul-warming nature found here with a big Cabernet, a Valpolicella, or go really big with a good Amarone with its raisiny, dry fruit. Or CONTRAST with a Bordeaux, big Rioja, California Meritage, or a Barolo (my favorite). These dry, big red wines with wonderful tannins enhance your dining experience.

Prepare the Lamb

Ingredients

- 6 lamb shanks, approximately 1 lb. each
- 2 tablespoons mustard seeds
- 1 tablespoon fennel seeds
- 1 teaspoon cayenne pepper
- 1 teaspoon garlic powder
- ½ teaspoon caraway seeds
- 2 tablespoons paprika
- 1 tablespoon ground white pepper
- 1 tablespoon ground cumin
- ½ teaspoon Ceylon cinnamon
- ½ cup extra-virgin olive oil
- 2 tablespoons honey
- 2 red Comice pears, peeled and chopped
- ½ cup dark rum
- 1 cup water
- ½ cup olive oil
- 2 medium carrots, chopped into ½"-pieces
- 1 medium red bell pepper, chopped into ½"-pieces
- 2 cups celery root, chopped into ½"-pieces
- 1 medium white onion, chopped
- 1 small fresh fennel bulb, trimmed and chopped into ½"-pieces
- 3 large garlic cloves, minced
- 2 clementines, zested (reserve the flesh for another use)
- 1 teaspoon chopped fresh thyme
- 1½ teaspoons chopped fresh rosemary
- 2 teaspoons chopped fresh sage
- 2 large fresh bay leaves
- 1, 28-ounce can whole San Marzano tomatoes
- 1 cup beef stock
- 1 cup dry red wine
- 2 tablespoons tomato paste
- 1 tablespoon sea salt
- 2 teaspoons ground black pepper

Directions

1 Place lamb shanks in a large dish and set aside.

2 Place the mustard seeds, fennel seeds, cayenne pepper, garlic powder, and caraway seeds into a spice grinder and process to a fine powder.

3 Transfer to a small bowl and add the paprika, ground white pepper, cumin, Ceylon cinnamon, extra-virgin olive oil, and honey.

4 Mix well and then rub all over the lamb shanks.

5 Cover and let marinate for at least 30 minutes or overnight.

6 In a small saucepan, combine the pears, dark rum, and water.

7 Bring to a boil over medium-high heat, then lower heat and continue to cook for 20 minutes.

8 Set aside.

9 After the lamb has marinated, add the ½ cup olive oil to the pressure cooker pot and place over high heat.

10 Once the oil is heated, add the lamb shanks and brown on all sides. *Note: You may have to do this in batches depending on the size of your pressure cooker.*

11 Remove the lamb shanks as they are browned and place on a platter.

12 Drain off all of the oil. Add the carrots, bell pepper, celery root, onion, fennel, and garlic to the pot.

13 Cook until the vegetables just start to soften, approximately 5 minutes.

14 Now add the remaining ingredients as well as the cooked pear mixture and mix well to combine.

15 Put the lamb back into the pot.

16 Place the lid on the pressure cooker and close according to the manufacturer's instructions.

17 Bring the pressure up to high and cook for 35 minutes.

18 Remove from heat and let the pressure come down naturally.

19 Once the pressure is released, remove the lid and adjust the salt and pepper if necessary.

20 Serve with the wheatberries.

Prepare the Wheatberries

Ingredients

- 1 cup wheatberries
- 2½ cups beef stock
- ½ teaspoon saffron
- Salt and pepper

Directions

1 Bring the wheatberries, stock, and saffron to a boil over medium-high heat in a medium saucepan.

2 Cover and simmer until wheatberries are softened.

3 Add salt and pepper to taste.

Note: Wheatberry cooking time will vary depending on the type you choose. Pearled or soft wheatberries (lower protein) cook faster, about 25 minutes. The type that are not pearled or hard (high protein) will take longer, about 60 minutes. Cook according to the package instructions.

Juice & Essence "Turducken"

J&E Time Signature

Birth & Balance

Serves 4 to 6

This is our take on a fairly new Thanksgiving tradition originating in Louisiana around 1985. This is so delicious; and although not made in the authentic Louisiana style, we are sure you will enjoy our health conscious modifications. We used only breast meat (save the chicken livers), lots of digestion-enhancing herbs, citrus, and minimal amounts of added fat. We chose the clay pot method for roasting to lock in flavor and moisture.

Juice & Essence

This is a true fall energizer! The turkey, with the addition of the duck and the chicken livers, will especially tonify your yin. This includes increased eye health, hair health, glowing skin, and healthy joints. The chicken builds energy and blood, warms insides, strengthens kidneys, and increases appetite. It also helps with intestinal issues. The duck moistens dryness, nourishes the stomach, treats dry cough, parched mouth, and night sweats. Celery used in significant quantity benefits the stomach and spleen/pancreas, calms an aggravated liver, improves digestion, purifies the blood, and assists with vertigo and nervousness. Onion lowers blood pressure and cholesterol while decreasing phlegm and inflammation of the nose and throat. Onion is a cure for the common cold. Corn nourishes the heart, heals the stomach, promotes healthy teeth and gums, strengthens the kidneys, and enhances fertility.

Complement or Contrast

CONTRAST – Pinot Noir will work. Pinot Noir is inherently flowery and herbaceous. It's rich and big enough to handle the liver and duck, mild enough to meld with the turkey and chicken. Something wonderful we found was a South African Pinotage/Cabernet blend. There are several options available in this family of wine.

Ingredients

- 3 lbs. whole skin-on boneless turkey breast
- 2 teaspoons sea salt
- 2 teaspoons freshly ground black pepper
- 2 tablespoons extra-virgin olive oil
- 1 teaspoon dried Herbs de Provence
- *Buttermilk Cornbread* (page 430)
- 1.85 lbs. duck breast, trimmed of all fat and skin
- 1 lb. chicken breast, trimmed of all fat and skin
- ½ lb. chicken livers
- 1 tablespoon extra-virgin olive oil
- 1 tablespoon unsalted butter
- 1 cup chopped celery
- 1½ cups chopped yellow onion
- 5 garlic cloves, minced
- ¼ cup minced green onion – green parts only
- 1½ tablespoons chopped fresh parsley
- 1 tablespoon chopped fresh thyme
- 1½ teaspoons chopped fresh rosemary
- 2 teaspoons chopped fresh sage
- 1 tablespoon sea salt
- 2 teaspoons freshly ground black pepper
- 2 teaspoons paprika
- 2½ cups chicken stock
- 4 whole carrots, trimmed
- 4 celery stalks, trimmed
- 1 lemon, sliced
- 1 tablespoon flour
- 2 teaspoons water

Special Equipment
clay pot roaster

Directions

1 Place the turkey breast skin side down on a cutting board.

2 Remove the tenders and set aside for the stuffing.

3 Make a lengthwise cut about 1"-deep down the middle of each breast.

4 Cover with plastic wrap and pound the breast evenly to about 1½"-thickness using the smooth side of a meat mallet.

5 Season both sides of the turkey with the 2 teaspoons sea salt, 2 teaspoons freshly ground black pepper, 2 tablespoons extra-

virgin olive oil, and the teaspoon of Herbs de Provence.

6 Wrap turkey in plastic and place in refrigerator (can be prepared 1 day in advance).

Make the Stuffing

Directions

1 Prepare the cornbread recipe and set aside to cool (can be prepared 2 days in advance).

2 Cover and leave at room temperature.

3 Once the cornbread has cooled, cut it into 3"-chunks and toast in a 350°F. oven for 10 minutes.

4 Set aside to cool.

Juice & Essence "Turducken" ~ *continued*

5 Using the food grinder attachment on a stand mixer, grind the duck breast, chicken breast, turkey tenders, and chicken livers.

6 Set aside.

7 Heat a large sauté pan over medium-high heat.

8 Add the tablespoon of olive oil and butter to the pan.

9 Next add the celery, onion, and garlic.

10 Sauté until the vegetables just begin to soften.

11 Add the green onion, parsley, thyme, rosemary, sage, salt, pepper, and paprika.

12 Stir to combine and transfer to a large bowl.

13 Now add the ground meats to the pan and sauté until the meats are cooked through.

14 Add to the bowl with the vegetables and mix well.

15 Set aside at room temperature to cool for 20 minutes and then cover and place in the refrigerator (can be prepared 1 day in advance).

16 Submerge the clay roasting pot in water for 15 minutes.

17 Once the toasted cornbread has cooled, crumble ⅔ of it into the meat mixture.

18 Stir to combine.

19 Open up the turkey breast, skin side down, on a cutting board.

20 Spread 2½ cups of the stuffing onto the turkey breast.

21 Beginning with one long side of the breast, roll the turkey into a cylinder as tightly as possible.

22 Tie the turkey crosswise at 1" intervals with kitchen twine, then place one tie lengthwise to hold the turkey together.

23 Cut off excess twine.

24 Remove the clay pot from the water.

25 Add 1½ cups of the chicken stock, the whole carrots, celery, and lemon slices to the bottom of the clay pot.

26 Place the turkey breast, seam side down, on top of the vegetables.

27 Put the cover on and place on the center rack of a cold oven.

28 Turn the oven on to 450°F.

29 Roast for 70 to 80 minutes until turkey is cooked through and lightly browned.

Meanwhile, while the turkey is roasting:

30 Crumble the remaining cornbread into the meat stuffing.

31 Add the remaining 1 cup chicken stock.

32 Mix well and place the mixture into a 2-quart baking dish and cover.

33 When turkey is done, lower the oven temperature to 350°F. and bake the stuffing until heated through, about 30 minutes.

34 Place the turkey breast on a carving board and cover lightly with foil to keep warm while it is resting.

35 Place the drippings from the clay pot into a saucepan.

36 In a small bowl, mix together the flour and water until combined with no lumps.

37 Whisk into the drippings and heat the mixture over low heat until thickened.

38 Remove the kitchen twine from the turkey breast.

39 Cut the turkey crosswise into 1"-slices.

40 Serve with the stuffing and gravy.

Juice & Essence Best Chili Ever

Birth & Balance

Serves 8

This protein-on-protein mix is a beautiful way to distribute iron and fiber to the body. When it is cold outside, the body needs warmth and our blood needs to be enriched. Chili has long been a dependable companion to the long distance journeyman. Most of the goods can be from a dried source and the live protein can be caught in the wild. Our Juice & Essence approach is one part wild and one part tame. So we have given you venison and beef: balancing the common with the unexpected and showing you a new take on an old technique.

Juice & Essence

Venison: sweet and warm, nourishes the liver and kidney, as well as strengthens joints and bones. Treats lower back and knee soreness and weakness as well as male fertility issues. Additional benefits from beans include diuretic qualities that will assist with edema and swelling and lung tonifying qualities that will assist with promoting beautiful skin. The balanced herb combinations in this dish relieve gas and ease digestion of this high protein meal. Bell peppers improve the appetite and resolve stagnant food in cancer cases where digestion is very poor. They also reduce inflammation, promote circulation, and are rich in vitamin C. There is a cooling nature to bell peppers which helps to balance the hot and spicy nature of our *J&E Best Chili Ever*. We used cocoa for its high antioxidant, warm nature. In this case, the bitter nature of cocoa works well in balancing the sweet/sour of the tomato and hominy. Hominy is dried corn and is beneficial to the heart, lung, spleen, liver, stomach, gallbladder, and bladder. Corn strengthens lung function, calms the heart, regulates the digestion, assists with poor and frequent urination, and helps heal the gallbladder thereby assisting with gallstones, jaundice, hepatitis, and hypertension. All of the ingredients work to foster a blood building, energizing bowl of healing goodness.

CONTRAST – Malbec, Zinfandel, Shiraz, Syrah, Because of the chili peppers /heat, vinegar and the tomatoes which bring sweetness and acid. The overall tart aspect will require a wine with some fruit forwardness and depth. It will have to be powerful enough to tangle with the chili spice. These wines will match the spice with spice.

Prepare the Beans

Ingredients

- 1 cup each dried navy beans, dried pinto beans, dried kidney beans
- Water

Directions

1   Place the dried beans into three separate bowls.
2   Pour 3 cups of water into each of the bowls over the beans.
3   Cover and let the beans soak overnight. (Soaking the beans overnight helps to aid the body in digesting the beans.)
4   Drain the navy beans and place in a pressure cooker.
5   Add enough fresh water to just cover the beans.
6   Lock the lid onto the pressure cooker.
7   Place the pressure cooker over high heat.
8   Once the steam starts coming out on the lid, cook the beans for 5 minutes.
9   Release the pressure and drain the beans.
10 Set aside.
11 Continue cooking the remaining beans using the same process. Adjust the cooking times as follows: pinto beans = 10 minutes and kidney beans = 10 minutes.
12 Reserve all the kidney beans and 2 cups each of the navy and pinto beans for the chili.
13 Save the remaining navy and pinto beans for another use.

Prepare the Venison

Ingredients

- ½ cup minced sweet onion
- 1 large garlic clove, minced
- ½ cup extra-virgin olive oil
- ¼ cup red wine vinegar
- 2 tablespoons chopped fresh culantro
- 1 tablespoon minced fresh chives
- 1 teaspoon sea salt
- ½ teaspoon ground black pepper
- ½ teaspoon dried Mexican oregano
- 1 teaspoon dried jalapeño pepper powder
- 1 teaspoon ground New Mexican chili pepper
- 1 teaspoon ground chipotle chili pepper
- 1 teaspoon ground ancho chili pepper
- 1½ lbs. venison tenderloin, trimmed and chopped into ½"-cubes

Directions

1   Combine the onion, garlic, oil, vinegar, culantro, chives, salt, pepper, oregano, jalapeño, New Mexican chili, chipotle chili, ancho chili, and venison together in a bowl.
2   Cover and let marinate at room temperature for 30 minutes.

Assembly

Ingredients

- 2 tablespoons olive oil
- 1 yellow bell pepper, diced
- 1 green bell pepper, diced
- 1 orange bell pepper, diced
- 4 large garlic cloves, pressed
- ½ cup chopped sweet onion
- 1 teaspoon freshly ground black pepper
- 1 tablespoon paprika
- 1 tablespoon celery salt
- ¾ cup Knob Creek bourbon
- 1½ lbs. lean ground sirloin
- 2, 28-ounce cans whole tomatoes (crush tomatoes by hand)
- 1, 15-ounce can yellow hominy
- ½ cup diced sundried tomatoes
- 1 teaspoon cayenne pepper
- 2 teaspoons freshly ground Himalayan salt
- 1 tablespoon cocoa powder
- 4 sprigs of fresh thyme

Directions

1   Heat the olive oil in a large stockpot over medium-high heat.
2   Add the peppers, garlic, and onion.
3   Sauté until the vegetables are softened, about 8 to 10 minutes.
4   Add the black pepper, paprika, and celery salt.
5   Stir in the bourbon and continue to cook until the bourbon is nearly evaporated, stirring occasionally.
6   Add the ground sirloin and cook until browned.
7   Then add the venison along with the marinade and cook until the meat is browned.
8   Add the remaining ingredients along with the reserved beans.
9   Cover and cook on medium heat, stirring occasionally for 10 minutes.
10 Remove cover and reduce heat to low.
11 Continue cooking for another 45 minutes.
12 Serve with cornbread.

Koa's No-Chill Chowder

Birth & Balance

Serves 4

This is the best clam chowder each of us has ever had…although we are biased! On this special day, Dr. Ken's son, Koa, was born. There was a chill in the air that was conducive to a belly-warming concoction. In this case, everything was last-minute inspiration fulfilled to perfection by Carol while Dr. Ken was welcoming Koa to this earth. Our unique process and approach utilized cardamom pods to balance the dampness of the heavy cream. This was our first use of cardamom and beer in a J&E dish.

Juice & Essence

The use of cardamom pods is to balance out the dampness of the heavy cream and dairy products. Dampness is an energetic description used frequently in traditional Chinese medicine to mean a heavy, clogged feeling present in the human body when there is an imbalance in circulation of overall fluids and energy known as "qi." Cardamom is warming and drying so it will make for easier digestion and assimilation of the energy found in dairy products. Clams, as one of the main ingredients, are a yin tonifying food, helping to moisten overall dryness and facilitate proper body fluid distribution. Health benefits include help with edema, hemorrhoids, reproductive organ issues, and goiter. Mussels strengthen the liver and kidneys, build blood, increase kidney essence, treat low back pain, knee weakness, impotence, and vertigo. Potatoes benefit the spleen/pancreas and increase energy. Potato lubricates the intestines and enhances the yin aspects of the kidneys. Celery purifies the blood and is used in excess heat conditions such as burning urine, blood in urine, acne, and canker sores. Celery is beneficial to the stomach and spleen/pancreas. Fennel harmonizes digestion and also benefits yin and balances the cooling aspects of the body. Overall blood tonifying, energizing, warming, and immune system boosting qualities are to be had in this classic comfort soup.

Complement or Contrast

CONTRAST – To truly enrich the dining experience, this complex briny seafood dish with tons of herbs needs to be embraced by a fresh dry California Chardonnay with creamy aromas, notes of pear, apple, citrus, and a little bit of butter. My hands-down recommendation is Cakebread.

Ingredients

- 2 dozen mussels, scrubbed
- 2 dozen middle neck clams, scrubbed
- 1½ cups Dogfish Head, Miles Davis Bitch's Brew Ale brewed with honey and gesho (African root)
- Water
- 2 tablespoons extra-virgin olive oil
- ¼ lb. pancetta, diced
- 1 cup minced fresh fennel bulb
- 1 cup minced celery
- 1 cup minced yellow onion
- 4 garlic cloves, minced
- ½ teaspoon dry mustard
- ½ teaspoon celery salt
- ½ teaspoon paprika
- ½ teaspoon freshly ground black pepper
- 1 pint shrimp stock (purchased from fish monger)
- ½ sprig of fresh rosemary
- 1 sprig of fresh thyme
- 2 sprigs of parsley
- 1 lb. Yukon Gold potatoes, diced
- 1 lb. fresh cod cut into 1"-chunks
- 1 teaspoon freshly ground Himalayan salt
- 1 cup half & half
- 1 cup heavy cream
- 8 cardamom pods
- ¼ teaspoon freshly ground black pepper
- ¼ teaspoon crushed red pepper flakes
- Publix Rosemary Peppercorn bread toasted and buttered

Directions

1. Place cleaned mussels and clams into two separate medium-size saucepans.
2. Add ½ cup of the Miles Davis Bitch's Brew to the pan with the mussels and add 1 cup to the pan with the clams.
3. Add enough water to each pot to just come to the top of the shells.
4. Cover each pot and cook over medium heat until the shells open, about 15 to 20 minutes.
5. Remove the cooked mussels and clams from each pan, discarding any shells that have not opened.
6. Strain the stocks separately into heatproof bowls and set aside.
7. Remove the meat from the mussels and coarsely chop.
8. Remove the meat from the clams and combine with the mussels.
9. Set aside.
10. In a medium-size stockpot, heat the olive oil and add the pancetta.
11. Sauté for 10 minutes over medium heat until the pancetta is golden brown.
12. Add the fennel, celery, onion, and garlic and continue to cook until the vegetables begin to soften.
13. Now add the dry mustard, celery salt, paprika, and black pepper.
14. Measure out 2 cups each of the mussel and clam stocks (reserve the leftover stocks for another use).
15. Add to the stockpot along with the prepared shrimp stock.
16. Tie the fresh herbs together in a bundle with kitchen twine and add to the pot.
17. Add the potatoes and bring to a boil.
18. Continue to cook for about 15 minutes, or until the potatoes are tender.
19. Turn heat down to a simmer and, using an immersion blender, puree about ½ of the potatoes.
20. Now add the chopped cod, clams, mussels, and salt.
21. Continue to simmer the soup while preparing the cream.
22. In a small saucepan, combine the half & half, cream, cardamom pods, black pepper, and crushed red pepper.
23. Bring just to a boil and then simmer for 10 minutes.
24. Remove the cardamom pods and add the cream mixture to the soup.
25. Stir to combine and continue to cook for another 5 minutes.
26. Serve with the toasted and buttered Rosemary Peppercorn bread. Yum!!!

Harvest Festival Soup

Birth & Balance

Serves 8 to 10

Harvest says it all!!! Up to this point we were still settling into using life experiences to create new expressions of health enhancing cuisine. This harvest season ushered in confirmation that we had done more than settled. We had arrived! The thoroughly gratifying three-page holiday spread in our local paper that followed would cement our newly paved path. The ingredients for this second course in our holiday dinner were strongly influenced by Carol's trip to Jamaica, causing us to reflect on new ways to employ pumpkin. In West Indian culture, the characteristics of pumpkin become the key in many soups and stews, secretly bringing them to new levels. In this case, we were able to disguise the lamb flavor to the point that a table of nine individuals could not discern the significant lamb bone base!

Juice & Essence

Lamb, and in this case lamb marrow, is soothing and warming to the stomach, benefits the kidneys and spleen, and is helpful in relieving low back and knee weakness. The combination of white onion, garlic cloves, thyme, and bay leaves make this soup immune boosting with circulation qualities. The pumpkin detoxes while reducing inflammation and assisting with pain relief.

CONTRAST – Lamb broth has an earthy sweetness that will respond to the earthy acid of Chianti. This very dry wine with mild tannins and low fruit will give you a clean break between bites. Chianti is also very good as a settling factor to the gaminess you get from lamb. My absolute favorite is Canonica a Cerreto.

Lamb Stock

Ingredients

- 2 lbs. lamb neck bones
- 3 tablespoons olive oil
- 1 large white onion, chopped
- 4 large garlic cloves, chopped
- 2 tablespoons tomato paste
- 2 bay leaves
- 1 large sprig of fresh thyme
- 8 cups water
- 1 teaspoon whole allspice
- ½ cup Wild Turkey bourbon
- 1, 15-ounce can pumpkin puree
- Salt and pepper to taste

Directions

1 Lightly salt and pepper the lamb neck bones.

2 Place a large stockpot over medium-high heat.

3 Add 2 tablespoon of the olive oil.

4 When the oil is hot, sear the lamb bones until very brown on all sides.

5 Once browned, remove from the pan to a large plate and set aside.

6 Add the remaining 1 tablespoon of olive oil to the stockpot.

7 Sauté the onions and garlic until softened, about 8 to 10 minutes.

8 Reduce the heat to medium and move the vegetables to the side to create a clear space in the center of the pot.

9 Add the tomato paste to the cleared spot and cook the paste until it is lightly browned and caramelized, stirring often.

10 Combine with the onions and garlic.

11 Return the lamb bones to the pot and add the bay leaves, thyme sprig, and water.

12 Cover and bring to a boil.

13 Lower the heat and simmer for 5 hours, stirring occasionally.

14 After the stock has simmered for 5 hours, add the allspice and bourbon.

15 Raise the heat to medium, cover, and continue to cook for another hour, stirring often.

16 Let cool slightly, then refrigerate in the pot overnight.

17 The next day, remove from the refrigerator and skim off the fat that has congealed on the top of the stock.

18 Return the pot to the stove and gently bring to a simmer.

19 Continue to cook until the stock is heated through. Meanwhile, prepare the *Chanterelle~Spaghetti Squash Medley.*

Harvest Festival Soup ~ *continued*

Chanterelle~Spaghetti Squash Medley

Ingredients

- 1 lb. spaghetti squash
- 1 tablespoon olive oil
- 1½ cup fresh chanterelle mushrooms, sliced
- 1 large garlic clove, minced
- 1 teaspoon minced fresh sage
- ½ teaspoon minced fresh oregano
- 1 large tomatillo, chopped into large chunks
- 1 yellow tomato, chopped into large chunks
- Salt and pepper to taste

Directions

1 Preheat the oven to 400°F.

2 Cut the spaghetti squash in half lengthwise and clean out the seeds.

3 Cover a baking sheet with sides with foil.

4 Sprinkle 2 tablespoons of water on the foil.

5 Place the squash halves, cut side down, on top of the foil.

6 Bake the squash for 40 to 45 minutes until it is fully cooked.

7 Once the squash is cool enough to handle, use a fork to flake the strands of "spaghetti" into a bowl.

8 Set aside while cooking the mushrooms.

9 Heat a medium sauté pan over medium-high heat.

10 Add the olive oil, mushrooms, and garlic.

11 Sauté until the mushrooms are just cooked through.

12 Add the sage and oregano.

13 Remove from heat and add to the bowl with the spaghetti squash.

14 Mix in the tomatillo, tomato, salt and pepper and stir well to combine.

15 Set aside and finish preparing the stock.(Medley can be prepared 4 hours in advance.)

16 Cover and set aside at cool room temperature.

Assembly

1   Remove the bones from the pot and discard.

2   Strain the remaining vegetables and herbs from the stock into a smaller pot, discarding the solids.

3   Stir the pureed pumpkin into the stock.

4   Add salt and pepper to taste.

5   Heat the soup to a simmer.

6   Continue to cook for 20 to 30 minutes to blend the flavors.

7   Ladle some of the stock into soup bowls and top with a scoop of the *Chanterelle~Spaghetti Squash Medley.* Serve immediately.

Autumn Accompaniments

Chapter 3
Autumn Accompaniments

These accompaniments are gorgeous mates to the flavor notes and visual canvases of Juice & Essence entrées. These accompaniments are a fresh take on vegetable combinations that, as is customary with Juice & Essence, have an unpredictably delicious twist!

Rosemary Garlic Whole Wheat Crackers

Birth & Balance

Serves 4

Making your own crackers, although at first seeming odd if you do not bake, can still be a satisfying accomplishment. It is easy to go into a box, rip open a package, and start munching. We served these homemade crackers with pride knowing that every ingredient was well thought out.

Juice & Essence

These tasty crackers filled with rosemary and garlic have anti-viral and antibacterial qualities with benefits to the stomach and lungs. The two main ingredients help with food and drink accumulation and stagnation; i.e., that uncomfortable full feeling or indigestion. Other benefits of this simple cracker are warming chilly bodies, getting rid of extra water, swelling, parasites, and symptoms of the common cold.

Ingredients

- 1¼ cups whole wheat flour
- ½ teaspoon sea salt
- 1 tablespoon chopped fresh rosemary
- 1 teaspoon pressed garlic
- 4 tablespoons extra-virgin olive oil
- 6 tablespoons water
- 1 egg white
- 2 tablespoons water
- *Toppings*: coarse sea salt, coarsely ground black pepper, grated Parmesan, feta cheese, sesame seeds

Directions

1 Preheat oven to 400°F.

2 In a large bowl, mix together the flour, salt, rosemary, and garlic.

3 Add the oil and 6 tablespoons of water.

4 Mix well until a compact ball of dough is formed.

5 Lightly sprinkle a piece of parchment paper (large enough to fit on your baking sheet) with flour.

6 Place the dough on the parchment paper.

7 Using a floured rolling pin, roll the dough to ⅛"-thickness.

8 Once the dough is rolled thinly, use a pizza cutter to cut the dough into squares.

9 Transfer the parchment paper with the dough on it to a baking sheet.

10 Combine the egg white and the 2 tablespoons of water to make an egg wash.

11 Brush the wash onto the dough.

12 Sprinkle with one of the suggested toppings.

13 Bake for 10 to 15 minutes, or until the crackers are lightly browned and crisp.

Seeded Flax, Oat & Wheat Bread

Birth & Balance

Makes 2 loaves

The endeavor was to make a delicious seed-rich, high-protein, vitamin-packed bread. The cold rise process was used to reduce rise and overall baking time. We learned about this technique and adapted this recipe from the *Healthy Bread in 5 Minutes a Day* cookbook.

Juice & Essence

A tonic of a bread with oats helping to energize, balance hormonal activity, lower blood cholesterol levels, cleanse, assist in protecting against bowel cancer, and possessing antidepressant qualities. Flax also aids in treating stress and nervous disorders. Enjoy the anti-inflammatory actions available in the flax in this bread. While relieving fatigue, tonifying kidneys, and encouraging healing, wheat is one of the few foods which Chinese medicine attributes to directly nourishing the heart and mind. Wheat calms and focuses the mind and can be used for heart palpitations, insomnia, irritability, menopausal difficulty, and emotional instability.

Ingredients

- ⅛ cup ground flaxseed
- ⅛ cup organic oat flour
- 3½ cups organic whole wheat flour
- 2¼ teaspoons granulated yeast
- 1½ teaspoons sea salt
- ⅛ cup vital wheat gluten
- 1½ cup plus 6 tablespoons lukewarm water
- ¼ cup toasted sunflower seeds,
  plus more for topping
- ¼ cup toasted pumpkin seeds,
  plus more for topping
- ⅛ cup sesame seeds,
  plus more for topping

Directions

1 To the bowl of a stand mixer fitted with the paddle attachment, add the flaxseed, oat flour, whole wheat
   flour, yeast, salt, and wheat gluten.

2 Mix just to incorporate.

3 Add the lukewarm water and the seeds.

4 Mix just until a dough is formed.

5 Transfer to a dough rising container and cover.

6 Let rest at room temperature until it rises and collapses (or flattens on top), approximately 2 hours.

7 Transfer the container to the refrigerator overnight, or up to 10 days in advance.

8 When ready to bake, dust the surface of the refrigerated dough with flour and divide in half.

9 Quickly shape each half into a ball by stretching the surface of the dough around to the bottom on all four sides, rotating the ball a quarter-turn as you go. (This is the method used in the cookbook for making this wet type of dough.)

10 Let the loaves rest, loosely covered with plastic wrap, on a pizza peel coated with cornmeal for 90 minutes.

11 Meanwhile, place an oven rack at the bottom of the oven and one at the very top.

12 Place a pizza baking stone on the bottom shelf of the oven and preheat to 450°F.

13 30 minutes prior to baking, place an empty baking pan on the very top shelf.

14 When ready to bake the bread, brush the top of the dough with a little water and sprinkle with some of each of the seeds.

15 Cut three parallel ¼"-deep slashes across the top of each loaf.

16 Prepare 1 cup of very hot tap water and have on hand.

17 Slide the loaves directly onto the hot pizza stone.

18 Quickly pour the hot tap water into the baking pan on the top shelf and close the oven door to keep the steam inside.

19 Bake for 30 to 35 minutes until the loaves are nicely browned and firm.

20 Remove to a wire rack to cool.

Buttermilk Cornbread

Birth & Balance

One 8"×8"×2" pan

Included as a Thanksgiving treat and utilized in our own *Juice & Essence "Turducken"* (page 412) recipe, this is as down to earth as home-style cooking gets! It is a basic, solid, simple cornbread recipe that tastes phenomenal!

Juice & Essence

Cornmeal is tonifying, energizing, and nourishing and settling to the heart, lung, kidneys, spleen, liver, gallbladder, and stomach. Cooking with corn is a simple way to assist with moistening the intestines, stopping hiccups, remedying constipation caused by dryness, treating gallstones, jaundice, hepatitis, and hypertension.

Ingredients

- 1 cup yellow cornmeal
- 1 cup all-purpose flour
- 1½ tablespoons sugar
- ½ teaspoon baking soda
- 1 tablespoon baking powder
- 1 teaspoon salt
- ¾ cup buttermilk
- 3 large eggs
- 4 tablespoons unsalted butter, melted

Directions

1   Preheat oven to 425°F.

2   Grease an 8"×8"×2" pan.

3   Mix together in a large bowl the cornmeal, flour, sugar, baking soda, baking powder, and salt.

4   In a small bowl, combine the buttermilk, eggs, and butter.

5   Add to the dry ingredients.

6   Stir just to combine. *Do not over mix!*

7   Pour into the prepared pan and bake for 20 to 25 minutes until the top is pale golden and a tester comes out clean.

8   Cool in the pan on a rack for 10 minutes.

9   Remove from pan and place on the rack again to cool completely.

Use in the **Turducken** *stuffing or serve with butter and honey.*

Three-Bean Salad

Birth & Balance   Serves 6 to 8

This is a really complex three-bean salad; however, worth every minute of your time. In the end, we changed the nature and nutrition content by selecting black soy beans, navy beans, and haricot vert rather than the traditional wax, string, and kidney beans. Our selection of herbs, veggies, citrus, and our own orange-infused oil pushed this salad over the top.

Juice & Essence

All of these beans have a blood building, energizing quality to them and tonify the spleen, pancreas, kidneys, and lungs. The iron and protein content are great for building strong muscles. We have used the proper combination of herbs and spices to aid with proper digestion and assimilation of the many medicinal elements available. Black soybeans are especially helpful as a diuretic and removing toxins from the body. Their uses range from treating rheumatism to kidney disease and kidney-related conditions such as low back pain, weak bones, and painful knees. String beans can be useful in diabetic-related complaints such as frequent urination and thirst. Navy beans are beneficial to the lungs and promote beautiful skin.

Ingredients

- ½ cup grapeseed oil or other neutral oil
- 1 orange, zest removed in strips from whole orange (reserve orange for another use)
- 16 ounces haricot vert French beans, steamed
- 1, 15-ounce can black soy beans, rinsed and drained well
- 1, 15-ounce can navy beans, rinsed and drained well
- ½ cup sliced celery
- ½ cup halved and thinly sliced radishes
- 6 baby bell peppers, sliced into thin rings
- 2 tablespoons minced shallots
- ½ cup finely diced fresh fennel
- 1 teaspoon chopped fresh fennel fronds
- 2 sprigs of fresh parsley
- 1 sprig of fresh oregano
- 1 sprig fresh thyme
- 10 fresh chives
- 4 large basil leaves
- ½ teaspoon freshly ground black pepper
- ½ teaspoon sea salt
- 1 teaspoon orange zest
- ¼ cup champagne vinegar

Directions

1 Put grapeseed oil and orange zest strips into a small saucepan and bring to a simmer.

2 Simmer for 5 minutes, then set aside to cool.

3 Once cool, strain out the orange zest strips and discard them. Set the oil aside.

4 Place the cooled haricot vert in a bowl.

5 Cover and refrigerate.

6 Place the black soy beans, navy beans, celery, radishes, bell peppers, shallots, fennel, and fennel fronds in a large bowl.

7 Mix together well.

8 Remove the leaves from the parsley, oregano, and thyme and finely chop.

9 Finely chop the chives and basil.

10 Add all of the chopped herbs to the bowl with the vegetables.

11 Add the cooled orange-infused oil, pepper, salt, orange zest, and vinegar.

12 Mix together well.

13 Cover and refrigerate.

14 About 1 hour before serving, add the haricot vert to the vegetable mixture. *Leave out at room temperature until ready to serve.*

Farro~Lentil Stuffed Cabbage

Birth & Balance

Serves 4

Our mission to create a more healthful stuffed cabbage was based on the desire to incorporate cleansing grain, legume, and seed. This is a great dish for the beginning of fall where the body focus is the liver and large intestine.

Juice & Essence

Traditionally used for anti-inflammatory properties and cancer prevention, cabbage deserves its place in the vegetable hall of fame. This dish with the protein giant lentils and superstar cabbage will benefit the heart, spleen, stomach, large intestine, and kidneys. Uses for this dish combine blood cleansing with the ability to resolve alcoholic thirst. Furthermore, the treatment of constipation, sluggish adrenal system, and circulation are some of the healing qualities found in lentils. This is a mixture of sweet, slightly bitter, and cooling natures, energies, and properties.

Stuffed Cabbage

Ingredients

- ⅓ cup baby red bell pepper, halved and sliced
- ⅓ cup minced onion
- ½ teaspoon ground cumin
- ½ teaspoon ground cinnamon
- ½ teaspoon ground coriander
- 2 cups cooked green lentils
- 2 cups cooked farro
- ½ cup roasted sunflower seeds
- 1 cup chicken broth
- ½ teaspoon salt

Directions

1 Sauté the sliced red bell pepper, minced onion, cumin, cinnamon, and coriander in a small sauté pan until the vegetables are wilted.

2 Place the green lentils and the farro in a medium saucepan.

3 Add the sautéed vegetables, sunflower seeds, chicken broth, and salt.

4 Bring to a boil and then reduce to a simmer.

5 Cover and cook for 15 minutes.

6 Remove from heat and set aside until ready to stuff the cabbage.

Sauce

Ingredients

- 1, 28-ounce can San Marzano peeled tomatoes, drained, tomatoes coarsely chopped
- 1 tablespoon minced fresh oregano
- ½ teaspoon salt
- ¼ teaspoon crushed red pepper flakes
- ⅛ teaspoon ground cayenne pepper
- ⅛ teaspoon freshly ground black pepper
- ¼ cup Merlot wine

Directions

1 Combine all of the sauce ingredients in a medium-size saucepan.

2 Bring to a boil over medium-high heat.

3 Turn the heat down to a simmer and continue to cook for 20 minutes.

4 Set aside until ready to assemble stuffed cabbage.

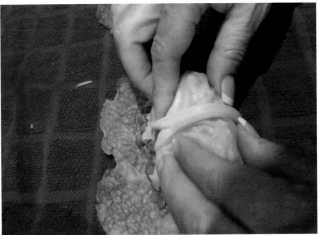

Assembly

Ingredients

12–14 Napa cabbage leaves, wilted in boiling water to soften

Directions

1 Preheat the oven to 400°F.

2 Spoon ½ cup of the sauce in the bottom of a 2-quart baking dish.

3 Take 1 cabbage leaf and place ¼ cup of the farro mixture in the center.

4 Roll the cabbage leaf around the farro mixture, bringing in the sides to totally enclose the farro.

5 Place in the baking dish, seamed side down, and continue with the rest of the cabbage leaves and farro mixture.

6 Drizzle the cabbage rolls with some more of the sauce just to moisten.

7 Cover with foil and bake for 20 minutes, or until heated through.

8 Top with the rest of the sauce and serve.

Kabacha Squash Brûlée

Birth & Balance

Serves 6

Making a brûlée sounded fun! The healthful approach came with choosing the Kabacha squash. Certain aspects of this dish took on a creative substitution as with the almond and goat's milks instead of cow's milk and brown sugar instead of white sugar. It was a tasty delight not recognizing the substitutions in the flavor while still receiving the nutritious benefits!

Juice & Essence

Warming nature with sweet flavor makes this flavorful fall dish lovely in its qi increasing, circulation assisting, pain alleviating, and strengthening powers. This is a very beneficial dish for the spleen/pancreas and stomach with anti-inflammatory properties. This squash in particular contains a generous amount of natural sugars, carbohydrates, and vitamin A. The seeds can be saved and eaten in order to rid the intestines of parasitic worms.

Ingredients

- 3 lbs. Kabacha squash
- ¼ teaspoon ground allspice
- 1 tablespoon minced shallots
- 1 teaspoon olive oil
- 2 teaspoons minced fresh tarragon
- ¾ cup goat's milk
- ¾ cup unsweetened almond milk
- 4 large eggs
- 1 tablespoon all-purpose flour
- Salt and pepper to taste
- 6 teaspoons light brown sugar

Directions

1 Preheat oven to 400°F.

2 Cut the Kabacha squash in half and scoop out the seeds and strings.

3 Line a baking sheet with foil.

4 Sprinkle the inside of the squash with the allspice.

5 Sprinkle 2 tablespoons of water on the foil-lined baking sheet.

6 Place the squash, cut side down, over the water on the foil.

7 Bake on the middle rack in the oven for 40 minutes, or until the squash is cooked through.

8 Remove the flesh from the shell and place in a large mixing bowl.

9 Mash to a smooth consistency.

10 Set aside.

11 Heat a small sauté pan over medium-high heat.

12 Add the olive oil and the shallots.

13 Sauté for 3 to 5 minutes until the shallots are softened.

14 Mix in the tarragon and add to the mashed squash.

15 In a small mixing bowl, whisk together the goat's milk, almond milk, eggs, flour, salt, and pepper.

16 Add to the squash and mix together well.

17 Place 6 buttered ramekins (1-cup size) on a baking sheet.

18 Divide the squash mixture evenly in the ramekins.

19 Bake for 25 to 30 minutes in a 400°F. oven until puffed and light golden brown on top.

20 Sift 1 teaspoon of the brown sugar over the top of each ramekin.

21 Using a kitchen torch, brown the sugar until it is caramelized. Serve immediately.

Escarole & Bean Purée

Birth & Balance   Serves 4

We both enjoy a good traditional Escarole & Bean! With the inspiration for this version birthing from our *Candied Blood Orange Veal Tenderloin* (page 408) dish, it seemed appropriate to consider altering the texture to complement the veal. Hence, pureeing the white kidney beans!

Juice & Essence

Escarole as a lettuce will act as a diuretic and sedative due to the naturally occurring sedative lactuarium. Escarole also assists in drying damp conditions such as edema, digestive ferments, and yeasts. White kidney beans are rich in iron and blood building yin enriching elements. According to their Five Element color of white, legumes benefit the Metal Element organs, which are the lungs and the large intestine.

Ingredients

- 1 large garlic clove, pressed
- 1, 19-ounce can white kidney beans, rinsed and drained
- ⅓ cup plus 1 teaspoon extra-virgin olive oil
- ⅓ cup water
- 1½ teaspoons minced fresh sage
- Salt and pepper
- 2 heads escarole, cut into 2"-pieces
- 2 tablespoons extra-virgin olive oil
- ½ teaspoon crushed red pepper flakes

Prepare the Bean Puree

Directions

1. Sauté the garlic in 1 teaspoon of the extra-virgin olive oil just until softened.
2. Add to the bowl of a food processor fitted with the chopping blade.
3. Add the beans, ⅓ cup olive oil, water, and sage.
4. Process until the mixture is a smooth consistency.
5. Season with salt and pepper to taste.
6. Place the puree into a small saucepan and warm up over medium-low heat.
7. Heat the 2 tablespoons of olive oil in a large sauté pan until hot.
8. Add the crushed red pepper flakes and the escarole.
9. Sauté for 6 to 8 minutes until the escarole is cooked through.
10. Add salt and pepper to taste.
11. Place the bean puree on a serving platter and top with the escarole. Serve immediately.

Jerusalem Artichokes

Birth & Balance

Serves 4

Poetically speaking we matched the root to the seed of the sunflower making for a tasty, healthy, full-flavored, nutritious side dish!

Juice & Essence

The Jerusalem artichoke as the root of the sunflower is energizing and blood building, however they contain no starch. This delicious side offers healing qualities for the intestines and the liver while helping to lower blood sugar, relieving asthmatic conditions and treating constipation. The seed of the sunflower benefits the spleen/pancreas and acts as a tonic to lubricate the intestines, and to treat constipation due to intestinal dryness.

Ingredients

- 1 tablespoon extra-virgin olive oil
- 1 teaspoon minced shallots
- ½ teaspoon blood orange zest
- 1 teaspoon chopped fresh thyme
- 1 lb. (16 ounces) Jerusalem artichokes, peeled and cut into ½"-slices
- ¼ cup roasted sunflower seeds
- Salt and pepper

Directions

1 Heat the olive oil in a large sauté pan over medium-high heat.

2 Add the shallots, zest, thyme, and artichoke slices and sauté for 10 to 15 minutes until softened.

3 Mix in the sunflower seeds and salt and pepper to taste. Serve immediately.

Broccoli Corn Salad with Scallion Dressing & Pumpkin Seeds

Birth & Balance   Serves 6 to 8

Perfectly thrown together to nourish our souls while working on our J&E Thanksgiving meal. This salad fits anywhere at any time and has an attractive taste and texture not easily forgotten.

Juice & Essence

Pumpkin seeds increase breast milk, kill parasites, and regulate urination. Broccoli brightens eyes, treats red painful eyes, and tonifies lungs. Corn strengthens the heart. All of the ingredients combined treat whooping cough, laryngitis, bronchitis, hypertension, dizziness, vertigo, and headache.

Ingredients

- 1 tablespoon Dijon mustard
- 1 teaspoon minced fresh thyme
- ¼ cup red wine vinegar
- ½ cup extra-virgin olive oil
- Salt and pepper
- 1 cup broccoli florets cut into ½"-pieces
- 2 ears of fresh corn, kernels removed from cob
- ½ cup sliced celery
- 6 scallions, sliced, white and green parts separated
- 1 cup grape tomatoes, cut in half
- ½ cup grated carrot
- 6 cups mixed greens
- ¼ cup roasted, salted pumpkin seeds

Directions

1 Combine the mustard, thyme, green parts of scallion, and vinegar in a small bowl.

2 Gradually whisk in the olive oil.

3 Season the dressing with salt and pepper to taste.

4 In a large salad bowl, combine the broccoli, corn, celery, white parts of scallions, tomatoes, carrot, and mixed greens.

5 Top with the pumpkin seeds.

6 Toss salad with enough dressing to coat. Serve immediately.

Mashed Butternut Squash & Sweet Potato Topped with Cranberry Compote & Oatmeal Streusel

Birth & Balance

Serves 8 to 10

Is this a side dish or a dessert? You call it!! We made a very special combination of fall favorites for you. The task we gave ourselves was to properly combine two Thanksgiving favorites under the umbrella of an oatmeal streusel and hidden medicinals: juniper berries, currants, and lavender flowers.

Juice & Essence

Pumpkin (butternut squash) is a clean energy booster, encourages healthy circulation, is a natural mild anti-inflammatory and pain reliever, increases kidney health, and detoxifies. Helps with chronic urinary infections and discourages kidney stones. Lowers blood cholesterol, balances hormones, and enhances male libido. Helps with asthma, prevents digestive-related cancer, skin cancer, anxiety, and depression, and is rich in fiber. Sweet potato, with its sweet flavor, strengthens the spleen/pancreas, promotes qi energy, removes toxins from the body, increases kidney yin thereby treating dry and inflamed conditions of the body. Cranberry adds a kidney and urinary benefit by helping with urinary bladder infections. The lavender is considered a cure-all and therefore can benefit the body on many levels including inflammation, pain relief, detox, and indigestion. Juniper berry is warming and helps ward off colds, boosts the immune system, and rids the body of excess phlegm. Oatmeal restores nervous and reproductive systems, increases energy, and strengthens the spleen/pancreas. Oats remove cholesterol from the digestive tract and arteries while strengthening cardiac muscles.

Butternut Squash & Sweet Potato

Ingredients

- 4 lbs. butternut squash, peeled, seeded and cut into 1"-cubes
- 2 lbs. sweet potatoes, peeled and cut into 1"-cubes
- 1 teaspoon ground allspice
- ½ teaspoon ground cloves
- ½ teaspoon ground ginger
- ½ cup buttermilk

Directions

1 Cook the butternut squash and sweet potatoes in a large pot of boiling salted water until tender, about 15 to 20 minutes.

2 Drain.

3 Return the squash and potatoes to the same pot and add the allspice, cloves, ginger, and buttermilk.

4 Mash mixture until smooth.

5 Pour into a buttered 13"×9" glass baking dish.

Cranberry Compote

Ingredients

- 2, 12-ounce bags of fresh cranberries
- 1 cup water
- 2 tablespoons dried currants
- 1 tablespoon juniper berries
- ½ tablespoon dried lavender flowers
- ½ cup port wine
- 1 cup brown sugar

Directions

1 Place all of the compote ingredients into a large saucepan.

2 Cover and bring to a boil.

3 Reduce heat to simmer and cook, stirring occasionally, until the cranberries pop, about 40 to 45 minutes.

4 Remove from heat and set aside while preparing the streusel.

Oatmeal Streusel

Ingredients

- ½ cup old-fashioned oatmeal
- ¼ cup all-purpose flour
- ⅓ cup light brown sugar
- ¼ teaspoon sea salt
- 4 tablespoons cold unsalted butter, diced
- ¾ cup chopped pecans, toasted

Directions

1 Stir together the oatmeal, flour, brown sugar, and salt in a medium bowl.

2 Add butter, rub in with fingertips until the mixture holds together in moist clumps.

3 Stir in the pecans.

Assembly

Directions

1 Spread the cranberry compote over the mashed butternut squash and sweet potatoes.

2 Sprinkle the streusel on top of the cranberry compote.

3 Bake in a 350°F. oven for 20 to 30 minutes, or until heated through.

Juice & Essence Collard Greens

Birth & Balance

Serves 6 to 8

This is a pretty straightforward recipe. Soul plus ingredients equals damn good!!! We can only take credit for the measurements and the love. Otherwise, the preparation is a classic collard greens recipe.

Juice & Essence

Collard greens are a great blood tonifier that help to settle the heart, prevent and assist with relieving gallstones, jaundice, hepatitis, and hypertension. They are also a great source of detoxifying and intestinal healing properties. Ham adds additional blood building and energizing properties.

Ingredients

- 2 smoked ham hocks
- 8 cups water
- 1 teaspoon freshly ground black pepper
- 3 lbs. collard greens, washed, stemmed, and coarsely chopped
- 1 teaspoon Himalayan salt
- 1 teaspoon garlic powder
- 1 teaspoon onion powder
- 1 teaspoon paprika

Directions

1. Place ham hocks, water, and black pepper in a large stockpot.
2. Cover and bring to a boil over high heat.
3. Lower heat to a simmer and cook for 1 hour.
4. Then add the salt, garlic powder, onion powder, and paprika.
5. Stir into the broth.
6. Add the chopped collard greens and stir to combine.
7. Cover and continue to cook for 2 hours more until the collard greens are very tender and the ham falls off the bone.
8. Serve the collard greens with the ham and broth.

Autumn Desserts

Chapter 4
Autumn Desserts

The surprisingly astounding Juice & Essence dessert world is an amazing place! We feature satisfying and creative inventions with nutritionally balanced and in most cases gluten-free ingredients. Enjoy!

Apple~Pear & Mascarpone Strudel

Birth & Balance

Makes 2 strudels

This dessert really exemplifies our ability to take fresh, living ingredients and put them center stage while properly placing the supportive players. In this case, precious spices, walnuts, natural sugars, and liquors are used as support. We minimize additional calories in the carbohydrate area by choosing phyllo dough, thereby making this one of the best strudels you will ever taste!

Juice & Essence

Pear is one of the most delicious forms of medicine for stopping certain cough complaints and loss of voice associated with dry, hot lungs. Apples are very useful in the removal of cholesterol and toxic metals such as lead and mercury and the residues of radiation. There are additional benefits for low blood sugar conditions and the emotional depression associated with them. Apples are cleansing and beneficial to the liver and gallbladder.

Ingredients

- ¾ cup walnut halves, toasted and finely ground
- ¼ cup whole wheat panko breadcrumbs
- ⅛ cup currants
- ¼ cup Cointreau liquor
- 1 tablespoon clarified butter
- 2 Granny Smith apples, peeled, cored, and thinly sliced
- 2 ripe Bartlett pears, peeled, cored, and cut into 1"-cubes
- ½ teaspoon ground cinnamon
- ⅛ teaspoon ground cardamom
- ⅛ teaspoon ground ginger
- ⅛ teaspoon freshly ground nutmeg
- ¼ cup granulated sugar
- ½ cup clarified butter, melted
- 10 sheets phyllo dough
- ½ cup mascarpone cheese

Directions

1 Preheat oven to 400°F.
2 In a small bowl, combine the ground walnuts and panko breadcrumbs.
3 Set aside.
4 Combine the currants and the Cointreau in a small saucepan.
5 Bring to a simmer and then set aside to steep for 10 minutes.
6 Drain well.
7 Place a large sauté pan over medium heat and add the 1 tablespoon of clarified butter.
8 Once heated, add apples and sauté for 5 minutes.
9 Add the pears, cinnamon, cardamom, ginger, nutmeg, and sugar.
10 Combine well and then add in the currants.
11 Continue to sauté for about another 5 minutes, or until the apples are just cooked through.
12 Remove from heat and set aside to cool slightly.
13 Open the phyllo dough and place on a work surface.
14 Cover with plastic wrap and a damp cotton towel so it will not dry out.
15 Take one piece of the dough and place it on a piece of parchment paper (long side facing you).
16 Brush lightly with a little melted clarified butter.
17 Sprinkle the dough with 1 teaspoon of the walnut-panko mixture.
18 Take another piece of dough and place it on top of the first one.
19 Brush again with a little of the clarified butter and sprinkle with 1 teaspoon of the walnut-panko mixture.
20 Continue this procedure four more times.
21 You will have 6 sheets of the phyllo dough stacked together.
22 Now take half of the apple-pear mixture and place it down the center of the dough leaving a 2" border on each of the short ends of the dough.
23 Spoon half of the mascarpone cheese on top of the apple-pear mixture.

24 Wrap the dough, tightly, around the filling, using the parchment to help you.
25 Tuck the ends of the dough under the strudel and place on a parchment-lined baking sheet (leaving room for the second strudel).
26 Brush the top and sides with a little more of the clarified butter.
27 Follow the same procedure using the remaining ingredients.
28 Place next to the other strudel.
29 Bake the strudels for 25 minutes, or until they are nicely browned.
30 Set aside to cool for about 15 minutes before slicing.
31 The strudel can be made ahead of time and kept at room temperature.
32 Serve at room temperature or reheat in a 400°F. oven for 10 minutes.

Juice & Essence Spiced Walnuts

Birth & Balance

Makes 5 cups

This is the first Juice & Essence labeled dish. We made this spice combo from scratch and birthed perfection. Used as a snack or garnish for desserts and salads; however, if they are already made, they can serve as a topping for anything.

Juice & Essence

Walnuts are sweet and warming and are beneficial to the kidneys and lungs. They are a beautiful way to strengthen kidneys thereby increasing vitality, fertility, and virility. Also helps treat low back pain and lower leg weakness, frequent urination, irregular breathing, and wheezing. These nuts assist with digestion anytime, especially after dinner.

Ingredients

- Whites from 2 large egg whites, at room temperature
- 1 cup packed brown sugar
- 1 teaspoon freshly ground nutmeg
- ¾ teaspoon freshly ground caraway seeds
- ½ teaspoon ground ginger
- ¾ teaspoon cinnamon
- ¼ teaspoon ground cayenne pepper
- ¼ cup butter, melted
- 4 cups walnut halves (pecans are also great)

Directions

1 Preheat the oven to 275°F.

2 Cover a half-sheet pan with heavy-duty aluminum foil.

3 Using an electric stand mixer fitted with the whisk attachment, beat the egg whites until soft peaks form when the beaters are lifted.

4 Combine the brown sugar, nutmeg, caraway, ginger, cinnamon, and cayenne.

5 Gradually add to the egg whites and continue beating until the whites are stiff and glossy.

6 Stir in the melted butter and the walnuts.

7 Mix well so that the nuts are coated with the meringue.

8 Spread the nuts out in a single layer on the prepared half-sheet pan.

9 Bake for 1 hour, or until the meringue is dry, stirring every 15 minutes to separate the nuts.

10 Cool completely in the pan.

11 Store in an airtight container at room temperature.

Honey Roasted Pears with Juice & Essence Spiced Walnuts

Birth & Balance

Serves 6

This health-driven dessert comes from an ancient Chinese food therapy recipe. We simply spiced it up with the *Juice & Essence Spiced Walnuts*…no pun intended! The Chinese used pears for dry lung issues and the honey offers a multi-faceted array of health benefits.

Juice & Essence

This dish benefits the lungs, kidneys, and digestion. Pears are great for lung issues of all sorts; this includes shortness of breath and dry coughs. You will find a toning effect will be had for those with low back and knee weakness. Walnuts offer tremendous medicinal benefits to complement the pears' lung moistening attributes. This dish can be kept in mind when addressing pain and inflammation, wheezing, chills, coldness, poor functioning kidneys and adrenals, and painful back and knees.

Ingredients

- 6 Bosc pears
- 6 tablespoons clover honey
- 24–30 whole cloves
- ¼ cup cognac
- ¼ cup water
- 1 tablespoon clover honey
- 1½ tablespoons light brown sugar
- ½ teaspoon vanilla extract
- Freshly grated nutmeg and fresh mint sprigs for garnish
- 1 cup *Juice & Essence Spiced Walnuts* (page 452)

Directions

1 Preheat oven to 350°F.

2 Cut off 1" from the top of each pear and core them.

3 Add a tablespoon of clover honey to each cored out portion of the pears and place the top back on.

4 Stick 4 to 5 whole cloves around the outside of each pear.

5 Place the pear on a sheet of foil and enclose tightly so none of the juices will escape while baking.

6 Once all of the pears are wrapped, place them in a glass baking dish so they are standing up.

7 Bake them in the center of the oven for 60 to 80 minutes, or until the pears are cooked through.

8 Keep the pears covered in the foil while they cool to room temperature.

9 Prepare the sauce: combine the cognac, water, clover honey, brown sugar and vanilla in a small saucepan.

10 Bring to a boil and cook for 10 minutes.

Serving

1 Unwrap the pears and place in individual serving bowls.

2 Drizzle with the sauce and the *Juice & Essence Spiced Walnuts.*

3 Garnish with fresh mint sprigs and a grating of fresh nutmeg.

Apple Surprise

Birth & Balance

Serves 6

Apples and fall go together. We decided on a dessert that, while creative, would also hit home on a warming level. Hence a spice-topped baked apple custard! Healthier choices were made by selecting goat's and almond milks. Super-duper spices along with organic Golden Delicious apples further enhance this simple yet satisfying fall dessert.

Juice & Essence

Apples benefit the lung, stomach and large intestine by moistening the lungs, providing a good source of fiber and cooling the body especially from summer heat and alcohol toxicity. Additionally there is some immune system enhancing qualities to be found via the generous seasonings. Eggs are very energizing and blood building. Eggs will assist women that have a tendency to miscarry. They are helpful in cases of diarrhea and dryness of the lungs, throat and eyes. Both almond milk and goat's milk are blood and bone building. They are great for fertility and beneficial to the yin aspects of the body. However, goat's milk is one of the best fluorine sources. It is nearly ten times higher than cow milk. Dietary fluorine helps build immunity, protect teeth and strengthen bones. Unfortunately fluorine is lost in pasteurization.

Ingredients

- 2 Golden Delicious apples, peeled, cored, and thinly sliced
- ½ cup Frangelico liquor
- ¼ cup unsalted butter
- ½ cup sliced almonds, finely ground in a spice grinder
- 3 tablespoons Sugar-in-the-Raw
- ⅛ teaspoon freshly ground nutmeg
- ¼ teaspoon ground ginger
- ¼ teaspoon ground allspice
- ¼ teaspoon ground cinnamon
- 2 tablespoons unsalted butter
- 8 large egg yolks
- 4 large whole eggs
- 1 cup goat's milk
- 1 cup unsweetened almond milk
- Zest of 1 orange
- Zest of 1 lemon

Directions

1   Preheat the oven to 350°F.
2   Place apples, Frangelico, and butter in a sauté pan.
3   Cook over medium-low heat until softened, about 15 to 20 minutes.
4   Divide the apples evenly into ¾ cup ramekins.
5   Place the ramekins into a 13"×9" baking pan leaving space between each ramekin.
6   Set aside.
7   In a small bowl, combine the almonds, sugar, nutmeg, ginger, allspice, and cinnamon.
8   Heat a small frying pan over low heat.
9   Add the 2 tablespoons butter and the almond mixture.
10   Sauté, stirring often, until the almonds are nicely toasted.
11   Remove from pan, spreading the almond mixture evenly on a plate.
12   Set aside to cool.
13   In a large bowl, combine all of the eggs, milks, and zests.
14   Pour evenly into each ramekin.

15   Place the baking pan on the middle rack of the preheated oven.
16   Carefully pour enough water into the baking pan to come halfway up the sides of the ramekins. Be careful not to splash any water into the custard.
17   Bake the custards for 20 to 30 minutes, or until the custard is just set.
18   Remove the ramekins from the water to a wire rack.
19   Top each with some of the almond mixture, pressing lightly to adhere.
20   Cool completely.
21   Cover and refrigerate for at least 8 hours and up to 2 days.

Chocolate, Orange & Hazelnut Biscotti

Birth & Balance

Makes about 36

Twice baked goodness!!! If there was ever an interesting, complex biscotti…this is it! Each ingredient was selected with meaning providing a depth and interest in flavorscapes never before seen in a dessert cookie. The scope of these biscotti offers a hint of sophistication for the more mature palate. This is our serious dessert for the discerning connoisseur. We matched hazelnuts with Frangelico and espresso to enhance the dark chocolate and orange zest to complement them all.

Juice & Essence

Orange zest is a spleen and stomach tonifier that is beneficial for weak digestion. Chocolate is a blood tonifier and circulatory invigorator that will brighten eyes, boost strength and energy, as well as benefit qi. Orange peel is helpful in the areas of chronic diarrhea and pediatric diarrhea.

Ingredients

- 1¼ cup hazelnuts, toasted and skins rubbed off
- 6 ounces milk chocolate candy bar, chopped
- 2 cups all-purpose flour
- ⅓ cup unsweetened cocoa powder
- 1 tablespoon powdered espresso
- 1 teaspoon baking soda
- ⅛ teaspoon sea salt
- ¼ teaspoon freshly ground black pepper
- ¾ cup organic sugar
- 1 teaspoon orange zest
- 1 teaspoon vanilla extract
- 2 tablespoons Frangelico liquor
- 3 large whole eggs
- 1 large egg white

Directions

1 Preheat oven to 300°F.

2 Line a baking sheet with parchment paper.

3 In the bowl of a food processor fitted with the chopping blade, place ½ cup of the toasted hazelnuts and the chocolate bar.

4 Set the mixture aside.

5 In a large bowl, mix together the flour, cocoa, espresso, baking soda, salt, pepper, and sugar.

6 Add ¼ cup of the flour mixture to the hazelnut and chocolate in the food processor.

7 Process until the nuts and chocolate are chopped fine and powdery.

8 Add to the bowl with the rest of the flour mixture along with the orange zest and remaining hazelnuts.

9 Stir to combine.

10 Lightly beat together the vanilla extract, Frangelico, and the 3 eggs in a separate bowl.

11 Add to the flour mixture and mix together by hand using a wooden spoon.

12 Keep mixing and pushing the ingredients together until you get a cohesive dough. Don't be tempted to use your hands. The heat from your hands will melt the chopped chocolate.

13 Divide the dough in half.

14 Shape each half into a log that is about ¾" thick, 10" long, and 2½" wide.

15 Place on the parchment-lined baking sheet being sure to have them at least 4" apart since they will spread.

16 Lightly beat the egg white in a small bowl.

17 Brush each log on the top and sides with the egg white.

18 Bake the logs for 50 minutes.

19 Remove from the oven and immediately reduce the temperature to 275°F.

20 Transfer the logs to a cutting board.

21 Cool for 5 minutes; then using a thin sharp knife cut crosswise into ½"-wide strips.

22 Place slices standing upright on the unlined baking sheet.

23 Bake the slices for 35 minutes.

24 Cool on a wire rack.

Anise, Almond & Cherry Biscotti

Birth & Balance

Makes about 36

This was created to serve as a stocking stuffer for our "Haute and Healthy" Holiday Dinner for the *Palm Beach Post*. The process is fun and great for family involvement. We used anise and dried cherries for the sweet aroma and yumminess. Almonds added a gentle crunch. You'll find the combination of spices and Chambord to resonate harmoniously.

Juice & Essence

Almond is beneficial to the spleen, heart, lung, and kidneys with attributes that include increased qi and nourished blood. Almond is the only nut to alkalize the body. All other nuts acidify. Cherries improve circulation and provide relief for sore throats, acute types of paralysis, and numbness. Uses of this dish include settling the heart and stomach before bed and gently relieving complaints of constipation. Cherries are helpful in relieving gout, rheumatism, and arthritis.

Ingredients

- 3 cups all-purpose flour
- 2 teaspoons baking powder
- ¼ teaspoon sea salt
- ¾ cup organic sugar
- 1 tablespoon anise seeds
- ¼ teaspoon freshly grated nutmeg
- 1½ cups blanched almonds, toasted and coarsely chopped
- ⅔ cup diced dried cherries
- 3 large whole eggs
- 2 tablespoons Chambord liquor
- 1 teaspoon vanilla extract
- 2 tablespoons extra-virgin olive oil
- 1 large egg white

Directions

1 Preheat oven to 350°F.

2 Line a baking sheet with parchment paper.

3 In a large mixing bowl, combine the flour, baking powder, salt, sugar, anise seeds, nutmeg, almonds, and dried cherries.

4 In a separate smaller bowl, lightly mix together the 3 whole eggs, Chambord, vanilla, and olive oil.

5 Add the egg mixture to the flour mixture and stir together with a wooden spoon or your hands until a thoroughly combined dough forms.

6 Divide the dough in half.

7 Shape each half into a log that is about 11" long, 2½" wide, and ¾" thick.

8 Place on the parchment-lined baking sheet being sure to have them at least 4" apart since they will spread.

9 Lightly beat the egg white in a small bowl.

10 Brush each log on the top and sides with the egg white.

11 Bake the logs for 30 minutes, or until golden brown.

12 Remove from the oven and immediately reduce the temperature to 325°F.

13 Transfer the logs to a cutting board.

14 Let them cool for 10 minutes.

15 Then, using a thin, sharp knife cut crosswise into ¾"-wide strips.

16 Place slices standing upright on the unlined baking sheet.

17 Bake the slices for 20 minutes.

18 Cool on a wire rack.

Juice & Essence Spicy Spice Log with Cardamom Cream

Birth & Balance   Serves 10

This was a tightrope of a dessert approached on a wing and a prayer with total faith that love would follow through and compensate where the science of baking might fail us! The key to the preparation was not over-baking the cake portion. The birth of this holiday dessert emerged from creating our healthy take of a Buche de Noel.

Juice & Essence

This dessert is warming and nourishing. The combination of spices, ginger, cardamom, cinnamon, cloves, and allspice are all beneficial tonics to the stomach that will assist with indigestion while also relieving nausea. This cake is a gentle preventative for after dinner bloating, abdominal distention, and pain.

Ingredients

- ½ cup all-purpose flour
- 1 teaspoon baking powder
- 1 teaspoon ground ginger
- ½ teaspoon roasted cinnamon
- ¼ teaspoon ground cloves
- ¼ teaspoon ground cardamom
- ¼ teaspoon ground allspice
- 4 large eggs, yolks and whites separated
- 1 teaspoon vanilla
- Organic granulated sugar separately measured into ⅓ cup and ½ cup
- 1¼ cup heavy cream
- 7 cardamom pods
- 1 tablespoon organic granulated sugar
- ¼ teaspoon vanilla bean paste
- Confectioners' sugar
- *Juice & Essence Spiced Pecans* (page 452)

Directions

1 Preheat oven to 375°F.

2 Grease a 15½"×10½" jelly roll pan.

3 Line the bottom and up two sides with parchment paper letting the paper hang over the edge of the pan.

4 Grease and flour the parchment paper. Set aside.

5 In a small bowl, mix together the flour, baking powder, ginger, cinnamon, cloves, cardamom, and allspice. Set aside.

6 In a stand mixer using the paddle attachment, beat the egg yolks and vanilla together at high speed until thick and lemon colored, about 5 minutes.

7 Gradually add the ⅓ cup of sugar.

8 Beat on high until the sugar is almost dissolved, about 5 minutes more.

9 Remove mixture to another bowl.

10 Thoroughly wash and dry the mixer bowl.

11 Add the egg whites to the cleaned bowl.

12 Install the whisk attachment to the stand mixer.

13 Whip the egg whites at medium speed until soft peaks form.

14 Gradually add the ½ cup of sugar and continue to beat until stiff peaks form.

15 Gently fold the egg yolk mixture into the egg whites.

16 Then sprinkle the dry ingredients over the egg mixture folding gently until combined.

17 Spread the batter evenly into the prepared pan.

18 Place on center rack of preheated oven and bake for 12 minutes.

19 Cake should spring back when lightly touched.

20 Remove from the oven and immediately loosen the edges of the cake from the pan.

21 Turn the cake out onto a cotton towel sprinkled with confectioners' sugar.

22 Remove the parchment paper from the bottom of the cake.

23 Gently roll the cake and the towel, jelly-roll style, starting from the short end of the cake.

24 Cool the rolled-up cake in the towel on a wire rack.

25 Meanwhile, prepare the cardamom cream.

26 Bring the heavy cream and cardamom pods to a simmer for 2 minutes.

27 Remove from the heat and let cool in the pan for 20 minutes.

28 Strain out the pods from the cream and place the cream into a mixing bowl.

29 Refrigerate until very cold.

30 Once cream is cold, whip it with the 1 tablespoon of sugar and the vanilla bean paste until it is firm but not grainy.

31 Unroll the cake.

32 Spread the cream to within 1" of the edges.

33 Roll up the cake as tightly as possible.

34 Place seam side down on a serving platter.

35 Cover and refrigerate overnight to allow the favors to blend.

36 About 30 minutes before serving, remove the cake from the refrigerator.

37 Lightly sprinkle some confectioners' sugar over the cake.

38 Decorate with the *Juice & Essence Spiced Pecans* and some fresh greenery for the holiday.

39 Slice and serve. Enjoy!!!

Autumn Sauces, Spices, Marinades & Rubs

Chapter 5

Autumn Sauces, Spices, Marinades & Rubs

Juice & Essence Sauces & Spices are meant to be the perfect complement to our Juice & Essence recipes. This chapter will guide you through this part of the creative cooking process.

Three-Peppercorn Encrusting Rub

Birth & Balance

Makes 1 cup

We loved that we could incorporate a spice group that came in three different colors with three different distinct tastes but with similar shapes and textures. Making them into a rub seemed like: *Why haven't we heard of this before?* So we did it and rubbed our way to dietary ecstasy...

Juice & Essence

Peppercorns, when freshly ground, are less irritating to the digestive tract and carry the wonderful prevention traits that come with healthy circulation and toned digestion. Peppercorns, especially black peppercorns, warm the abdomen treating diarrhea, food poisoning and thereby indigestion. Peppercorns open the pores for sweating and are helpful at the onset of the common cold. They are beneficial to the lungs in such a way as to help protect against simple viral infections such as colds and flus. Sea salt, in moderation, is very appropriate for fall and winter since the action of salt is to strengthen digestion, soften and remove abdominal swellings and intestinal obstructions thereby assisting with bowel movements. This will come in handy during the holiday richness associated with foods during these seasons. Sea salt, depending on its source, contains many trace minerals.

Ingredients

- ¼ cup pink peppercorns
- ¼ cup white peppercorns
- ¼ cup black peppercorns
- ¼ cup sea salt

Directions

Put all of the peppercorns and salt into a spice grinder and process to a fine powder.

This rub may be used on beef, pork, poultry, fish, and seafood.

J&E Mediterranean Marinade

Birth & Balance

Makes about 1¼ cups

Created for use with our *Mediterranean Grilled Lamb Chops* (page 398), this marinade is classically Mediterranean. No new tricks here…save J&E's loving touch and a bit of finely ground mustard seed. Gotta love it!

Juice & Essence

Olive oil is a healthy fat that also lubricates the digestive tract and aids in ridding the gall bladder of stones. This oil topically and internally is great for skin health. Rosemary is a natural antibacterial and antiviral with a drying nature that helps with bloating caused by yeast and dampness. Rosemary is also beneficial to the mind and helps with clarity and memory. Use rosemary for common colds, headache, indigestion, and menstrual pain. Garlic benefits the spleen, stomach, and lungs. Use garlic for parasites, bloating, diarrhea, whooping cough, dysentery, and cold pain. Lemon helps get rid of phlegm in the lungs thereby assisting with cough. Lemon also benefits the spleen and stomach, helps regulate blood pressure, and assists in alkalizing the body. Black pepper benefits circulation and adds to the digestive benefits of this marinade.

Ingredients

- 1 cup extra-virgin olive oil
- Zest and juice of 1 lemon
- 6 garlic cloves, pressed
- 2 teaspoons sea salt
- 1 teaspoon freshly ground black pepper
- ½ teaspoon fresh mustard seed, finely ground
- 1 teaspoon paprika
- 1 teaspoon chopped fresh rosemary

Directions

Combine the oil, lemon zest and juice, garlic, salt, pepper, ground mustard seed, paprika, and rosemary in a large bowl.

Use this marinade on everything from meats, poultry, fish, seafood, and vegetables.

Life-Changing Rub

Birth & Balance

Makes about 1½ tablespoons

Integrating this rub into our *Life-Changing Oxtail & Root Vegetable Soup* (page 400) served as the perfect foundation. The flavor of our oxtails was crucial as they are the back bone…no pun intended. This poetic meld of herbs and spices was constructed with one of the hardest meat choices in the culinary world in mind: oxtail.

Juice & Essence

The ground red and white peppers generate heat in the body, boost digestive energy and circulation. Cumin assists with riding the body of gas. Cloves benefit the kidney, spleen, and stomach. They also treat hiccup, abdominal pain, diarrhea, infertility, and impotence.

Ingredients

- ¼ teaspoon ground red pepper
- ½ teaspoon paprika
- ¼ teaspoon white pepper
- ½ teaspoon onion powder
- ½ teaspoon garlic powder
- ¼ teaspoon cumin
- ½ teaspoon celery salt
- ¼ teaspoon ground cloves
- ¼ teaspoon ground allspice
- 1 teaspoon sea salt

Directions

Combine the ground red pepper, paprika, white pepper, onion powder, garlic powder, cumin, celery salt, cloves, allspice, and sea salt in a small bowl.

This rub can be used on meat, poultry, fish, seafood, and vegetables.

Mmmmm-Mmmmm Marinade

Birth & Balance

Makes about 1 cup

This was created with lamb shanks in mind. The marinade transported divine flavor straight to the bone. We love the balance of spice, sweet, and pungent found within this concoction. Enjoy!

Juice & Essence

Mustard seeds, cayenne, and cinnamon target circulation, warmth, and heart health. Mustard is a key element in strengthening digestion and ridding the lungs of phlegm. Caraway seeds benefit the liver, kidney, and stomach; treat indigestion, bloating, nausea, hiccup, poor appetite, vomiting, and menstrual pain. Fennel seeds are useful in promoting kidney, spleen, liver, and stomach health. Use fennel to treat flatulence/gas, bloating, poor appetite, vomiting, and menstrual pain. Olive oil lubricates the intestines and benefits the lungs. Its moistening nature treats dry sore throat and dry cough.

Ingredients

- 2 tablespoons mustard seeds
- 1 tablespoon fennel seeds
- 1 teaspoon cayenne pepper
- 1 teaspoon garlic powder
- ½ teaspoon caraway seeds
- 2 tablespoons paprika
- 1 tablespoon ground white pepper
- 1 tablespoon ground cumin
- ½ teaspoon Ceylon cinnamon
- ½ cup extra-virgin olive oil
- 2 tablespoons honey

Directions

1 Place the mustard seeds, fennel seeds, cayenne pepper, garlic powder, and caraway seeds into a spice grinder and process to fine powder.

2 Transfer to a small bowl and add the paprika, ground white pepper, cumin, Ceylon cinnamon, extra-virgin olive oil, and honey.

This is a great marinade for lamb and beef.

J&E Chili Starter

Birth & Balance

Makes enough for 3 lbs. of meat

Using three different types of chili seemed exciting at the time. In the end, we simply joined a festival of spices that would work well with the venison we used in our version of chili. We are confident that this starter will be stunning with most meats and poultry. Enjoy!

Juice & Essence

Use onion for lung, spleen, liver, and large intestine issues as it warms internally, invigorates circulation, and treats common cold, diarrhea, and worms. Garlic benefits the spleen, stomach, and lungs while resolving toxins, treating bloating, and helping rid the body of worms. Oregano is an antiseptic with warming, drying, and pungent properties. Oregano has antiviral and antifungal properties and can be used to assist in treatment of colds, flus, candida, fungi, and muscular pain including arthritis and fibromyalgia. Culantro adds to the health benefits of this starter by increasing digestive health and immunity. Culantro has natural anti-inflammatory and analgesic properties.

Ingredients

- ½ cup minced sweet onion
- 1 large garlic clove, minced
- ½ cup extra-virgin olive oil
- ¼ cup red wine vinegar
- 2 tablespoons chopped fresh culantro
- 1 tablespoon minced fresh chives
- 1 teaspoon sea salt
- ½ teaspoon ground black pepper
- ½ teaspoon dried Mexican oregano
- 1 teaspoon dried jalapeño pepper powder
- 1 teaspoon ground New Mexican chili pepper
- 1 teaspoon ground chipotle chili pepper
- 1 teaspoon ground ancho chili pepper

Directions

1   Combine the onion, garlic, oil, vinegar, culantro, chives, salt, pepper, oregano, jalapeño, New Mexican chili, chipotle chili, and ancho chili together in a bowl.

2   Add your beef, venison, lamb, pork, or poultry that has been cut into 1"-cubes to the bowl with the starter.

3   Let marinate for at least 30 minutes.

4   Continue on with your favorite chili recipe while incorporating all of the meat and marinade.

Cranberry Catsup

Birth & Balance

Makes about 2 cups

In thinking that the cranberry flavor would go great with pork and kraut, we expanded and added the sweetness of orange, fig, and pear. We then chose to add Lemoncello to help the flavors mingle. In the end, we couldn't believe how much this reminded us of catsup and named it thusly. It played a trick on our eyes and respectively a trompe l'oeil of the mouth!

Juice & Essence

The elements of the cranberry catsup are packed with vitamin C and antioxidants. Cranberries benefit the kidneys, urinary bladder, and urinary tract as an anti-adhesive to certain bacteria. Figs fortify the spleen and benefit the stomach and large intestines. Use figs for constipation, sore throat, dry cough, and sluggish appetite. Orange benefits the lungs and stomach; helps lessen excessive drinking of alcohol, stops thirst, and certain types of vomiting.

Ingredients

- 1 navel orange
- 1 tablespoon orange zest (from the navel orange)
- 2 Bosc pears, peeled, cored, and diced
- 15 dried Black Mission figs, stemmed and chopped
- 1, 12-ounce bag fresh cranberries
- ½ cup light brown sugar
- ½ cup Lemoncello liquor

Directions

1. Zest the orange and then peel and coarsely chop the flesh.
2. Put the zest and the orange into a large saucepan.
3. Add the pears, figs, cranberries, brown sugar, and Lemoncello to the saucepan.
4. Cover and cook over medium-low heat for 20 minutes, stirring occasionally.
5. Reduce heat to simmer and continue to cook, stirring occasionally, for another 40 minutes, or until the fruit is very soft.
6. Use an immersion blender to puree the fruit until it is completely smooth.
7. Let the catsup cool to room temperature.

Can be stored in the refrigerator in an airtight container for a week.

Support

We live in an amazing time, with the vast customs, creations, and delicacies of the world at our fingertips.

With so many options of health-inspired items to choose from, it is our goal to fill your life, kitchens, and cabinets with thoughtfully selected products. Our Juice & Essence "Support" section is a delightful, essential addition to daily routines.

Have fun accentuating your unique style as you celebrate the indelible benefits of holistic living.

We appreciate:

www.gardenoflife.com

> "I wanted to take a multi made from the same organic, nutritious foods I eat in my daily diet."

Alicia Silverstone
Actress, NY Times Best Selling Author,
Health Advocate

Garden of Life® introduces a multivitamin made **USING ONLY REAL FOOD!**

Kind Organics multivitamins are packed with the nutritious power of over **30 organic fruits, vegetables and herbs.** With Kind Organics, you get a high daily value of nutrients in a **Certified USDA Organic, Non-GMO Project Verified, vegan** tablet made with our patented "Clean Tablet Technology™."

Feed your body with real, nutritious organic, whole food nutrients every day. Make Kind Organics a daily part of your plan to achieve Extraordinary Health. Discover the entire Kind Organics line at OrganicMulti.com.

Empowering Extraordinary Health®

Bibliography

- "Chinese System of Food Cures, Prevention & Remedies" by Henry C. Lu

- "Healing with Whole Foods – Asian Traditions and Modern Nutrition" by Paul Pitchford

- "The Tao of Healthy Eating – Dietary Wisdom According to Chinese Medicine" by Bob Flaws

- "Pocket Atlas of Chinese Medicine" by Marnae C. Ergil and Kevin V. Ergil

- "Chinese Natural Cures – Traditional Methods for Remedy and Prevention" by Henry C. Lu

- "The Illustrated Encyclopedia of Healing Remedies" by C. Norman Shealy M.D., Ph.D.

http://www.coconutresearchcenter.org

http://www.yinyanghouse.com

http://www.acupuncture.com

http://www.tcmhealthbc.com

http://www.ezinearticles.com

http://www.articlebase.com

http://www.livestrong.com

http://www.oilbenefits.net

http://www.webmd.com

http://www.thedailygreen.com

http://foodiecure.wordpress.com

Health Systems Index

The Health Systems Index consists of recipes that will address the following main organs and their operations.

- Lung / Sinus / Allergy / Cough / Skin

- Stomach / Spleen / Digestion / Metabolism

- Kidneys / Adrenals / Fatigue / Immune System / Fertility / Libido/Back Pain

- Liver / Joints / Tendons / Stress / Inflammation

- Heart / Mental / Emotional / Insomnia / Vertigo

About the Authors

Juice & Essence *is* Carol Maglio and Dr. Ken Grey, Holistic Physician.

For us it is not about subtractions as much as knowing how and where to add the Juice & Essence of life and the abundance it can offer. We promote balance in every sense of the word. Deprivation, excess, moderation, variety, and exercise are equally important. Take any of our recipes in our "HEALTH in *Balance*" cookbook series and you will see that we are not pigeonholed into any particular culinary approach. We happily embrace all foods, all cultures, and promote the use of healthy, appropriate substitutions where nature permits. At our core, we'd like to expand the "Food Pyramid" way of thinking into the "Energy and Property" way of thinking. As we recognize the purpose, place, and energy of foods, be it medicinal or otherwise, then we can apply this knowledge as it pertains to our health and well-being. Becoming in-tune with your body and building your awareness of nature's harmony can offer a sense of peace, joy, and lightness. "HEALTH in *Balance*" will be your aid by expanding your food vocabulary and introducing you to nature's healing code. Come with us on an amazing journey. You will experience "HEALTH in *Balance*."

Meet the Authors

Carol Maglio

Carol Maglio is a Health & Wellness Coach certified at The Goal Imagery® Institute. While under the care of co-author Dr. Ken, her Doctor of Oriental Medicine, Carol modified her already healthy habits to a balanced lifestyle that would address the mind, body, and spirit, helping her with her fight against cancer. Carol conquered cancer and in the process upgraded her lifestyle using the methods she has written about in the HEALTH in *Balance* cookbook series. Carol is enthusiastic to share how she is able to maintain an active and happy life. As co-author of the holistic cookbook series HEALTH in *Balance*, Carol finds incredible joy creating unique, healing, and life-changing recipes based on the concept and the principles of Oriental medicine with Dr. Ken Grey.

As a Health & Wellness coach, Carol expands her repertoire of life experience and recipes for success into a life-fulfilling joy ride of self-development. Carol is a devout potential seeker with an eye for individually designed, goal-oriented systems that work. For Carol, the path to a healthy life and a prosperous life are one. Her well-rounded holistic approach exemplifies HEALTH in *Balance*.

Resonating with the attractive nature that true well-being can inspire has caused a ripple affect around Carol. Her friends and family are where her passion for sharing is most evident. From dietary goals, which may include weight loss, to physical goals, which are multi-tiered and will address emotional, physical, and mental growth, her coaching provides the hand holding, cheerleading, and accountability needed to see through even the most insurmountable goal.

Ken Grey, DOM, AP

Ken Grey, DOM, AP Holistic Physician, obtained his masters in both Acupuncture and Oriental Medicine from the Atlantic Institute of Oriental Medicine and enjoys being both a physician and an educator.

He has extensive experience in creative education teaching those with special needs, including individuals with Parkinson's, Alzheimer's, and Autism. His unique approach to holistic healing has taken him abroad to lecture in Germany and treat sports professionals in Hawaii and France and locally onsite at the Honda Classic as well as at his office where he is sought after by golfing and tennis greats.

Dr. Grey has lectured on Acupuncture, Qi Gong, Tai Qi, Reflexology, and Women's Health in relation to Traditional Chinese Medicine, Food Therapy, and uses his experience in Acupuncture and Oriental Medicine to collaborate with physicians of Western medicine in treating the whole patient. Dr. Grey has been on staff at Jupiter Medical Center for over 6 years where he has helped create a new paradigm in integrative medicine.

He has been interviewed on several primetime news specials and ABC Dr. Oz segments for his groundbreaking efforts in the integration of holistic medicine and surgery, alternative treatments for arthritis, and the co-authoring of several books on food therapy aptly named HEALTH in *Balance* with Carol Maglio. His alternative successful treatments for arthritis and pain management magnetized and magnified Dr. Grey's practice, creating significant collaborations with some of the best MDs and surgeons from the award-winning Jupiter Medical Center and Cleveland Clinic.

Now with great honor he travels, lectures, explores, and hosts exquisite dinners whenever possible with co-author Carol Maglio sharing the wonderful world of Juice & Essence Inc. "It's what everything in life boils down to." Please visit our site at www.juiceandessence.com.

Notes

Notes

Notes